The Affinities and Medieval Transposition

Music: Scholarship and Performance
Thomas Binkley, General Editor

The Affinities and Medieval Transposition

Dolores Pesce

INDIANA UNIVERSITY PRESS
Bloomington and Indianapolis

Manufactured in the United States of America

Library of Congress Cataloging-in-Publication Data

Pesce, Dolores.
The affinities and medieval transposition.

(Music--scholarship and performance)
Bibliography: p. ISBN: 978-0-253-30460-5
Includes index.
1. Musical intervals and scales. 2. Transposition (Music). 3. Music--Theory--500-1400. 4. Music--Theory--15th century. 5. Music--Theory--16th century. I. Title. II. Series.
ML3812.P28 1987 781.6'42'092 86-45398

1 2 3 4 5 91 90 89 88 87

To My Loving Parents

Contents

Figures

Music Examples

Abbreviations

AM — *Antiphonale monasticum pro diurnis horis*. Paris: Desclée & Co., 1934.

AR — *Antiphonale sacrosanctae Romanae ecclesiae*. Paris: Desclée & Co., 1949.

AS — Frere, Walter, ed. *Antiphonale Sariburiense. A Reproduction in Facsimile of a Manuscript of the Thirteenth Century, with a Dissertation and Analytical Index*. London: Plainsong & Mediaeval Music Society, 1901-24; reprint ed., London: Gregg Press Limited, 1966.

CS — Coussemaker, Edmond de. *Scriptorum de musica medii aevi*. 4 vols. Paris, 1864; reprint ed., Hildesheim: Georg Olms, 1963.

GB — *Le Codex VI. 34 de la Bibliothèque capitulaire de Bénévent (XIe-XIIe siècle): Graduel de Bénévent avec prosaire et tropaire*. *Paléographie musicale* 15. Tournai, 1937; reprint ed., Bern: Herbert Lang, 1971.

GR — *Graduale sacrosanctae Romanae ecclesiae*. Paris: Desclée & Co., 1952.

GrS — Frere, Walter, ed. *Graduale Sariburiense. A Reproduction in Facsimile of a Manuscript of the Thirteenth Century, with a Dissertation and Historical Index*. London: Bernard Quaritch, 1894; reprint ed., London: Gregg Press Limited, 1966.

GS — Gerbert, Martin. *Scriptores ecclesiastici de musica sacra potissimum*. 3 vols. St. Blasien, 1784; reprint ed., Hildesheim: Georg Olms, 1963.

JAMS Journal of the American Musicological Society

LA Antiphonaire monastique; XIIe siècle: Codex 601 de la Bibliothèque Capitulaire de Lucques. Paléographie musicale 9. Tournai, 1906; reprint ed., Bern: Herbert Lang, 1974.

LR Liber responsorialis pro festis I. classis. Solesmes, 1895.

LU The Liber usualis with introduction and rubrics in English. Tournai: Desclée & Co., 1961.

MGG Die Musik in Geschichte und Gegenwart. 14 vols. Edited by Friedrich Blume. Kassel: Bärenreiter Verlag, 1949-68.

OHS Officium hebdomadae sanctae et octavae Paschae. Rome: Desclée & Co., 1962.

PM Processionale monasticum ad usum congregationis Gallicae. Solesmes, 1893.

SYG Le Codex 903 de la Bibliothèque Nationale de Paris (XIe siècle): Graduel de Saint-Yrieix. Paléographie musicale 13. Tournai, 1925; reprint ed., Bern: Herbert Lang, 1971.

WA Antiphonaire monastique; XIIIe siècle: Codex F. 160 de la bibliothèque de la cathedrale de Worcester. Paléographie musicale 12. Tournai, 1922; reprint ed., Bern: Herbert Lang, 1971.

The Affinities and Medieval Transposition

Introduction

Definitions of mode that survive from the ninth century are vaguely worded.[1] Yet we can surmise that modal classification was based at least in part upon the similarity of motives or formulae found in one group of chants as compared to another. This is evident from the fact that the earliest medieval chant books, tonaries, contain short formulae, set to the syllables *noeane* or some variant thereof, which were intended to represent the melodic characteristics of the various modes.[2]

By the end of the ninth century, theorists had assumed the task of reconciling an inherited chant repertory that was steadily growing with a theoretical system still in the process of development. Coincident with the formulation of a tonal system, the gamut, theorists began to discuss the importance of a melody's final note in modal classification.[3] They located the four modal finals on the notes rendered today as *D*, *E*, *F*, and *G*, which are associated with the *maneriae protus*, *deuterus*, *tritus*, and *tetrardus* respectively.[4] In almost the same breath, they analyzed the gamut to discover how it might embody mode. It is at this point that the concept of *affinitas* arises, described as the similarity of melodic movement shared by certain tones in the gamut. The most frequently cited affinities exist between *D*, *E*, and *F* and notes a fifth above, *a*, *b-natural*, and *c*, respectively.

It is significant that what the theorists were describing was a pitch relationship, a linking of two tones by virtue of their identical surrounding intervals. But in order to discuss the relationship, they used note designations. Consequently, we find the affinities defined sometimes with reference to "pitches," sometimes with reference to "notes," and sometimes with reference to both. As the act of notating and reading music became progressively a more vital part of musical contemplation, some theorists tended not to differentiate _vox_ from _nota_. Accordingly, the reader will find varying degrees of specificity in the use of the terms by the theorists under consideration here. I have tried in my translations to render the sense behind each author's choice of wording, acknowledging that, in some cases, there is inconsistency.[5]

The history of the concept of the affinities entails an interaction between theory and practice. Extant discussions of the concept suggest that theorists were trying to reconcile certain problematic chants to the eight-mode system in terms of both classification and notation; they stipulated that such chants might end on a note in affinity with a standard modal final (hence, the term _affinalis_), and they gave reasons why this should occur.

The reason most often singled out by scholars of today is that the concept of the affinities provides for a means of notating certain intervals of a chant that cannot be accommodated at the position of the normal final.[6] The medieval gamut allowed for the inflection of only one pitch, _b_, as either _b-natural_ or _b-flat_. Apparently some chants contained other inflected pitches, principally _E-natural_-_E-flat_ and _F-natural_-_F-sharp_. In transposing all or some of a chant to the position of the affinities, aberrant tones such as _E-flat_ and _F-sharp_ could be changed, perhaps with the aid of _b-flat_, to ones belonging to the diatonic gamut. In effect, the ending on the _affinalis_ preserved the modal identity through the resemblance of the intervallic motion around it to that around the regular final.

How did use of the affinities as a notational device have bearing on performance? Was a chant notated a fifth above its usual final necessarily sung at a higher level? Some theorists seem to say that the voice will rise to a higher range as a result of transposition to the affinities; but, in the absence of definite knowledge concerning levels of pitch, both absolute and relative, it is not possible to determine the extent to which such a practice occurred.

The word _transpositio_ plays an important role in discussions of the affinities, frequently used by theorists to describe (or prescribe) the transfer of part or all of a melody to a related position in the diatonic gamut. Although, to the medieval mind, the term transposition had this basic connotation, as early as the eleventh century another sort of transposition was proposed. Some theorists perceived a modal identity between a regular final and the note a fourth above, a limited identity that could be extended if _b-flat_ were included as an admissible note at the higher position. On account of the powerful influence of Guido of Arezzo, however, a number of theorists considered such transpositions to the fourth above to be objectionable: Guido advocated the avoidance of any non-diatonic tone in notation, even including *b-flat*, normally a legitimate part of the gamut. A number of his interpreters applied this apparent dictum to the positioning of modes a fourth above their usual finals. To them, *protus* (final *D*) transposed to *G* using *b-flat* would transform the identity of *G* as a *tetrardus* final into *protus*. Likewise, *deuterus* (final *E*) transposed to *a* using *b-flat* would distort the diatonic association of *a* with *protus* (as an affinity at the fifth above).

Both the theorists' statements and manuscript evidence attest to the fact that transposition of chants to the upper fourth nevertheless occurred, mainly of *deuterus* chants to *a* and of *tetrardus* chants to *c*. The principal reason for this seems to have been the same one that resulted in the transposition of many melodies to the diatonic affinities -- the desire to notate aberrant tones within the diatonic confines of the gamut. Confronted with a practice which they essentially condoned, yet lamenting its concomitant distortion of the tonal system as they conceived it, a number of theorists engaged in a verbal battle over the relative merits of *transpositio* versus *transformatio*. Transposition, which was associated with the affinities, maintained an unquestionably favored status throughout the eleventh and twelfth centuries.

When eleventh-century theorists described the common movement around a final and its *affinalis*, they said that it occupied the range of a sixth. The characteristic interval structure of each *maneria* could then be located either within the diatonic segment *C* to *a* or *G* to *e*. Guido of Arezzo (and shortly after Hermannus Contractus) explained *affinitas* in terms of these six-note diatonic segments. From this followed Guido's six-syllable pedagogical tool, known today as the hexachord. While Guido did not expressly link his hexachord syllables with the transposable diatonic segments he described, one may infer from his discussion of the affinities that the two concepts were related. Guido's explanation of alternative modal positions foreshadows later hexachord theory. The *C* to *a* segment is, in essence, the natural hexachord, and the *G* to *e* segment, the hard hexachord.

By the thirteenth century, hexachord terminology pervaded theorists' discussion of modal finals. The syllable *re* could refer either to the normal *protus* final on *D* or to its *affinalis* on *a*, because those notes occupy analogous positions within their respective hexachords. At this time, theorists came to recognize that a similar correspondence occurs at a third point in the gamut, within the segment *F* to *d*, the so-called soft hexachord. In *protus*, for example, a *G* final has the syllable *re*, assuming the *F* to *d* segment incorporates *b-flat*. But this modal position, located a fourth above the normal one, is the same one that was said to cause *transformatio* two centuries earlier.

Although the label eventually was discarded, theorists showed continued reluctance to accept this third modal position. Only in the fourteenth century did a few theorists tentatively acknowledge the usefulness of *b-flat* in modal constructions, in spite of its distortion of a strictly diatonic tonal framework.

The fourteenth century witnessed an increasing number of theoretical explanations of practices related to the composition and performance of polyphony. The theory of *coniunctae* concerning the use of altered tones, both written and implied, emerged and was associated with the concept of the affinities. A group of writers, beginning with the anonymous author of the Berkeley Manuscript, defined a *coniuncta* as making a tone into a semitone and vice versa. These same theorists then expanded this concept to allow for the generation of transposed hexachords beyond the usual number permitted by the theory of affinities. These result when a *coniuncta*, in effect a half step, is located at any selected point in the gamut. The first note of the *coniuncta* is called *mi* and the second *fa*; a hexachord may then be constructed by adding notes corresponding to *ut* and *re* before the *mi* and notes corresponding to *sol* and *la* after the *fa*. For example, the *coniuncta* *F-sharp*-*G* implies the formation of a *D* - *b-natural* hexachord. This expanded concept assumes significance for the history of the affinities: a number of theorists offer the *coniuncta* as an alternative to the limited process of transposition that had hitherto provided the solution to the problem of notating chromatically altered tones in chant. Although a superficial reading of these discussions suggests that the practical use of the affinities was coming to an end, closer examination reveals that the theorists did not intend their expanded theory of *coniunctae* to apply to chant, but instead to polyphony.

The sixteenth century witnessed a significant change in theorists' definition of mode. They now regularly linked a given mode to a particular octave segment within the gamut. Certainly this awareness of octave species had been evident in theory treatises intermittently since the *Alia musica* of the ninth century, but only with the humanistic thrust of the sixteenth century did such an approach to mode become prevalent. Just as the Greeks had discussed modes as octave species, so would their humanist emulators. On the other hand, the theoretical emphasis on octave species may also have resulted as a direct response to polyphonic practice. For a number of generations, one- and two-flat signatures had appeared in polyphonic compositions. To some extent, these signatures accounted for accidentals needed to prevent horizontal and vertical tritones. In some contexts, they might also account for tones altered to achieve an exactly corresponding interval pattern in imitative parts. Perhaps in an attempt to explain what they observed in polyphonic compositions, theorists began to emphasize the fact that a mode's exact interval arrangement, as defined within a diatonic octave species, could be found at an alternative position within the gamut other than at the affinity. That position was at the fourth above the final, the location once said to harbor "transforming" effects because of its integral use of b-flat, in other words, what we now call a flat transposition once removed. The rise of octave species theory eventually made possible transposition in the modern sense. Undoubtedly, the rejection of a modal concept founded on a flexible but limited correspondence of modal nucleus and the adoption of one founded on octave-species correspondence ultimately influenced the recognition of fully functional tonality in the seventeenth century.

Because the history of the affinities is linked to the interaction of theory and practice, I have attempted wherever possible to make correlations between a theorist's statement concerning a particular chant and the version of it transmitted by the extant sources. In some instances, a surviving version corresponds exactly to his description, while in others, all the available versions differ to the extent that only a hypothetical correlation can be made. For the most part, I have limited my examination of chant sources to those listed in Bryden and Hughes' An Index of Gregorian Chant,[7] except in the cases where a more extensive comparison of the sources is readily available.

This study brings together the statements made by theorists on the concept of related tones from the end of the ninth century through the mid-sixteenth century. A chronological approach has been chosen to illustrate the subtle, gradual evolution of these ideas, as well as to provide the materials in a readily accessible fashion.

It is hoped that my work might rectify certain misunderstandings about, or neglect of, the concept of the affinities observed in modern scholars' discussions of mode. Too often affinalis is confused with tenor, dominant, or reciting tone, functional terms in psalmody, or else the concept is dismissed, because the writer takes into account only certain sixteenth-century theoretical discussions in which the term affinalis had come merely to stand for the note a fifth above the final. In the earlier centuries, the concept of affinitas played a fundamental role in the practice of classifying and notating chants within the eight-mode system. Furthermore, its conceptual basis gave rise to that indispensable tool of the medieval and renaissance musician -- hexachord solmization. Perhaps most significantly, the linking of modal identification to the concept of affinitas caused a long-delayed recognition of the modern concept of transposition.

I. From Hucbald to Guido: Origins of the Concept

The earliest surviving sources of Western music theory that discuss relationships among the tones of the gamut are thought to have originated in the late ninth century. Theorists present this concept as part of their overall attempts to understand their tonal system, but some of their explanations also reflect a concern for the practical -- how can the affinities aid in the task of notating chants whose content in some way conflicts with either the gamut or with their assumptions about mode or with both? This chapter traces the development of the concept of the affinities, as expressed in both abstract and practical terms, from the rather vague mention of it by Hucbald through the extended exposition by two eleventh-century authors, Berno of Reichenau and Guido of Arezzo.

Hucbald's De harmonica institutione

The earliest known treatise to mention the affinities is De harmonica institutione by Hucbald.[1] Yves Chartier has speculated that the treatise may have been written between 893 and 899 for the cathedral school of Rheims.[2] The organization of Hucbald's treatise marks it as a school text; it follows a cyclical curriculum, in which the same topics are presented three times. It appears that Hucbald sought to improve chant practice through his explanations of and suggestions for new pitch notations. Even more significant, he attempted to outline a tonal system that would correspond to chant practice. Specifically, Hucbald structured the medieval gamut to reflect the principle of modal classification operative in the late ninth century, based upon the system of four "finals."

In Hucbald's words, the four finals are so called because "everything that is sung ends among them."[3] Hucbald names the finals using the Greek designations equivalent to D, E, F, and G,[4] and further discusses the four finals as a tetrachord with an interval arrangement of tone-semitone-tone. This tetrachord becomes the basic structural unit used to divide the gamut as follows:

A B C D E F G a ♮ c d e f g aa

Hucbald was proceeding from tradition, since the Greeks had divided their gamut, the Greater Perfect System, into tetrachords, but in the pattern tone-tone-semitone beginning with their equivalent of _aa_ and descending. Hucbald in fact discusses the Greek tetrachord division as transmitted through Boethius. By juxtaposing the Greek system with his own tetrachord division reflecting chant practice, he reveals a conscious adaptation of an inherited theoretical tradition.

In addition to the four diatonic tetrachords shown in the diagram above, Hucbald mentions a _synemmenon_ tetrachord, spelled _G_ _A_ _b-flat_ _c_,[5] after which he acknowledges the use of _b-flat_ as well as _b-natural_ in chant practice:

> While examples of the tetrachord of the synemmenon are often encountered in all the modes, or tones, they can be seen especially in the authentic and plagal tritus so ubiquitously that in these scarcely any melody is found without a mixture of the tetrachords of the synemmenon and the diezeugmenon.[6]

As later discussion will show, the acceptance or rejection of _b-flat_ is a major factor in the approaches to modal classification adopted by eleventh- and twelfth-century theorists. Hucbald next makes this observation about his theoretical system (I have adopted Warren Babb's reading of this passage -- see n. 7):

> . . . the notes a fifth above each of these four finals respectively are joined with them in such a bond of similarity that one will generally find that melodies can close on these notes a fifth above without offending either one's judgement or ear. They remain entirely within the same mode or trope, as though according to some principle. In this relationship are linked the lichanos hypaton [D] with the mese [a], the hypate meson [E] with the paramese [♮], the parhypate meson [F] with the trite diezeugmenon [c], and the lichanos meson [G] with the paranete diezeugmenon [d], they being respectively a fifth apart.[7]

This appears to be the earliest reference in extant medieval Latin treatises to what later came to be known as the concept of _affinitas_. Hucbald uses the term _socialitas_ to describe the relationship of tones a fifth apart, or in other words, of tones similarly placed in two tetrachords.[8]

Hucbald's statement is clear, concise, but rather abstract. Was his observation about the relationship between the finals and tones a fifth above a conceptual extension of his notions of a tetrachord division as derived from Boethius, or was it simply his attempt to classify chants as they were sung in his time? His next statement suggests that he was describing phenomena he observed in the current chant practice:

> The four finals also possess somewhat of a like relationship to the notes a fourth below, and in certain cases a fifth below, but such notes are used for beginnings, not endings. For the limit for beginnings extends down to these notes. Thus related are: the proslambanomenos [A] to the lichanos hypaton [D]; the hypate hypaton [B] to the hypate meson [E], *but this only rarely*; the parhypate hypaton [C] with the parhypate meson [F]; and the lichanos hypaton [D] with the lichanos meson [G]. Moreover, when the lichanos meson [G] is the final, the beginning is *sometimes* placed as low as the parhypate hypaton [C], a fifth away, but *this is very rare* with the other finals. (emphasis added)[9]

In this paragraph, Hucbald refers to the relationship between each of the finals and the respective tone in the lowest tetrachord A B C D. Although he dismisses these tones as possible modal endings, he imputes to them another function, that of providing a lower limit for the beginning of chants. Significantly, he supports this discussion by including a list of chant examples showing all the possible starting notes for each *maneria*. For *protus*, *deuterus*, and *tritus*, respectively, A, B, and C are the lowest beginning notes, while for *tetrardus*, he allows C.

In contrasting fashion, Hucbald does not include chant examples to elucidate his exposition on related sounds at the upper fifth. The lack of examples is particularly notable since he provides them for practically every other concept in the treatise.[10] Furthermore, this discussion of related tones betrays a disturbing feature in that Hucbald links D and a, E and ♮, F and c, *and* G and d. This last pair is omitted by many later writers discussing the affinities, presumably because G and d share only one common ascent, by tone, after which the ascent from G proceeds by tone and that from d by semitone (G⌴a⌴♮◡c; d⌴e◡f⌴g where ⌴ = tone, ◡ = semitone) In practical terms, the "similarity" of movement around G and d is too limited to accommodate chant ranges, which usually proceed more than a step above the final.[11]

Thus, the first mention of the affinities is apparently rooted in a speculative inquiry about the tonal system, and to judge by the lack of clear details, that inquiry rested in a preliminary stage.

Musica enchiriadis and *Scolica enchiriadis*

These,[12] like Hucbald's work, discuss the tetrachord of the finals as a basic unit in the tonal system. Where Hucbald superimposes the tetrachord upon the traditional gamut from *A* to *aa*, the *Enchiriadis* author presents it as the basic structural unit of an unusual formulation of a gamut (expressed here in letter notation rather than in the daseian signs peculiar to the *Enchiriadis* treatises):

Γ A B♭ C D E F G a ♮ c d e f♯ g aa ♮♮ cc♯

Varying interpretations have been offered for why the anonymous author projected a unique system that sometimes lacks octave duplication and is composed entirely of disjunct tetrachords. Otto Gombosi supposes that the author may have borrowed this disjunct division from medieval Byzantine sources.[13] A more widely held viewpoint suggests that the author was accounting for the practice of parallel organum at the fifth, which he discusses at some length, since this gamut precludes the occurrence of anything but perfect fifths.[14]

One other explanation for this particular gamut seems plausible -- the author seeks to support his discussions of organum by reference to relationships inherent in the modal system, that is, to the affinities. Specifically, he takes a melody of limited range beginning on *D*, "Tu patris sempiternus es filius," and moves it successively to a higher starting point in the gamut until it reaches *a*. Referring to the melody a fourth removed from *D*, he states:

> . . . if [you make it higher] by three [spaces], the fourth mode arises. If it is carried still one space higher it will be first [mode] again in the fifth position.[15]

Thus, while exposing the change of mode effected by a transposition to the fourth above,[16] he recognizes a modal identity at the fifth above, that is, in the same position within the higher tetrachord as in the lower one.[17] He reinforces his discovery by applying the names of the four *maneriae* - *protus*, *deuterus*, *tritus*, and *tetrardus* - to the four respective members of each tetrachord in his gamut. Based on this means of identification, it was possible to describe a perfect fifth as occurring between the respective *deuterus* members of two tetrachords. The appeal of such symmetrical labeling by no means ended with the *Enchiriadis* author, as later discussion will show. In the context of the *Enchiriadis* treatises, the symmetry of modal names that exists between tones a fifth apart reinforces the author's apparent preference for organum at the fifth rather than at the fourth.

Apart from the question of the gamut, the author provides a clear statement of the concept of _sociales_ or related final tones. Following his discussion of modal differentiation through tone-semitone arrangement, he stresses the importance of the final in determining the mode of a particular melody:

> Principally, indeed, the character of any _tropus_ appears to depend on any final sound for this reason, that the _tropus_ will have existed [only] by ending on it. This, however, is added, that the same final sound and its more usual related sounds (_sociales_) are found at the end of _commata_ or _cola_. Each sound has its related sounds (_sociales_) not only at the fifth positions, but it seeks other sounds related to it (_compares_) also at the fourth positions, which is the location of the third consonance [i.e., the diatessaron]. Accordingly, in phrases which are parts of a song, the _cola_ or the _commata_ nearly always proceed towards these _socialitates_ in the raising and lowering of sounds, and either arsis or thesis seek to reach them.[18]

The author thus states that melodies show the use of _sociales_. Specifically, the finals and their related sounds occur at the end of _commata_ and _cola_, that is, at the conclusion of phrases. Based on the meanings of these two words in their original grammatical context, it would seem that the author is referring to internal phrases and not to the final division of the work.[19] Nowhere does he explicitly state, as Hucbald did, that a chant may end on a _socialis_.

The quotation also reveals that the author accepts another related sound besides the _socialis_; he employs the distinguishing word _compar_ for this tone located a fourth above the final. By virtue of the order in which they are mentioned, the _socialis_ stands in a closer relationship to a final than does the _compar_. This precise linkage of relationships of the fifth and fourth with the terms _socialis_ and _compar_, respectively, resurfaces in the work of Berno of Reichenau. The _Enchiriadis_ author refers to them collectively, however, when he ends the paragraph with a generalization about phrase endings at the _socialitates_.

Taken alone, this passage allows us to conclude only that the author observed phrase endings a fifth and a fourth removed from a given final. Is there any intimation that he knew of or sanctioned transposition of a melody to one of these related positions? One little-known passage in the _Scolica enchiriadis_ suggests that he was describing such a practice:

> It ought to be known, however, that the first concord is that which is used in the previously stated manner [unison] to direct the melody. There is another concord of less importance, when,

> wishing to lessen a difficulty of excessive height or to raise up an excessive lowness, we force [it] by a fifth transposition into a higher or lower position. There is also a third concord which comes at the eighth position of sounds, that is, when we shift a melody for a young or higher voice. And through these associations, a certain harmony of songs can be preserved. Otherwise it cannot, unless perchance any melody is totally changed into another mode by transposition. If you transpose any melody whatsoever in the same series of sounds, one, two, or three spaces higher or lower, the mode of the *tropus* moves at the same time to another species.[20]

Although ambivalent in many respects, this statement describes three acceptable transpositions, a fifth higher, a fifth lower, and an octave higher.[21] Even though the author prescribes transpositions of the fifth as a way to deal with excessive range within a given melody, he does not specify whether part or all of such a melody would be transposed. He also acknowledges that musicians transpose a melody to the octave to accommodate "young or higher voices." In his final reference to the way the mode of a melody is changed when it is transposed using the interval of a second, third, or fourth, he reinforces the concept that modal identity is preserved at the fifth and octave -- hence, that affinities exist in the tonal system.

The author of the *Enchiriadis* treatises was interested in describing a practice of his time -- that of organum at the fifth. At the same time, he sought to prescribe a tonal system according to the tetrachord of the finals, as did Hucbald. In spite of the inherent defects of the author's particular system, to which his immediate successors sometimes alluded, it is clear that he saw beyond the confines of his artificial gamut and accepted the changes that were necessary to reflect chant as it existed. This attitude is particularly evident in his discussion of *absonia* or altered tones.[22] Such acknowledgements and references to sight-singing and note-reading exercises lend support to the idea that the author was not engaged in mere abstractions about a quadrivial science, but rather was aware of and knowledgeable about musical practices of his time. Thus, his references to finding "related sounds" (a fifth and a fourth distant from the final) at phrase endings are credible, and a hypothesis that he was prescribing transpositions of a fifth and octave seems reasonable.

Dialogus de musica

A discussion of the affinities that is not tied to tetrachord divisions occurs in the treatise entitled *Dialogus de musica*, written at approximately the beginning of the eleventh century, possibly by an anonymous Benedictine monk in the province of Milan.[23]

The purpose of the treatise is clearly stated at the outset: to provide rules by which "boys and simple persons" could learn to sight-sing chant quickly. The authors' primary contribution to this end is his presentation of a letter notation which allows for octave duplication within the gamut:

Γ A B C D E F G a b ♮ c d e f g aa

By means of this system, which has remained the basis for letter notation to the present day, the author explains a limited number of concepts essential to chant performance - division of the monochord, intervals, and modal classification.

The author states the raison d'être of mode: "A tone or mode is a rule which classes every song according to its final."[24] He is the first writer to state explicitly that the arrangement of tones and semitones around the final distinguishes one mode from another, and accordingly, he includes both a word description and diagram of each mode's tone-semitone organization.[25] Although the diagrams allow for a basic octave with an added tone on one or both ends, there is no suggestion that the author associated a mode with an octave species as later writers were inclined to do.[26]

An interesting point comes to light in the course of the mode-by-mode exposition. For several of the eight modes, the author includes b-flat and not b-natural as the normal inflection on that degree of the gamut.[27] Hucbald had alluded to the frequent occurrence of both inflections in tritus melodies,[28] but this author considers b-flat as part of the regular internal arrangement of protus (authentic and plagal) and tritus (authentic and plagal), as well as plagal deuterus.[29]

His descriptions are partially verified in the passage that most concerns us here, in which the magister relates each step of the gamut to the modes.[30] Specifically, he confirms that F modes are constructed with b-flat by attributing to tritus the ascent of tone-tone-semitone from C; by analogy, the ascent from F would be F G a b-flat.

The total spectrum of modal "likenesses" (his word similitudo, -ines) recognized by the author becomes apparent in his diagram, shown below in Figure 1. Roman numerals I through VIII represent modes one through eight as described in footnote 27.

Fig. 1. Modal "likenesses" according to the Dialogus author.

VII	I		V	I	III	V	VII	III I		V	I	III	V	VII	I
Γ	A	B	C	D	E	F	G	a	♮	c	d	e	f	g	aa
VIII	II	IV	VI	II	IV	VI	VIII	II	IV	VI VIII	II	IV	VI	VIII	II

The coupling of notes with modes reveals a relationship at the fifth: for modes one and two, D with a, for mode four, E with b, for modes five and six, F with c. The refusal to link G with d for modes seven and eight shows the author's practical approach to his tonal system. He suggests that he considers their common ascent of only one step too limited to warrant a modal identity.[31]

The diagram also reveals a recognition of related sounds at the interval of a fourth. Notably, a is related to the final of mode three following this arrangement: ". . . if you consider it in connection with the first ninth [step], b-flat, it will have in descent a tone, but in ascent a semitone and three tones . . ." And, further, c is related to the final of mode eight since ". . . if it is deprived of the second ninth [step], b-natural, it will have below it a tone, a semitone, and two tones, but above it two tones and a semitone . . ."[32] Thus, the author accepts that, through the use of b-flat, additional points of correspondence arise in the gamut.

What end do these correspondences serve? Noting that b-flat has no "likeness," the author states, "Consequently, you will find that neither a song nor a distinction (phrase) may have a beginning or end on it, unless it happens by a fault."[33] By extension, he seems to say that the notes named as "likenesses" could begin or end a song or distinction in that mode. In an earlier statement he specifically says that the several pairs of related notes may serve as potential finals; however, he does not clearly explain why that may occur. In the context of his discussion of the seventh mode, he offers this leading statement: "Again, if through only one distorted sound it ends on the eighth [step] a, it again becomes first [mode] throughout . . ."[34] The allusion to a "distorted" sound could simply mean that the singer has miscalculated an interval at some point and consequently ends on a instead of G. Or, it could refer to an integral tone in a chant which does not ordinarily occur in the mode and thus appears distorted. If the latter were his meaning, the use of a related final could provide a means to notate the incongruous tone, as will be explained below. Whether he was considering this solution is difficult to determine, since earlier, in Chapter Six, he had taken no notice of an opportunity to offer exactly this solution to a chant with a tone "departing from the mode."

Referring in that chapter to the antiphon "Domine qui operati sunt," he notes a semitone at the words "in tabernaculo tuo" that detracts from its sixth-mode character.[35] Strunk, in a footnote to this passage, includes the version found in the Liber responsorialis as well as in the Lucca and Worcester antiphoners.[36] A comparison of these versions reveals that an E-flat is called for at the words quoted by the Dialogus author, and elsewhere in the chant an E-natural. To avoid E-flat, which was not a part of the theoretical gamut, the Worcester antiphoner transposes the chant up a fifth to its related position where the E-flat becomes a theoretically acceptable b-flat. The reasoning behind this solution is not disturbed by the presence of a whole step below the tritus final (F to E-flat), rather than the normal half-step (F to E). For the Dialogus author, however, the whole step below the final is a characteristic feature of tetrardus, not tritus (Example 1), and therefore a notational solution to the E-flat is alone not sufficient. He recommends beginning the chant on G, not F, and classifying it as tetrardus.[37]

Ex. 1. Illustration of melodic movement in tritus and tetrardus modes.

"Domine qui operati sunt" is the only chant example with a modal deviation cited by the author. In his discussion, he clearly prefers a modal reclassification to an emendation that would change the essential intervallic structure of a traditional melody. His solution for "Domine," transposition by one step, is understandable since he recognizes tritus with b-flat and thus its parallel construction to tetrardus except for the subfinal. If he were willing to account for, and thus accept, deviations in other modes by transposition to related notes a fourth or fifth above, he gives no clear indication of it in this treatise. One must keep in mind, however, that the author intended to present little more than an introduction to the basic rules of the tonal system. Little is said concerning exceptions to the rules, aside from warnings that they exist.

Berno's Prologus in tonarium

While Berno of Reichenau's Prologus in tonarium,[38] contains borrowings from earlier writers, such as Aurelian, Hucbald, and Regino, it also reveals a particular preoccupation of eleventh- and twelfth-century German monastic theorists with the relationships of species of fourths, fifths, and octaves to the plainchant gamut and to the modes.[39] This latter approach differs from that of the Dialogus author and, as we shall show, of Guido, for both of whom the intervallic movement around the final was of sole importance in determining mode. Ultimately, Berno likewise recognizes the final as the primary modal determinant, because, in spite of the space he devotes to enumerating the species associated with each of the modes, he admits that the chant repertory does not uniformly reflect pure modal species. In discussing problematic chants, Berno expounds the concept of the affinities.

Berno reveals his familiarity with both Hucbald's work and the Enchiriadis treatises by paraphrasing their passages on related sounds.[40] Throughout his discussion, he adopts the Enchiriadis' terms sociales and compares, respectively, for the tones a fifth and a fourth above the finals. Not only does Berno view the sociales and compares as "regular" endings, but he also gives the first clear explanation with examples for why they might be so used. The first reason reads as follows:

> . . . for example, this responsory "Factum est dum tolleret" which, indeed, since it begins regularly, but ascends contrary to the rule beyond the ninth into the tenth sound, by no means terminates on its final lichanos hypaton [D], but on its socialis mese [a]. In the same way are ended the responsory "Terribilis est" and the communion "Cantabo Domino."[41]

Berno describes the first-mode responsory "Factum est" as ending on a instead of D after it has ascended beyond the range of a ninth usually allowed to authentic modes. Once the responsory is in the higher range, it does not return to the final, but instead ends on its socialis.[42]

Berno adds that the responsory "Terribilis est" and the communion "Cantabo Domino" end on a. Although he is unclear as to whether they end there for the same reason that "Factum est" does, there is evidence that suggests he did intend this reason to apply to them at least in a general sense. Several later theorists describe "Terribilis est" as ending on a related note after it had lingered too long in the higher region. Although the precise reference to an ascent of a tenth is missing, this description agrees with Berno's reason.[43]

Several of the extant sources of "Cantabo Domino" strongly suggest why Berno included it with the other two named chants. In one case, the melody moves around a from the outset and ends there -- Graduale Romanum (323). The Graduale Sariburiense (143) preserves the same version a fifth lower, except for the first phrase which is set a fourth lower. If that first phrase were also transposed down a fifth, E-flat would result.[44] As will be discussed below, the use of the affinities to legitimize pitches not found in the gamut was a known practice, one that would explain the use of the a region in GR. Berno, however, comments only upon the ending of the communion in that region. Therefore, one can only conclude that he recommends an ending on _a_ for all three chants because they had moved or been moved to the higher region sometime during their melodic unfolding.

Berno's second reason for using related endings is to preserve the intervallic character of a chant when it contains pitches not otherwise available in the medieval gamut:

> . . . a good number of melodies, if begun on their [proper] final -- or at some other tone above or below it -- do not come out well because of the lack of semitones; if, however, they are begun at the higher level, then they continue smoothly _without detriment to any pitch_ and close properly on the related final. (emphasis added)[45]

The underscored expression _absque ullius soni diminutione_ is paraphrased later as _absque neumarum dispendio_ or "without the loss of melodic segments." Clearly, Berno views the use of related notes as a means of avoiding emendation, just as the _Dialogus_ author had similarly viewed the whole-tone transposition of "Domine qui operati sunt." As previously observed, however, the _Dialogus_ author insisted on modal reclassification to account for the anomalous tone even as he sought to preserve it. For Berno, the basic modal identity is not disturbed by such tones, insofar as the normal tone-semitone movement associated with the final predominates. He, in fact, cites "Domine qui operati sunt" as a chant in the sixth mode transposed to the upper fifth to preserve its interval structure.

Berno does not offer a systematic discussion of _sociales_ and _compares_ to the extent of naming all related notes and defining the limits of the relationship. His aim, rather, is practical -- to provide a notational solution for problematic chants apparently known by his readers. In addition to a number of fourth-mode chants which will be discussed below, he also cites the communion "Beatus servus" in mode three and the communion "De fructu operum" in mode eight, each transposed to its respective _compar_ a fourth above (for modes three and four, from _E_ to _a_, for mode eight, from _G_ to _c_).[46] Finally, he mentions "Domine qui operati sunt" and "Alias oves habeo" as sixth-mode antiphons tranposed from _F_ to _c_.[47]

The emphasis on _a_ and _c_ in this second explanation of alternative finals is understandable. In the area of these two tones the gamut offers two forms of a pitch, _b-flat_ and _b-natural_; this theoretically acceptable double position can serve as a _musica recta_ location for chromatic tones found elsewhere in untransposed chant. Thus, the _E-flat_ of "Domine" becomes _b-flat_ when the chant is transposed up a fifth, while the normal *E-natural* becomes *b-natural*. Analogously, transposition up a fourth would legitimize *F-sharp* as *b-natural*. In this instance, however, the normal modal inflection of *F-natural* becomes *b-flat* with the result that *b-flat* is now integral to the mode. Significantly, Berno allows two inflections of a pitch in the course of a single chant. The *sociales* and *compares* are thus valued not only because they preserve a basic modal identity at another position (the *sociales* through *b-natural* and the *compares* through *b-flat*), but also because they offer the possibility of deviating from the modal norm while remaining legitimate in terms of the orthodox gamut. Berno's treatise represents the first time this concept is fully elucidated.

Berno devotes most of his discussion concerning the preservation of chromatic tones by means of transposition to fourth-mode antiphons, in particular, "Factus sum," "O mors ero," "Sion renovaberis est," "Sion noli timere," "Vade iam," "Ad te Domine levavi," and "Ex Egypto vocavi."[48] Throughout the Middle Ages, all of these antiphons are referred to in discussions of the problems of modal classification. They all belong to Gevaert's "theme 29," one of the most common melodic prototypes found in the antiphoners.[49] The characteristics of the prototype are shown in Example 2, as found in the antiphon "Rorate caeli".

Ex. 2. The antiphon "Rorate caeli" (*AM* 213).

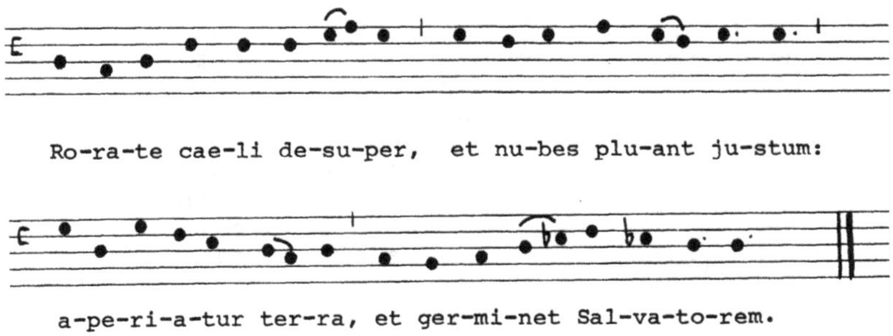
Ro-ra-te cae-li de-su-per, et nu-bes plu-ant ju-stum:
a-pe-ri-a-tur ter-ra, et ger-mi-net Sal-va-to-rem.

The fourth distinction reveals a clear *deuterus* pattern of movement around the final, and the total ambitus, consisting of an ascent of a fifth and descent of a third, suggests the plagal form of that *maneria*. Another feature, however, the resemblance of "Rorate's" beginning to that of chants in mode seven, caused classification problems for several theorists before Berno. Referring to chants within this prototype by name, Regino of Prüm in *De harmonica institutione* and pseudo-Hucbald in *De modis* stated that they begin in the seventh mode and end in the fourth mode.[50] This feature does not seem to have bothered Berno, as will become evident below.

Berno tells us instead that these chants contain a semitone not available in their regular gamut position. Based on his description, Berno had before him a version of the chants that resembles the model of "Rorate caeli" -- that is, with b-natural in the third distinction, and b-flat in the fourth distinction, F-sharp and F-natural, respectively, at the lower level. He advises his reader that both inflections can be preserved if the chants are transferred from E to a, and thus he indicates that he was not disturbed by the presence of the anomalous F-sharp in a *deuterus* chant.

With regard to two of these chants, "Ad te Domine levavi" and "Ex Egypto," Berno states:

> Certain people, less attentive to this, claim that these [antiphons] and similar ones are ruled by the seventh rather than the fourth mode, although they do not deny that the same ones close in the fourth.[51]

In this statement, he implies that some theorists did not consider his transposition to the upper fourth as a solution to the modal ambiguity of these chants, even though it offers a solution to the problem of notating them. Furthermore, his wording suggests that these theorists took note of the opening melodic figuration in identifying the mode, while he looks instead to the tone-semitone movement of the ending. An examination of the tonary that accompanies Regino's treatise reveals that he conforms to Berno's description; indeed, Regino classifies a number of problematic chants that begin in one mode and end in another according to their beginning melodic configuration.[52]

Berno's discussion of the fourth-mode antiphons clearly shows that his priority lay in preserving the melodic character of chants he had inherited, rather than in molding them to an *a posteriori* system of classification. For these chants and for the others he discusses, related notes provide a solution to the problem of notating pitches not found in the gamut (principally E-flat and F-sharp). With regard to Gevaert's theme 29 antiphons, however, the alternative notation fails to eliminate the modal ambiguity that had disturbed theorists for several centuries.

Micrologus and *Epistola* by Guido of Arrezo

The writings of Guido of Arezzo (b. c. 991, d. after 1033) provide the most comprehensive exposition of musical practice encountered up to his time. While these writings show Guido to have been a knowledgeable practitioner in both chant and polyphony, they also reveal a theorist who prescribed usages amenable to a well-defined system. This latter trait bears on his approach to the affinities. He cannot allow this concept to encompass as many relations of notes as did

Berno, for example, because, from his standpoint, the basic clarity of the modal system might be disturbed.

Guido's primary work, the *Micrologus*, dates from c. 1026-33.[53] For any discussion of the affinities, a second significant writing is the *Epistola Guidonis Michaeli Monacho de Ignoto Cantu*.[54]

Chapter Seven of the *Micrologus*, entitled "De affinitate vocum per quattuor modos" or "Concerning the Affinity of Pitches through the Four Modes [i.e., *Maneriae*],"[55] reveals that Guido uses the term *affinitas* for the relationship designated *socialitas* by Hucbald. Throughout his discussion, Guido does not directly quote or paraphrase any earlier writer, but certain aspects of his theory hark back to ideas expressed by the *Enchiriadis* author. When Guido begins discussing related pitches, he tells us that each pair shares a *modus vocum*, a "modal quality or pattern":

> The first *modus vocum* arises when a pitch descends by a tone and ascends by a tone, a semitone, and two tones, as do *A* and *D*. The second *modus* arises when a pitch descends by two tones and ascends by a semitone and two tones, as do *B* and *E*. The third is that which descends by a semitone and two tones but ascends by two tones, as do *C* and *F*. The fourth goes down by a tone but rises by two tones and a semitone, as does *G*.[56]

His labeling each tone in the gamut with a modal indicator seems to follow the *Enchiriadis* practice (see p. 9 above).[57] Another suggestive piece of evidence for Guido's familiarity with the treatise is found in the *Epistola*: Guido describes the change of mode that results when one begins a melody on different pitches, and his example, "Tu patris sempiternus," is the same one used by the *Enchiriadis* author in his related discussion.[58]

In any case, Guido enumerates the lower related tones, *A*, *B*, and *C*, in the passage quoted, but he remarks immediately thereafter that *affinitas* exists not only at the fourth below, but also at the fifth above.[59] In subsequent passages, he emphasizes the relationship at the fifth because of a practical consideration: the pitches located at the fifth above the normal finals offer an alternative modal site, for which Guido finds a use peculiar to his theory. His interest in *affinitas* is also grounded in a broader intent of providing an interpretation of the tonal system's makeup. Hucbald carried out the first step in the latter task by showing how the gamut embodied mode: it was divisible according to the tetrachord of the finals. Guido extended this finding, although he never analyzed the gamut in terms of tetrachords. Rather, he recognized the affinity of a final and the pitches a fifth above and fourth below, in that all are surrounded by identical tone-semitone movement within the range of a sixth. Thus, he called attention to identical segments within the gamut - *C* to *a*, *Γ* to *e* and *G* to *e*. What is striking about Guido's discussion is that he applies to these identical segments a modal significance. Each mode, excluding *tetrardus*, can be identified by the interval pattern surrounding its final or *affinalis* within the range of a sixth - the *modus vocum* (Figure 2). This definition of mode does not agree with that of his predecessors or contemporaries. In fact, any *maneria* can be distinguished from another by two ascents and one descent (*protus* T-S ascent, T descent; *deuterus* S-T ascent, T descent; *tritus* T-T ascent, S descent; *tetrardus* T-T ascent, T descent). Guido's linking of modal identity to a sixth is an artifice created to reflect a feature of the diatonic tonal system -- the affinity of certain six-note segments.

Fig. 2. The *Modi vocum* according to Guido of Arezzo.

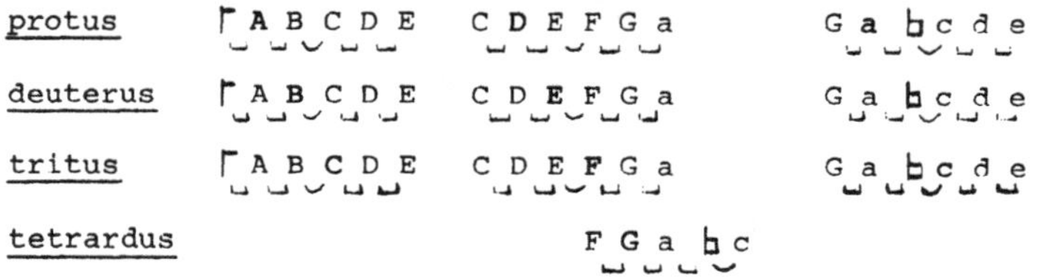
protus
Γ A B C D E
C D E F G a
G a ♮ c d e
deuterus
Γ A B C D E
C D E F G a
G a ♮ c d e
tritus
Γ A B C D E
C D E F G a
G a ♮ c d e
tetrardus
F G a ♮ c

Let us now consider Guido's peculiar use of these modal segments -- he prized them as a notational device for erasing *b-flats* from a given chant! A passage from Chapter Eight of the *Micrologus* is enlightening on this point:

> We use *b-flat* mostly in that song in which *F* or *f* recurs rather extensively, either low or high. Here *b-flat* seems to create a certain confusion and transformation, so that *G* sounds as *protus*, *a* as *deuterus*, whereas *b-flat* itself sounds as *tritus*. As a result, many make no mention of it, but the second ♮ has been acceptable in general. But if you wish not to have *b-flat* at all, alter the melodic segments in which it occurs, so that instead of *F G a* and *b-flat* you have *G a ♮ c*. *If it is the kind of melodic segment that, going up after D E F, wants two tones and a semitone--which causes b-flat--or going down after D E F, wants two whole tones, then instead of D E F use a ♮ c, which are of the same mode and regularly have the previously mentioned descents and ascents*. One removes the especially unfavorable confusion by clearly distributing ascents and descents of this type between *D E F* and *a ♮ c*. (emphasis added) [60]

In the *Epistola*, he elaborates his concern over the "transformation" caused by *b-flat* in discussing the use of either *b-flat* or *b-natural* after *a*:

> . . . namely, the first [*a*], if followed by a semitone, changes from *protus* to *deuterus*. If, however, it should be permissible for one pitch to belong to two or more modes, this art will appear to be marked off by no limit, confined by no definite boundaries.[61]

In rejecting all *b-flats*, not just the theoretically non-existent low *B-flat*, Guido obviously strove for a purely diatonic system, in which every pitch had a single modal identity: *D protus*, *E deuterus*, *F tritus*, *G tetrardus*, *a protus*, *♮ deuterus*, and *c tritus*. Thus, his reason for omitting *d* as a related note to *G* becomes evident, since *d* already has a *protus* identity. In the quotation from the *Micrologus*, he offers two solutions for avoiding *b-flats*. The first solution (not underscored) is to transpose the offending phrase containing *b-flat* a whole tone higher. This quoted passage is the first clear statement prescribing, or perhaps describing, partial transpositions in chant, that is, shifting of only parts of a chant to a different tonal level. The second solution (underscored) relies upon the related modal segment a fifth higher. Inflections involving low *B-flat* and small *b-flat* can be notated diatonically at the upper position:

B^b C D E F G a b = F G a ♮ c d e f

Berno had valued alternative modal positions for allowing some variety of melodic movement within the modal nucleus, hence the integral role of both *b-flat* and *b-natural*. Guido, however, apparently values the second site for allowing a flexibility outside the nucleus. A *protus* melody might, in sound, have a tone inflection above the nucleus C D E F G a ♮ or a semitone C D E F G a b. Under these particular circumstances, Guido harbors an aversion only to the notation of *b-flat*, not to its aural effects. On the other hand, he cautions that *b-flat* makes *G* sound *protus* (instead of *tetrardus*) and *a* sound *deuterus* (instead of *protus*), presumably when either of these pitches is serving as final. As remarked earlier, he seems to have demanded that each pitch have a single modal association, defined by its surrounding diatonic movement. The pitch *a*, located in the six-note diatonic segment *G* to *e*, possesses a *protus* character. Joining *b-flat* to it within the modal nucleus transforms it, undesirably, according to Guido, to *deuterus*.

But the use of *a* with *b-flat* was exactly the solution Berno offered for notating the *deuterus* chant "Beatus servus" -- he transposed it from *E* to *a*. There seems little doubt that Guido was unwilling to accept such a transposition to the fourth above. His statements on the transformation caused by b-flat are proof enough, but he also places the interval relationship a fourth above a final at the last position within his hierarchical scheme. That scheme places the octave relationship in a ruling position because only there is the "likeness" of melodic movement between two pitches complete.[62] The affinity relationship of a final and the pitch a fifth above (fourth below) comes next, discussed in full in the *Micrologus*, Chapter Seven. In Chapter Eight, Guido presents "other affinities" at the fourth above (fifth below), which share melodic movement in only one direction. In the case of *E* and *a*, it is a common descent by tone, tone, semitone; Guido does not extend their similarity by allowing b-flat in the ascent from *a*, and without the integral use of b-flat, a transposition to the fourth above would not be viable.

On the other hand, Guido might have sanctioned transposition to the fifth above to preserve the E-flat inflection of "Domine qui operati sunt." Although a disruptive b-flat would appear, the predominant b-natural would allow *c* to retain its *tritus* character within the diatonic set *G* to *e*. Is this an instance of what Guido calls "necessity"? In Chapter Ten, the following oblique reference appears:

> The place or mode where any melodic segment begins should be left to the experience of the singer, so that if it needs to be transposed (*si motione opus est*), he may search out related (*affines*) pitches. (emphasis added)[63]

In Chapter Thirteen he adds: "Moreover the plagals of the *protus*, *deuterus*, and *tritus* sometimes end by necessity on *a*, ♮, and *c* *acutae* respectively."[64]

The *Micrologus* and the *Epistola* are witnesses to the continuing theoretical interest, begun with Hucbald, in finding pitch relationships within the gamut. Although Guido discards the tetrachord divisions of his predecessors, he implicitly accepts the principle behind such a division: that the interval arrangement of the four finals can be found elsewhere in the gamut. He is unwilling, however, to accept an alternative position that would utilize b-flat, since his overriding concern is for the preservation of a strictly diatonic system in practice. Thus, in comparison to Berno, for whom the *compares* with their integral b-flat were a useful construct, Guido reveals himself to be a conservative thinker. He goes so far as to employ the affinities as a means of erasing b-flats that occur within the normal pitch location of a chant.

II. The Eleventh- and Twelfth-Century Commentators: Transposition and Transformation

The far-reaching impact of Guido's writings is reflected in the numerous commentaries on them from the second half of the eleventh century. Several anonymous writers seek to explain how Guido intended the affinities to be used, and perhaps more important, what he meant by the transforming effects of b-flat. The latter concern leads to controversy over the acceptability in theory and in practice of related notes that are not the diatonically conceived affinities of Guido.

In the eleventh century there flourished another group of writers who followed the German monastic tradition of discussing the gamut and modes in terms of species. Interestingly, in the matter of the affinities, these writers present a concept very close to Guido's even though they express it in their distinctive terminology. Each of the writers in fact acknowledges more or less directly his familiarity with Guido's theory. Because all the eleventh-century writings considered act at least in part as commentaries on Guido's concept of the affinities, I will present them within my chronological survey, rather than according to school of thought.

This chapter also treats a group of writings connected with the twelfth-century Cistercian chant reform. In the matter of the affinities, the Cistercians were among the most literal adherents of Guido's ideas, both in theory and in practice.

Liber argumentorum and Liber specierum[1]

Liber argumentorum is a brief exposition devoted primarily to definitions of consonances. Although it does not specifically treat the subject of modes and the affinities, it comments on Guido's passage about the confusion caused by b-flat:

> Likewise, Guido says that *b-flat* seems to create confusion and transformation, so that *G* sounds as *protus*, *a* as *deuterus*, whereas *b-flat* itself sounds as *tritus*, and *c* indeed, as reason shows, [sounds as] *tetrardus*. As a result, you hear from many ignorant people no mention of it. But as it seems that it ought not to be rejected by the ignorant, it ought to be accepted all the more by the learned.[2]

In stating that *b-flat* should be accepted in the formation of modes, this author seems to ignore Guido's insistence upon the single modal identity of each tone in the gamut. Instead, he explains that the objection of some persons to the lack of a consonant fourth above and of a fifth below *b-flat* can be met with an equally valid objection that *b-natural* lacks a consonant fifth above and fourth below. Although the *Liber argumentorum* does not mention the affinities *per se*, it would appear that Guido's use of the affinities to avoid *b-flat* was not adopted by all his readers.

Liber specierum is a more extensive treatise, which devotes a great deal of discussion to species of intervals, both in a general sense and as they relate to the modes. As such, *Liber specierum* sets out ideas similar to those of Berno, and as will be explained shortly, of Hermannus Contractus and Wilhelm of Hirsau. In addition, its author was familiar with Guido's *Micrologus*.

Near the beginning of its discussion of modes, the treatise includes a passage entitled "De finalibus vocibus" or "Concerning final pitches":

> On account of the ascents of authentic [modes] and the descents of plagal [modes], the final pitches of [authentic] modes and their plagals are fixed on *D*, *E*, *F*, and *G*. But sometimes plagal *protus* or *tritus*, *deuterus* or *tetrardus*, are ended in the *acutae* out of necessity.[3]

The author has combined ideas expressed in two chapters of the *Micrologus*. In Chapter Eleven, Guido stated that *D*, *E*, *F*, and *G* have been established as final pitches because their location on the monochord best corresponds to the ascents and descents most common to chant melodies. In Chapter Thirteen, Guido reported that "by necessity," plagal modes sometimes end on *a*, *♮*, and *c*. Like Guido, this author locates his alternative finals in the upper position, as expressed by his term *acutae*,[4] but unlike Guido, he includes one for *tetrardus*. It may be that he adds this related final for *tetrardus* to complete a theoretical symmetry, even though he uses Guido's descriptive words "sometimes end."

Musica by Hermannus Contractus

Hermannus Contractus' *Musica*, probably written between 1048 and 1054,[5] reveals its author's alignment with German monastic theorists who analyzed the gamut and modes according to species of fourths, fifths, and octaves. Like Berno, Hermannus bases his theoretical system on the tetrachord with interval arrangement tone-semitone-tone, and names the four diatonic tetrachords as follows:[6]

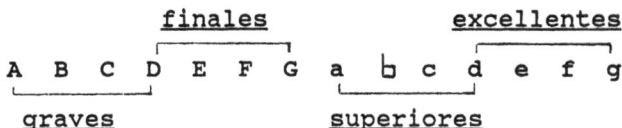

			finales							*excellentes*			
A	B	C	D	E	F	G	a	♮	c	d	e	f	g
graves							*superiores*						

Very early in his exposition of species of fourths, Hermannus relates the *graves* and *finales* tetrachords:

> . . . let us denote the pitches of the two tetrachords, namely those of the four modes in their two positions, by their appropriate letters in due order . . .

And immediately after:

> For while no one of the aforementioned pitches concords with another, although at the fourth place the same arrangement and therefore the same mode occurs; . . .[7]

Like Guido, Hermannus states that there are four basic *maneriae*, but whereas Guido located only three of them at two different positions in the gamut, Hermannus recognizes alternative positions for all four. Guido had emphasized octave identity within part of the gamut by stating that the related pitches a fourth below the finals, *A*, *B*, and *C*, had counterparts a fifth above the finals, on *a*, *♮*, and *c*. Hermannus, on the other hand, examines the entire gamut. He states that the two lower pitches related modally have octave duplicates in the two upper tetrachords of his system, and hence each *maneria* has four principal pitches. For *protus*, they are *A d a d*, namely, the first member in each of the four tetrachords. Similarly, *deuterus* takes the second member in each tetrachord: *B E ♮ e*; *tritus* the third member: *C F c f*; and *tetrardus*, the fourth member: *D G d g*. Hermannus further explains how the four given pitches form the constituent species of fourth, fifth, and octave, as well as their functional aspects as boundary tones, finals, and reciting tones, for that particular *maneria*.[8] Hermannus thus carries to its logical conclusion the concept first recognized by

Hucbald and the *Enchiriadis* author: that mode can be embodied in the gamut through successive division by the tetrachord tone-semitone-tone.

This particular passage is preparatory to the later discussion of the affinities that most concerns us here.[9] Nowhere, incidentally, does Hermannus use a word such as Guido's *affinitas* to describe the modal relationship of tones nor Berno's *sociales/compares* to describe the tones themselves. For him, related tones are the principal pitches of the *maneria*. He does, however, use the term *sedes troporum* or "seats of the modes" in reference to the related tones and their respective surrounding interval sets.

Hermannus states that a characteristic pattern of whole and half steps identifies each of the four *maneriae*, and like Guido, he calls that pattern a *modus vocum*.[10] When Hermannus outlines the basic melodic movement, one sees the limiting range of a sixth for all four *maneriae*, not just three, as in the *Micrologus*. Thus, *tetrardus* rises a tone and falls a fourth species fifth (i.e., descending tone-semitone-tone-tone = C␣D␣E‿F␣G␣a).

Hans Oesch finds no direct evidence that Hermannus knew Guido's work and therefore concludes that Hermannus came to this understanding of *modi vocum* independently.[11] Not only is the exact terminology *modus vocum* striking, however, but the opening sentence of Hermannus' discussion also casts doubt on Oesch's supposition:

> To begin with, let us look at one rule for recognizing the modes which has hitherto been dug out as a rough mass, so to speak, by previous writers, but not fully worked clear of dross . . .[12]

Later, referring to errors by these persons, Hermannus says:

> . . . they fixed the fourth mode finally on *G* alone, making it fall a tone and rise two tones and a semitone.[13]

This is exactly the formula for *tetrardus* offered by Guido. Thus, while it cannot be stated definitively that Hermannus took the idea of *modi vocum* from Guido, he does seem to have known it in the form presented by Guido.[14] Perhaps Handschin's remark on this matter is most appropriate: he states that since both Guido in Italy and Hermannus in Switzerland express the idea, we have an indication that it was indeed "in der Luft."[15]

In Hermannus' exposition, he explains how he arrived at the limiting sixth:

> Take any tetrachord you wish--say, that of the *graves*; add a tone at both ends; you then have the limits of the tonal patterns which form the basis of the modes.[16]

Hermannus had recognized that the corresponding interval structure found in every tetrachord is extended one step beyond the tetrachord in both directions. Accordingly, tones similarly positioned within their respective tetrachords are in affinity with one another within the range of a sixth. While Guido had linked A D and a by reference to interval relationships a fifth above and a fourth below the final, Hermannus simply called on tetrachord terminology -- A D a and d, the first members of their respective tetrachords, are related tones. Although their manner of expression differed, both Guido and Hermannus achieved the same goal, a further understanding of how the gamut is constructed. But like Guido, Hermannus went on to attach modal, and hence, practical significance to the six-note segments:

> The first tonal pattern (modus vocum) . . . is recognized in the Antiphon "Prophetae praedicaverunt," in the "In tuo adventu," and in similar ones which do not exceed six pitches in range. This pattern is recognizable on the principal pitches of protus, A, D, a, d.[17]

Thus, the protus modus vocum is found at multiple positions within the diatonic gamut (each a sedes troporum, according to Hermannus), and by extension, any protus melody of limited range can be placed at any of the four sedes. Hermannus goes on to name a deuterus chant "Gloria haec est" that shows the appropriate modus vocum; similarly, for tritus, "Modicum et non videbitis"; and for tetrardus, "Si vere fratres" and "Multi veniunt." Of all these chants, only one, "Modicum et non videbitis," appears in the available sources at different positions, namely, at F and at c.[18]

This latter discovery raises a question: did Hermannus actually condone the transposition of a chant to any of the four principal pitches he cited? His discussion of species of fourth earlier in the treatise hints at an answer:

> You may easily sing these species even on one pitch if you begin them with the customary melody of the saeculorum amen and conclude them with the appropriate endings. These endings may be sung fully and completely in the finales and the superiores; nevertheless the final neumes in any tetrachord are not discordant with their own mode.[19]

Hermannus gives preference to the finales D E F G and superiores a ♮ c d as "seats" of the modes, and thus agrees with the expositions on affinities we have encountered up to this time. Hermannus' reference to "endings" that can be sung in either position suggests he is allowing the transposition of psalm tones with their differentiae.

Apparently, Hermannus did not recognize an affinity of pitches at the fourth above the finals. With the tones of the *finales* tetrachord as starting points, he describes "formal" species of fourths which, he says, do not connect two tones of the same mode:

> . . . there will be the first form, *D*-*G*, but by false reasoning, for although *D* may, on account of its common function, be first, yet *G*, seventh in number and fourth in mode, can never be first. The second form beginning from *E* which is of *deuterus* ends on *a* which is of *protus*. The third, if nature be regarded, does not exist. The fourth, beginning on *G* which is of *tetrardus*, finishes on *c* which is of *tritus*.[20]

It seems that he did not follow Berno's instructions on *compares*. He does acknowledge in theory *synemmenon* formulations, however. He describes *F G a b-flat* and *G a b-flat c* as formal species of fourth created through the "irregular" *synemmenon*.[21]

A final characteristic of Hermannus' exposition on related tones is his failure to mention reasons for their use. The general context of his remarks suggests an explanation, for he is trying throughout the treatise to present the essentials of modal recognition, always eschewing too much detail. He devotes only enough space to the *modi vocum* to "work clear of dross" what other writers had said on the matter.

Musica by Wilhelm of Hirsau

Wilhelm of Hirsau's treatise *Musica* is closely aligned with that of Hermannus in dating and contents;[22] in fact, certain passages in *Musica* repeat Hermannus' text almost word-for-word. Wilhelm is no mere follower, however, and *Musica* reveals his tendency to reach his own conclusions after he presents selected arguments from other writers.

For the discussion of affinities, Wilhelm presents material according to Guido and Hermannus. His exposition of Guido's viewpoint begins during his defense of *D* and *d* as "*biformes*," serving both *protus* and *tetrardus*.[23] From this vantage point, he critiques Guido's chart from the *Aliae regulae* (see page 157 of this study) where, he says, *D* and *d* should receive the following modal designations:

	Wilhelm						Guido	
VII		I	VII		I		I	I
	D			d		vs	D	d
VIII		II	VIII		II		II	II

Wilhelm then paraphrases the seventh chapter of Guido's *Micrologus* on *modi vocum*, which includes the anomalous movement of *tetrardus* on *G* outside the range of the sixth. To Guido's exposition, Wilhelm adds a definition for modi vocum:

> Modi vocum are certain properties or characteristics of species of melody, that is, of modes.[24]

Beginning with Chapter Twenty-Seven, Wilhelm presents the reader with an explanation of modal similarities in the gamut according to Hermannus. Thus, Wilhelm states that a maneria ascends and descends equally from all its "principal pitches" within the range of a sixth, a premise that includes tetrardus on D G d g. This leads to a paraphrase of Hermannus' passage on modi vocum, which he later quotes almost word-for-word in Chapter Thirty-Eight, entitled "De modis vocum."

Wilhelm's Chapter Twenty-Eight presents an elaboration of a concept only mentioned by Hermannus, that of sedes troporum, the locations at which the modi vocum can be found. Like Hermannus, Wilhelm states that the sedes are created by adding a tone to both ends of a tetrachord. What is striking in this context is Wilhelm's listing of five tetrachords: the graves, finales, superiores, excellentes, plus the synemmenon G a b-flat c. The last is extended to the sedes F G a b-flat c d by adding a tone at either end -- the first evidence of what later became known as the F (soft) hexachord.

It seems doubtful, in fact improbable, that Wilhelm intended anything more than a hypothetical recognition of the F to d pitch set. In Chapter Thirty-Eight, he relates chant examples only to the principal pitches of the maneria, that is, to tones similarly placed in the four main tetrachords. Furthermore, he recognizes only four "legitimate" positions within his discussion of the sedes:

> The sedes or metae of the eight modes are recognized to be legitimate, however, only in four positions, that is, on C, on G, on a, and on c. Let us see, therefore, how many metae or intervals of metae can be made in the monochord, and why in the mentioned positions they are said to be legitimate more so than in others, as it was stated above.[25]

After examining each of the four main positions, he discusses the fifth, F to d:

> The fifth position placed in the middle is not accepted at all because of the less regular synemmenon.[26]

This statement provides proof that he did not consider tones a fourth above the finals with their attendant use of b-flat possible degrees on which to transfer the modi vocum.

In Chapter Thirty-Eight, "De modis vocum," Wilhelm presents Hermannus' passage on modi vocum, which he modifies slightly by adding authentic/plagal designations to the chant examples. Citing only the first of Hermannus' two protus antiphons, "Prophetae praedicaverunt," Wilhelm labels it authentic, but adds, "[The first] modus [vocum] is applied to protus without distinction."[27] The words "without distinction" suggest that the pattern of descent by one tone and ascent of a fifth could suit either authentic or plagal forms. Significantly, a number of medieval theorists refer to chants whose ambitus spans only the common fifth as difficult to classify. Furthermore, the manuscript sources reveal discrepancies in their modal attributions for such chants: the Lucca antiphoner classifies "Prophetae" as mode two, while a number of other sources classify it as mode one.[28]

Wilhelm calls the deuterus chant "Gloria haec est" plagal.[29] Hermannus had followed his analogous citation with "and similar ones, either authentic or subsidiary." When one considers the ascent of only a fourth within the deuterus modus vocum, Hermannus' addition of authentic chants is puzzling, since most definitions of authentic ambitus demand an ascent of at least a fifth above the final. Following the tritus chant example, "Modicum et non videbitis," which he calls plagal,[30] Wilhelm says of the tetrardus modus vocum:

> This modus [vocum] proves special among the others, because it can be recognized not only in the authentic antiphon "Si vere fratres," but also in this plagal antiphon "Multi veniunt."[31]

Inclusion of the authentic "Si vere fratres" by both Hermannus and Wilhelm is disturbing. The sources currently available present it with a range of G to e, which, as a sedes for the tetrardus modus vocum, should contain a final on d, yet in the sources it is on G.[32] It seems likely that these theorists include the chant since it has a range of a sixth, and they could not find many plagal chants such as "Multi veniunt" that contain the tetrardus modus vocum of ascent by tone and descent by a fifth from the final.[33]

Guido had stated that protus, deuterus, and tritus plagals sometimes end on a, ♮, and c. Wilhelm's statements in Chapter Thirty-Eight confirm Guido's basic premise, although his treatment of tetrardus examples remains puzzling.

In conclusion, Wilhelm, following the lead of Hermannus, proceeds with a speculative approach that examines all possibilities for modal formulations within the gamut. In doing so, he recognizes in theory the structural unit later known as the soft hexachord. Diatonic thinkers such as Wilhelm, and by implication, Hermannus and Guido before him, seem as yet unwilling to accept this construct in practice.

De musica by Aribo

Aribo's De musica has been dated between 1068 and 1078 and linked with Freising.[34] Like Hermannus and Wilhelm, Aribo presents a modal concept that emphasizes the species of fourth and fifth used within the characteristic octave of each mode. It is clear that Aribo also knew Guido's writings, since he includes a chapter "Utilis expositio super obscuras Guidonis sententias," a commentary on Chapters Fifteen and Seventeen of the Micrologus; he also refers to a passage in the Aliae regulae.[35]

Aribo does not devote a detailed discussion to the concept of the affinities, but he apparently understands it as a theoretical precept of his system. Like Hermannus and Wilhelm, he refers to the principales of each maneria:

> They are also called principal notes, because they are a foundation of the same pattern. I call pattern the likeness (similitudo) of ascent or descent or of both.[36]

The word similitudo or "likeness" was also used by the Dialogus author in describing ascents and descents from related tones in his gamut. Although initially Aribo reckons likenesses from the principales, he next discusses similarity of ascent or descent in the more general terms of relationship by fourth or fifth:

> . . . because such is the agreement not only at the fourth [positions], but also at the fifth [positions] above and below, so that it ascends to the middle of one and takes up the descent of another. If it is compared to the fourth above in elevation, it corresponds to the fifth above in descent; and on the contrary, with the fourth below in descent, it agrees with the fifth [below] in ascent, except deuterus of the graves and superiores . . .[37]

In this somewhat obscure statement, Aribo reveals that he understands the limitations imposed on melodic movement by the principle of related sounds, as presented according to Hermannus.[38] He attempts to find additional points of correspondence that will supply the ascending or descending movement that may be limited by the sixth framing each of the principales. We recall that Guido, too, spelled out the "other affinities" at the fourth and fifth after he had outlined his principal modal pairs (Micrologus, Chapter 8). Like Guido, Aribo apparently is making a theoretical observation on these additional relations.

Following the discussion of principal notes, Aribo turns to an exposition of authentic/plagal distinctions, which he represents through the vehicle of interlocking circles, as illustrated in Figure 3.[39] The circles show the five notes common to authentic and plagal as well as the notes particular to each. The four principales are designated with P. Furthermore, in some of the manuscript sources, one finds above the notes of the combined protus authentic/plagal spectrum, "The associated finals (sociales finales) are lower A through the diatessaron and higher A through the diapente," and similarly for the other three maneriae. The use of the word socialis is striking since it is not employed by either Hermannus or Guido, who seem to be the principal sources of Aribo's ideas.

Fig. 3. Representation of Protus from Aribo's De musica.

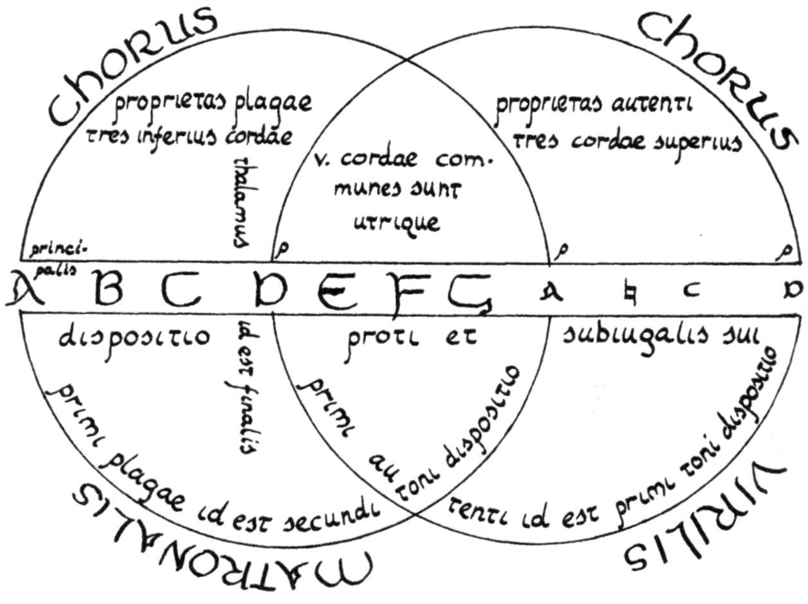

Taken as a whole, Aribo's treatise provides only a skeletal view of related sounds -- somewhat less than Hermannus and Wilhelm, who gave chant examples, and much less than Guido, who suggested functions served by such sounds.

Commentarius Anonymus in Micrologum Guidonis Aretini

Smits van Waesberghe has suggested that this anonymous commentary on Guido's Micrologus dates from approximately the same time as Aribo's Musica, because there is evidence that its author may have been engaged in a dispute with Aribo over the interpretation of Guido's Chapter Fifteen.[40] As to its place of origin, Smits van Waesberghe argues that it most likely came from Liège, but he allows that it might have been written in Bavaria.[41] In either case, the author had access to Aribo's work, and he incorporates German thinking on species into his modal discussion. In the main, however, his explanations resemble Guido's because of their emphasis on consonant agreement between tones in the diatonic gamut.

This anonymous treatise adds some details to the concept of the affinities as presented by Guido, showing how the concept had developed with regard to terminology and, to a degree, application, by the end of the century. After setting out the *modi vocum* according to Guido, the author adds a comment on how these patterns should be used:

> It ought to be known that these properties of descent or ascent, through which one distinguishes first from the second and other modes from one another, should be observed in songs *especially at the end of phrases or at the end of the songs themselves, so that it ascends or descends to the modal finals according to its natural properties* . . . (emphasis added)[42]

Whereas previous writers had made a general statement that the *modi vocum* aid in modal recognition, this author distinctly emphasizes their role at the end of phrases and of the chant proper. Since he makes this statement after describing the two principal locations where the *modus vocum* occurs -- the final and its affinity -- we witness the first clearcut reference to the connection between related tones with their modal patterns and their function as final notes.[43]

Accordingly, this author uses the substantive *affinalis*, emphasizing the related tone as a final. He also uses the form *affinitas*, as did Guido, but imparts to it a terminological fixity by repeatedly juxtaposing the expression *per affinitatem* with *per naturam*. Thus, " . . . these two pitches, *A* and *D*, belong to the first *modus [vocum]*, *D* through nature, *A* through affinity."[44] In addition, he employs the adjectival form *affinis* meaning "related," and at times, this assumes a substantive usage as "related [one]." Finally, in a few isolated instances, he refers to the related tone as the *socialis*.[45]

The anonymous commentator turns his attention to Guido's statement that the affinities are produced by the diatessaron and diapente. In keeping with this, he spells out the other affinities to show how tones related by a fourth above (or fifth below) can share similar ascent or descent, but not both. Like Guido, he touches upon the relationship between *F* and *b-flat*, from which he turns to a discussion of the confusion and transformation caused by *b-flat*. The author supplies a chant example:

> Just as in the antiphon "Urbs fortitudinis nostrae Sion," it [*b-flat*] causes the first phrase to be of the *protus* [mode], although it is still of the *tetrardus* [mode]; . . .[46]

According to available sources, "Urbs fortitudinis" uses *b-flat* of the *acutae*, but in the following remarks, the author implies that, in general, *b-flat* should be avoided: *B-flat* of the *graves*, since it is not found in the gamut, and *b-flat* of the *acutae*, since it is not in the "regular" (diatonic) arrangement after *D E F G a*. Following Guido, he affirms that the affinties allow one to retain the intervals created by *b-flats* in some cases. In his examples, he recommends transposition to the affinities to preserve *b-flat acuta* in mode six and *B-flat gravis* in mode two.[47] One notes that these *b-flats* fall outside of the respective *modus vocum*, and thus the modal identity is retained. When *b-flat* occurs in connection with *G*, however, it falls within the *tetrardus modus vocum* (F G a ♮ c) and transforms the mode. Although the author expresses disapproval of this in reference to "Urbs fortitudinis," he does not recommend any particular solution.

Finally, the author states that in chants containing both *b-natural* and *b-flat*, the affinity relationship cannot be used to avoid *b-flat*, since there is no other location in the gamut where a degree can be so inflected.[48] This is a qualification not mentioned by Guido.

The next comment on the use of the affinities is cited in full, since it seems to be a unique reference of this particular treatise:

> It ought to be known that the affinity of pitches as set forth is especially useful in instrumental music consisting of eight or seven pitches, as we find in bells or organs. Since truly there are not so many variations of pitches ascending or descending in turn, so that we cannot descend or ascend into the *acutae* after these eight pitches, since they are not there as order required, let us proceed likewise through their related sounds in the *graves*. For example, if in bells we ought to ascend through a diapente from final *G*, we will have the same species of diapente on its *affinalis C*. Therefore, in place of *G* let us use *C* and we will have the same song not inharmoniously. We will not find a song with *b-flat*, unless *b-flat* is in the same position, as it is placed by certain persons recently.[49]

The author's wording leaves it unclear whether he is describing or prescribing transposition to account for the limited range of bells.[50] In his monograph on bells, Smits van Waesberghe notes at least two manuscript references to transposition of single tones an octave higher or lower. The idea of transposing a melody down a fifth expounded by the anonymous commentator does not appear elsewhere, however, and we are further left to wonder whether he means that the entire melody or only the part ascending beyond the bells' range should be transposed.

What is striking in this passage is the direction to use *C* as affinity to *G*. Like Guido, this author had earlier stated that *G* and *C* share a partial affinity through ascent, but the context was a theoretical presentation of all affinities created through diatessaron and diapente relationships. This passage on bells is proof that at least one theorist who followed Guido's teaching rather closely accepted in practice an affinity other than at the fifth above (or fourth below). It should be noted, however, that in the context of bells, the author again only mentions the identity of the diapentes above *G* and *C*, both of which are strictly diatonic. The question then arises, would this author utilize a related position to the extent that *b-flat* appeared within the *modus vocum* at the transposed level? As was the case for Guido, we assume that he would not accept the *compares* where *b-flat* is integral; however, he does allude to a use of the proper affinities that might entail the appearance of a non-characteristic *b-flat* to account for a chromatic tone at the untransposed level. The context is a gloss of Guido's statement on transposition "by necessity":

> . . . they end by necessity on *a*, *♮*, and *c*, when they ascend to that place by a similar transposition, namely, either transposed in their entirety from the legitimate final to the affinity, as "Haec dies quam fecit Dominus" is transposed in its entirety from *D* to *a*, so that it is sung completely on *a*, or by transposition in part, as when a song, which ought to end on its legitimate final and has remained about it for awhile, transfers itself to the affinity in a playful manner and ends there, as in "Alleluia. Judicabunt." It ought to be noted that a free plagal, and not an authentic, allows transposition through the fifth above its proper final.[51]

In the first part of this statement, the author refers to the same gradual he cited earlier when discussing transposition to avoid low *B-flat*, "Haec dies." As mentioned in footnote 47, a number of extant versions of the transposed chant contain both *b-flat* and *b-natural acutae*, standing for *E-flat* and *E-natural* at the untransposed level. Although the anonymous author makes no mention of this particular inflection, we might conjecture that for him "necessity" includes the avoidance in notation of E-flat as well as of B-flat. Further support for this speculation is found in his gloss of another passage on "necessity" from the *Micrologus*:

> The place or mode where any melodic segment begins should be left to the experience of the singer, so that if it needs to be transposed (*si motione opus est*), he may search out related (*affines*) pitches.[52]

The commentator precedes it with:

> And because either through the fault of careless people or through the impropriety of *distorted pitches* a song is transformed, therefore, the singer opposing those faults should be skillful . . .[53]

And follows it with:

> I have said that there are four modes in which transformation and dissonance can arise by means of *irregularity of pitches* . . .[54]

Although it is not clear whether "distorted pitches" and "irregularity of pitches" are inherent to the chants or are the mistakes of singers, it would appear that the author recommends transposition to avoid them.

Let us return to the second part of the passage quoted on p. 35 where the author refers to partial transposition in connection with the "Alleluia. Judicabunt sancti." Earlier he had mentioned it as ending on its *affinalis* *a* instead of final *D*.[55] Karlheinz Schlager has identified a number of sources in which the verse "Judicabunt" does end on *a*. He attributes the ending in the higher region to the presence of a long melisma around *a* on the syllable "-gna-" of "regnabit"; the remaining words "illorum rex in eternum" are kept at the same tonal level. Significantly, those words move within the *protus* *modus vocum*, and thus can be sung at either the final or *affinalis* position. Schlager calls attention to two sources, Rome, Biblioteca Vallicelliana C 52 and London, Harleian 4951, in which the second half of the melisma is set a fifth lower, and the end of the verse therefore comes to rest on *D*.[56] The *Graduale Sariburiense* (199) presents a third version in which all of the melisma plus "illorum rex" moves around *a*, with "in eternum" shifting to the *D* level. The anonymous commentator knew a version ending on *a* and held the opinion that the concluding neumes had been transposed, hence, his designation "partial transposition." To judge by his tone, he apparently did not wholeheartedly approve of the practice, in spite of his including this use of the affinities under Guido's designation "by necessity."[57] A final point of interest in this passage is the reiteration of Guido's comment that plagal chants use transposition.

In conclusion, the anonymous commentary clarifies and supports Guido's thinking on the affinities, even as it provides glimpses of what others were doing in practices that the author declined to condone. Perhaps the most significant feature is its revelation of a tradition continuing from Guido, whereby transposition of chant material occurred for the apparent purpose of avoiding b-flat acuta, and thus preserving a strictly diatonic framework.

The Leipzig Treatise

Heinrich Sowa has considered the anonymous treatise found in Leipzig, Univ. Bibl. Codex 1492, to be of German origin, c. 1075.[58] The near word-for-word agreement between certain of its passages and those of the previously discussed anonymous commentary is striking, and suggests that both anonymi might have drawn upon the same source.[59] This author's distinctive contribution to the present issue lies in his attempt to reconcile some practice with the Guidonian concepts of transposition and transformation.

After he discusses formal as opposed to natural species of fourths, the author begins an exposition on the affinities. Interestingly, he does not spell out the modi vocum, but simply gives the related tones for each mode: "Primus modus sunt A et D, sed D per naturam, A per affinitatem."[60] Whereas the anonymous commentator from Liège first broached the use of affinities in his discussion of b-flat, the Leipzig author gives a broader view of their uses at the outset:

> . . . because of the lack of a ditone as you see in the "Haec" gradual, or because of the lack of a semitone as is seen in the introit "Exaudi domine," or because of the sharpening of a song. When it is sharpened so that it cannot turn back to its natural final, let it end on its affinity or gemina, as in the responsory "Terribilis," or by a simple transposition, . . .[61]

The author first emphasizes that the affinities accommodate certain tones not available around the normal final. The reference to the "lack of a ditone" in the "Haec" gradual apparently means low B-flat, since the anonymous commentator from Liège had referred to "Haec dies" as needing "two tones" in descent (below D). Like the anonymous commentator, this author does not mention an E-flat in the "Haec dies" graduals. In his second citation, however, the protus introit "Exaudi domine" which "lacks a semitone," there is a clearcut acknowledgement that the affinities could help preserve a chromatic tone.[62] Since the relevant tone, E-flat, falls within the modus vocum for protus, the author appears to adopt a less pure view of modal integrity than either Guido or the anonymous commentator from Liège.[63] A more significant departure from Guido's thinking is revealed in this author's failure to list avoidance of b-flat acuta as a reason for transposition.

The Leipzig author's third reason for use of affinities is "the sharpening of a song," and in this instance he names the responsory "Terribilis est." In the last paragraph of the treatise, he cites it again, this time as an example of partial transposition. This later paragraph follows, incidentally, almost word-for-word the anonymous commentator's statement regarding chants ending on a, ♮, and c, with its distinction between partial and total transposition.[64] By choosing the responsory "Terribilis est" in both instances, the Leipzig author ties Guidonian-oriented terminology ("partial transposition") to earlier statements by Berno ("sharpening of a song"), for Berno had cited "Terribilis est" as one of three chants for which he prescribed an ending in the affinities after they had moved, or been moved, to the higher range. Like Berno, the Leizig author favors the transposed ending, a fact that he confirms with his words, "Let it end on its affinity."

The author begins his discussion of transformation by quoting Guido:

> . . . transformation is when G sounds as protus, a sounds as deuterus, whereas b-flat itself sounds as tritus.[65]

He then cites an example for each transformation: a protus chant on G, "Angelus domini nuntiavit"; a deuterus chant on a, "Dum complerentur"; and a tritus chant on b-flat, "Vox clamantis in deserto." In the available sources, these antiphons appear respectively as protus, deuterus, and tritus ending on D, E, and F, with no feature that might necessitate their notation at another pitch level.[66] It is likely that the Leipzig author was merely recognizing that the named chants could be notated on G, a, and b-flat, for afterwards, he reflects that to do so would be an example of the second type of transformation, that which "takes place by absolutely no necessity," with the resultant b-flat causing confusion.[67]

Another type of transformation arises, however, "out of necessity":

> Transformation, therefore, takes place out of necessity when a song can neither be ended on its natural final by a regular method, nor be transposed to its equivoca, as is seen for example in the antiphon of the fourth mode "Apud dominum." In transformations of this type, let me say, not only does b-flat cause no confusion, on the contrary, it removes the greatest amount . . .[68]

The antiphon "Apud dominum misericordia" appears in available sources classified as mode four ending on a, where it contains both b-flat and b-natural.[69] This version corresponds to the melodic prototype that Gevaert called theme 29 and also agrees with the author's description of transformation of a into deuterus through the use of b-flat. Since "Apud" would contain F-natural and F-sharp at the lower pitch level, the author seems to say, however obliquely, that transformation is necessary to accommodate the F-sharp. (At the affinity position, the F-sharp would appear as an even more unacceptable c-sharp).

This description of transformation by necessity moves a step toward the acceptance of the serviceability of b-flat, a usefulness not acknowledged by Guido. In essence, the anonymous author describes transposition to the fourth above (Berno's transposition to the compares), by which a, and by projection, c, act as related tones to E and G, but only through the integral appearance of b-flat.[70] Labeling this procedure as transformation shows his deference to Guido for whom a given tone has a single modal identity defined by its surrounding diatonic interval set.[71] On the other hand, by distinguishing transformation "by necessity" and "by no necessity," he reveals that he does not consider Guido's theory wholly tenable in practice. In a case such as "Apud Dominum," his diatonic priorities are outweighed by his desire to preserve a chant's melodic character.

The Leipzig Tonary

In addition to the Leipzig treatise, the manuscript Univ. Bibl. Codex 1492 contains a tonary, which Sowa implies is written by the same theorist.[72] Based on the terminology, however, it would appear that different authors are responsible for the treatise and the tonary. In the tonary, the author introduces the noun translatio and the verb transfero when describing shifts to pitches both a fifth and a fourth above. He uses transformo only in the sense of changing mode within the four basic finals, a usage that is decidedly different from that of the treatise. Furthermore, though he uses affines for the pitches a fifth above the final as does the author of the treatise, he also employs the expression sociales finales for tones a fourth and fifth above at other times.[73] It is noteworthy that the tonary specifies, for each differentia within a given mode, which chants occur at related positions, and thus provides one of the longer lists of pertinent chants so far encountered.

Quaestiones in musica

Because of Rudolf Steglich's research, this treatise has been primarily attributed to Rudolf of St. Trond.[74] P. Cölestin Vivell has suggested another author, however, Franco of Liège (1047-1093?), who is also favored by Smits van Waesberghe.[75] Vivell and Smits van Waesberghe believe that the author was associated with the area of Liège at the end of the eleventh century, citing the manuscript tradition and the presence of Liègois melodies within the text.[76]

Even more than the Leipzig treatise, the _Quaestiones in musica_ attempts to reconcile some of the disagreement emanating from Guido's statements on transposition and transformation. In a chapter entitled, "What are transformed and what are transposed modes, or why and in what way they are said to be transformed and transposed from their proper seats,"[77] the author presents transformation in Guido's terms, stating that the modal association of a given tone changes through the use of _b-flat_. Like the Leipzig author, he indicates that transformation includes transposition to the fourth above, and in fact explicitly states that it is the need to accommodate a semitone or tone that prompts such a shift, namely of _tetrardus_ to _c_ and of _deuterus_ to _a_. Whereas the Leipzig author takes a strong position in accepting this "transformation by necessity," the author of the _Quaestiones_ presents the various arguments in a manner far less doctrinaire than either Guido or the Leipzig author, thus lending a certain air of reasonableness to the discussion. Indeed, the acceptance or rejection of a transposition to the fourth depends on two possibly contradictory motivations: to preserve the character of a chant at all costs, or to preserve the usual interval structure of a mode, which rests in a diatonic framework.

In order to show that a choice is possible, the author of the _Quaestiones_ cites phrases from _tetrardus_ chants which need an _F-sharp_.[78] He states that some persons move the chants to _c_, while others keep them at _G_, ". . . because it is absurd and awkward that the seventh mode be transformed and corrupted into the sixth."[79] His implication is that the _F-sharp_ semitone movement below _G_ changes the _maneria_ to _tritus_, which regularly has a semitone below the final. He suggests that rather than legitimize this anomalous movement within _tetrardus_ by transposition to _c_, some persons emend the chant to eliminate the _F-sharp_. For both of the _tetrardus_ chants cited by the author, available sources transmit such an emendation.

Following his description of these two solutions to the problem caused by an _F-sharp_ inflection in _tetrardus_, the author states: "Which you choose of these two we leave to your judgement."[80] That he favors emendation is suggested by his words introducing that solution, "others plead more reasonably." He does, incidentally, rule out _b-flat_ as an alternative final for _tritus_; like the _Dialogus_ author, he points to its lack of consonant agreement with the fourth above and octave below.[81] The author's position with regard to *protus* on *G* is less clear. Like the anonymous commentator from Liège and the Leipzig author, he cites the antiphon "Urbs fortitudinis" as an example of the transformation of *G* into *protus*,[82] to which he adds a second example, the antiphon "Magnus sanctus," with no further comment.[83] One can only surmise that he, like the other authors discussed, did not favor this particular transformation.

The author's discussion of transposition proper -- Guido's transposition to a position a fifth above the final -- sets up broad categories to explain its use, categories different from those of the Leipzig author. The author begins:

> . . . the division of its [transposition's] causes is threefold, because it arises either by will or by necessity or by the two combined.[84]

For this author, "will" refers to Guido's transposition to avoid *b-flat*, and he quotes Guido's statement, "If you do not want to have it," etc. He links "will and necessity" with partial transposition:

> . . . will and necessity combined accompany partial [transposition]. . . . but [transposition] in part arises in this way: when a song indeed begins according to the rule of its proper final and for awhile remains about the same final; afterwards, by the will of the musician, playing naughtily in the *acutae*, it is raised up and remains [there] longer than it should have; then, since it is absurd that it be led back to its proper seat, by necessity, as if weary and panting, it turns aside into the nearest lodging of its companion (*socialis*).[85]

Thus, the author, while allowing that the will of a musician may prompt him to place part of a chant in the *acutae*, nevertheless considers it wise to end there.[86]

Having made a distinct category of "will and necessity," the author blurs the fine line of distinction through what follows. Within a passage that begins "And, indeed, by necessity . . .," he includes chants that others have described as ending on the *affinales* by choice and "because of the sharpening of a song," namely, the responsories "Terribilis est" and "Factum est." The full passage reads as follows:

> And, indeed, by necessity, the first mode is transferred in its entirety from *D* to *a*, its *compar*, which has two tones below it that its final [i.e., *D*] lacks, as in "Haec dies." [The first mode] is transferred in part, as in the responsory "Factum est." The second mode [is transferred] in its entirety for the same reason, as in "Te unum" at [the word] "trinitatem"; [it is transferred] in part, as in "Terribilis." The fourth mode is

> transferred in its entirety from its final *E* to its *socialis* ♮ because of three tones [below], which ♮ has, but *E* does not, as in the offertory "Domine fac mecum." . . . The sixth [mode] is sung entirely on *c* through *b-flat*, because *F* lacks a tone under itself, as in "Honor virtus."[87]

One is tempted to read into this passage a suggestion that the partial transposition of "Terribilis est" and "Factum est" occurs for the same reason as the total transposition of "Haec dies," that is, to provide a tone that is not available around the final. It seems more likely, however, that the author is presenting a loose paraphrase of the passage in the Liège anonymous commentary and/or Leizig treatise where both total and partial transposition are included under the leading phrase "by necessity" (See Appendix B). In either case, as to the other chants mentioned, the author states clearly that the *deuterus* offertory "Domine fac mecum" is transposed to accommodate *B-flat* (as *F*), and the *tritus* responsory "Honor virtus" to legitimize *E-flat* (as *b-flat*).[88] The Leipzig author also acknowledged the avoidance of *B-flat* and *E-flat* as a reason for transposition, although he did not specifically label the latter "by necessity."

Two other details of the *Quaestiones* author's discussion of transposition are noteworthy. First, he links his refined categories of transposition by "will," "necessity," and "will and necessity" to the idea of transposition in whole or in part. As mentioned above, he associates "will and necessity" with partial transposition, but he allows that transposition of an entire chant may occur by will or by necessity.[89] These associations are not consistently evident in his examples, as indicated above.

Second, he links certain authentic and plagal modes with transposition by will or by necessity. Of the chants he cites as transposed by necessity, he includes examples for modes one, two, four, and six. Immediately before that passage, he had stated:

> There are other(s) [modes], such as the third, fifth, seventh, and eighth, to which the natural arrangement of sounds has not everywhere given a full concord. Thus let those modes be transposed by will. . .[90]

While this particular association may be somewhat arbitrary, the division of the modes is important. By citing examples for only modes one, two, four, and six and at the same time setting transposition of modes three, five, seven, and eight apart as "by will," the author may be bearing witness to practice, at least as observed in his immediate locale. Even if the distinction is prescriptive, it is a step beyond Guido's pronouncement that, by necessity, the "plagals" sometimes end on a, ♮, and c. To these, the Quaestiones author has added authentic protus.[91]

In conclusion, the Quaestiones in musica is one of several treatises from the end of the eleventh century that proceed beyond the rather limiting statements of Guido on transformation and transposition of modes. Significantly, the author of the Quaestiones offers a choice with regard to accepting transposition to the fourth above the final. Whether or not it was his intention to do so, the author seems to reconcile both Berno's and Guido's viewpoints on the issue. As regards transposition to the fifth above the final, that is, to the affinity established through diatonic movement, the author broadens the acknowledged reasons for which such transposition occurs "by necessity."

Anonymous Wolf

Another author writing at the turn of the century seems to have the opposite aim from that of the Leipzig and Quaestiones authors -- to break down the distinction between transposition and transformation. He may be among those to whom the Leipzig author referred when he said, "There are many simple musicians . . . who judge that between transformation and transposition there is no difference."[92] His treatise is found in Codex Darmstadt 1988, fols. 182v-189v, and is called "Anonymous Wolf" after the edition of it by Johannes Wolf.[93] The relevant passage reads:

> First, however, it should be diligently considered whether a song of this type [beginning in one mode, ending in another] can be sung either in transposed or in transformed [positions]. For any mode has transformed or transposed phrases, so that if any song cannot proceed in the phrases of its finals because of the lack of semitones there, it can proceed properly in transposed or transformed [phrases], which the studious singer should diligently observe.[94]

The author then cites two chants, "Turba multa" and "Domine qui operati sunt," whose respective semitones A to B-flat and D to E-flat could be acceptably notated within the gamut by shifting them to the fifth above.[95] Since the author gives no further examples, the impression remains that the "or" between transpose and transform signifies that the terms possibly have the same meaning. In the early fourteenth-century treatise De musica by Engelbert of Admont, these terms also appear to refer to the same phenomenon:

> But when, indeed, because of some changed interval [brought about] through the meeting with a

> transferred semitone, we are compelled to begin or end a song of any mode, not in its proper and natural location, but in a consimilis, then the song or mode is called transformed or transposed as was stated above just now. It is called transposed, moreover, for that reason, that its beginning and ending are transposed from its natural seat to the consimilis. And it is called transformed, because from the point at which it has been transposed, it is not sung in the natural species of fourth, fifth, and octave of that mode, but in consimiles according to form . . .[96]

Shortly thereafter, Engelbert discusses the use of b-flat around a and c, again referring to transposition and transformation. It appears that his application of both terms to shifts of the fourth is what was intended by the Anonymous Wolf author as well, for the latter began his discussion with a reference to chants beginning and ending in different modes, chants for which others offered transposition to the fourth above as a solution.

If this conjecture is correct, one sees evidence of two authors working in a south German area (Engelbert in Admont and the Anonymous Wolf author most likely in Hirsau, according to Wolf, although possibly in Liège according to Smits van Waesberghe),[97] who countered the distinction Guido's followers made with regard to transpositions to the fourth and to the fifth. Anonymous Wolf and Engelbert did so in the most effective way -- by commingling the meanings of those earlier categorical designations, transposition and transformation. Both writers knew Berno's Prologus, as selected paraphrases show.[98] That both integrate his view on related tones at the fourth with a Guidonian view on transformation is evidence for Berno's influence in Germanic regions.

De musica by John

De musica, written by the monk, John, c. 1100, contributes to our knowledge of practice with regard to the affinities, a fact in keeping with the general orientation of the treatise as an aid to choirboys in performing chant.[99] In his discussion of the affinities, John uses the Latin terms affines and affinitas with a general meaning of related tones and relationship, but he also views the related tones as alternative finals: ". . . the related tones are substituted for the finals without incompatibility whenever it is necessary."[100] His exposition is brief:

> Now we call those pitches related (affines) which agree in descent and ascent; for example, D, the final of protus, agrees with a acuta. Indeed both descend by a tone and ascend by a tone and a semi-

> tone. _E_, the final of _deuterus_, likewise has an affinity with _b-natural_, since they descend and ascend similarly. And _F_, the final of _tritus_, agrees with _c acuta_ in descent and ascent.[101]

John outlines the similar ascent and descent from _D_ and _a_, but only within the range of a fourth, not a sixth. His failure to spell out the defining sixth as his predecessors did may point to a by-now understood, if not accepted, concept of _modus vocum_. But, as remarked earlier, two ascents and one descent from the final are sufficient to identify a mode, and therefore, John reveals his practical bent by citing the minimal melodic movement rather than Guido's _modus vocum_. It is also significant that John, like Guido, does not give a related tone for _G_.

John prefaces this passage with a statement on the purpose served by _affines_. He refers to an "irregularity" (_illegalitas_) which arises "from the fault of singers and is very often of undeniable antiquity."[102] Since John attributes certain irregularities in chant to singers' practices, he opens the way to eliminating these irregularities: he is among the most outspoken of commentators in the matter of confessing to his own emendations. Nevertheless, John accepts certain irregularities because the affinities can accommodate them. First, he enumerates two _protus_ chants transposed to _a_ because they would require _B-flat_ in their normal positions. In this context, he relates that there are musicians who notate low _B-flat_:

> Some people, however, who wish to avoid this [transposition] place between _A_ and _B_ a Greek _S_, which they also call _synemmenon_, that is, "connected," so that they may have a tone below _C_. Nevertheless they cannot corroborate this by any authority.[103]

Then he names four chants which require _E-flat_, including chants in _protus_, _deuterus_, and _tritus_.[104]

Later in the treatise, John sheds additional light on his own preferences and others' practices. In Chapter Twenty-Two, entitled "On rejecting corrupt usage and on the extra _differentia_ of some modes," John returns to the _affines_. After mentioning an introit "Exaudi domine vocem . . . alleluia" that is sung at the affinity, he states:

> . . . and the communion _Dicit Andreas_ ought to be sung on related pitches according to those who assign it to the _Hypolydian_, but according to those who attribute it to the plagal _tetrardus_, it sounds well in its natural range.[105]

The problem of classifying this particular chant has been examined by two authors, Urbannus Bomm and Keith Fleming.[106] Fleming's conclusion, based on manuscript study more extensive than Bomm's, is that the chant's unusual melodic shape precipitated the problem. Its first three phrases move around c, while the fourth emphasizes c and then drops to a final G. Faced with this lack of tonal coherence, several medieval scribes apparently emended the communion by either raising the final cadence to the c level or lowering the rest of the melody to the level of the final G cadence. Based on John's description, it would appear that he accepts both of these solutions. Hypolydian (mode six) sung at the affinity fits the first change, while plagal tetrardus (mode eight) in its natural range fits the second change. That John does not state a preference in this case is consistent with his earlier statement that chants in certain modes, namely authentic tritus and tetrardus and their plagals, resemble each other closely.[107]

Another reference, however, suggests that John did not favor tonal shifts of chant endings. With regard to the responsory "Terribilis est," he states:

> . . . many go wrong at the place where et porta coeli occurs. Indeed, they suddenly raise this, leaping up to the acutae, although it should preferably be sung around the final D.[108]

This is the same chant mentioned by a number of other writers as moving to the acutae at some middle point and then ending there at the discretion of the singer. The interesting feature of John's comment is that he seems to oppose the high positioning of any part of this chant. If the phrase beginning at "et porta coeli" did move in the higher region by design, as others suggest it did, then his recommendation to sing it at the D level marks him as susceptible to carrying out the unnecessary emendations of which he accused others. In any event, although John accepted the use of the affinities to accommodate chromatic tones found in some chants, he apparently did not sanction their use in instances where the chant's ending could be kept at its normal position.[109]

John also does not choose transposition as a solution for certain other chants that are usually found in the sources ending a fourth above the normal final, but rather prefers a simple emendation to eliminate their problematic tone(s). He first refers to the deuterus communion "Beatus servus," for which Berno recommended a transposition to a. According to John's description, at the word "invenerit," the untransposed melodic movement includes F-sharp to G, which he says should be changed to G-G.[110]

He follows with a statement on problematic semitones in antiphons of the fourth mode, such as "Custodiebant," "Ex Egypto" and "Sion renovaberis,"[111] again with the implication that he does not recommend preserving the semitones through transposition to the fourth, but instead chooses emendation.

In summary, John's attitudes on the affinities show the influence of Guido, even as they reveal him to be an independent thinker on certain questions of modality. He is adamant on the issue of the final as the modal determinant, and at times seems unconcerned with the modal unity of a chant. Further, he accepts anomalous semitone movement within the course of a chant if it can be notated at the affinity position. For John, like Guido, the affinities are related tones a fifth above the finals; he never mentions the relationship at a fourth which relies on b-flat, and his solutions for certain chants reveal that he probably did not subscribe to the possibility. His acceptance of emendation in such cases witnesses alternative practice a century after Guido implied his opposition to the use of b-flat.

The Cistercian Treatises

One further twelfth-century view of the affinities is offered by a number of writings emanating from the Cistercian chant reforms that occurred between c. 1140 and 1147. The goals of the reform were twofold: to bring the corrupt chant used by early Cistercians into closer agreement with that current throughout Europe, and to regulate the chant according to the norms set out by recent theorists. In connection with the second goal, the Cistercians set out to enforce the guidelines for modal unity, usual ranges, and diatonic preference which their predecessors had prescribed. To this end, they utilized the affinities, and their discussions of the concept include some detail not provided by other theorists.

The main writings related to the reforms are the *Regule de arte musica*, the *Prefatio seu tractatus de cantu*, and the *Tonale Sancti Bernardi*.[112] In spite of a number of differing attributions over the years, the *Regule* is now thought to be the work of Guy d'Eu, who may have been the individual chiefly responsible for the Cistercian reform of the chant repertory. Both the *Prefatio* and the *Tonale* derive in large part from the *Regule*.[113]

Both the *Regule* and *Tonale* discuss chants that do not show modal *proprietas*, a word that signifies a decisive tone-semitone arrangement around the final. (Aribo also used this term rather than *modus vocum* -- see n. 38.) It is significant that the Cistercian writers, like John, spell out the identifying movement only within the range of a fourth, (two ascents and one descent), and for the first three *maneriae*, they give two finals, while the fourth has only *G*.[114]

In their attempt at systemization, the Cistercians generalize about the correspondence between each of the two finals and plagal versus authentic chants. As presented in the Prefatio, D and a can serve both authentic and plagal protus modes. With regard to b-natural and deuterus chants, the author states:

> Though this latter note is capable of acting as the final of both authentic and plagal [chants], nevertheless you will find in the Antiphonary no authentic which you can end on it.[115]

The reason given for avoiding b-natural as an authentic final is its lack of a perfect fifth above, as would be needed generally in authentic chants. The author notes that others have created a recitation tone for mode three that falls a sixth above the final, and thus could be accommodated at the b-natural level. Although he grudgingly admits the usefulness of this recitation tone in connection with b-natural, he implies that the Cistercians have not adopted it.[116] Therefore, he bears witness to the use of b-natural as an authentic deuterus final, although it has no place in the Cistercian tradition.

Finally, F is assigned to the greater part of tritus authentic chants and c to almost all tritus plagal chants. In one section of the Regule, the author describes in detail how F serves chants requiring three tones above the final (most often, authentic), while c serves those needing two tones and a semitone (most often, plagal). Similarly, D serves protus chants needing b-flat and b-natural, while a accommodates those needing low B-flat or using b-flat acuta regularly.[117] We therefore encounter a viewpoint on modal identity similar to that held by Guido and some of his followers: a b-flat inflection is accepted in protus and tritus modes, but to the extent that the b-flat can be avoided in notation through the affinities, transposition is used. Thus, a maxim in the Prefatio:

> No chant should be notated with it [b-flat] which can be notated without it.[118]

The author indicates that the only chants which cannot be notated without b-flat are those that contain b-flat and b-natural.[119]

Aside from their dictum to avoid the notation of b-flat, the Cistercian treatises shun its transforming effects in connection with G, a, and c finals. G has a single identity as tetrardus, a as protus, and c as tritus; accordingly, the use of G as protus, a as deuterus, and c as tetrardus is rejected. The Cistercians do, however, offer a solution for the problematic chants which Berno positioned at the compares. Prefatio centers its discussion on fourth-mode chants ending on a, specifically those belonging to Gevaert's theme 29:

> The correction of all these chants ending on A, therefore, is necessary; for in them a false similarity smothers their real nature. Misshapen by a contradiction which disfigures the members of the composition, they suggest one mode at their beginning and another at their conclusion.[120]

For this author, these chants reveal a lack of modal unity,[121] as well as indecisive tone-semitone movement above the final. The Cistercian solution, he tells us, is emendation, an emendation more drastic than John's simple conversion of F-sharp to G. Since the melodic movement at the beginning of these chants resembles that of seventh-mode chants, the Cistercians change the final cadence to one belonging to mode seven.[122] Hence, the chants end on G and are designated *tetrardus*. Thus, although the Cistercians claimed as one of their goals the reconciling of their chant with that sung throughout Europe, they sometimes chose a separate path, at least in the matter of these fourth-mode chants, which others had handled by means of simple transposition to the *compar a*.

Also relevant to the the Cistercian use of the affinities is their theory about the proper range of chants -- they should stay within the range of a tenth.[123] According to Marosszeki, the explanation for this theory lies in the manner of performance at Citeaux. Since a few trained soloists no longer executed the chant, but rather a divided choir in alternation, a chant with a large ambitus was probably beyond the choir's capabilities.[124] In the treatises examined, there is no direct statement that links the affinities to the problem of excessive ranges. However, comparative chant studies centering on Cistercian sources reveal that transposition of individual phrases to the affinities was a solution, as was the excising of notes beyond the tenth range.[125]

III. Hexachords: Seats of the Modes

Guido apparently conceived the idea of six syllables associated with six pitches primarily as a pedagogical tool useful in teaching choirboys new chants. By the thirteenth century, theorists viewed the six-pitch unit, the hexachord, as a fundamental construct of their tonal system, with the result that hexachord, rather than tetrachord, divisions of the gamut began to appear in many treatises.[1] Because these theorists had recognized that the basic intervallic structure of the hexachord could be found on three different pitches of the gamut, on C, G, and F, they were able to distinguish hexachord *proprietates* or "properties": a hexachord on C was "natural"; a hexachord on G was "hard," because it encompassed *b-natural* (*b-durum*); and a hexachord on F was "soft," because it encompassed *b-flat* (*b-molle*) (Figure 4).[2]

Though the theorists never managed to integrate the systems of mode and hexachord in their writings, hexachord terminology did enter into discussions of mode;[3] in fact, reference to the hexachord became a way of identifying mode. Whereas Guido had spelled out a *modus vocum* as a series of ascents and descents within the range of a sixth, the mere naming of a hexachord syllable accomplished the same thing. It was sufficient to link *protus* with *re*, since in relation to its total set *ut* to *la*, *re*'s position allowed for the exact pattern of ascent and descent that Guido had ascribed to *protus* -- descent by tone (*re ut*) and ascent of tone, semitone, tone, tone (*re mi fa sol la*). Thus, mentions of the *modi vocum* as such disappear as the Middle Ages unfold.

Guido did not explicitly make this connection between his pedagogical syllables and modal nuclei. As was pointed out earlier, he did recognize that a given *modus vocum* was available at two points in the gamut -- at the final (interval set C to a) and at its affinity position (interval set G to e) -- and that melodic units could be transferred between them. It was Wil-

Fig. 4. A representation of the medieval hexachord system as found in a MS by Magister Antonius von Sint-Maartensdijk (Ghent, University Library 70, fol. 108r).

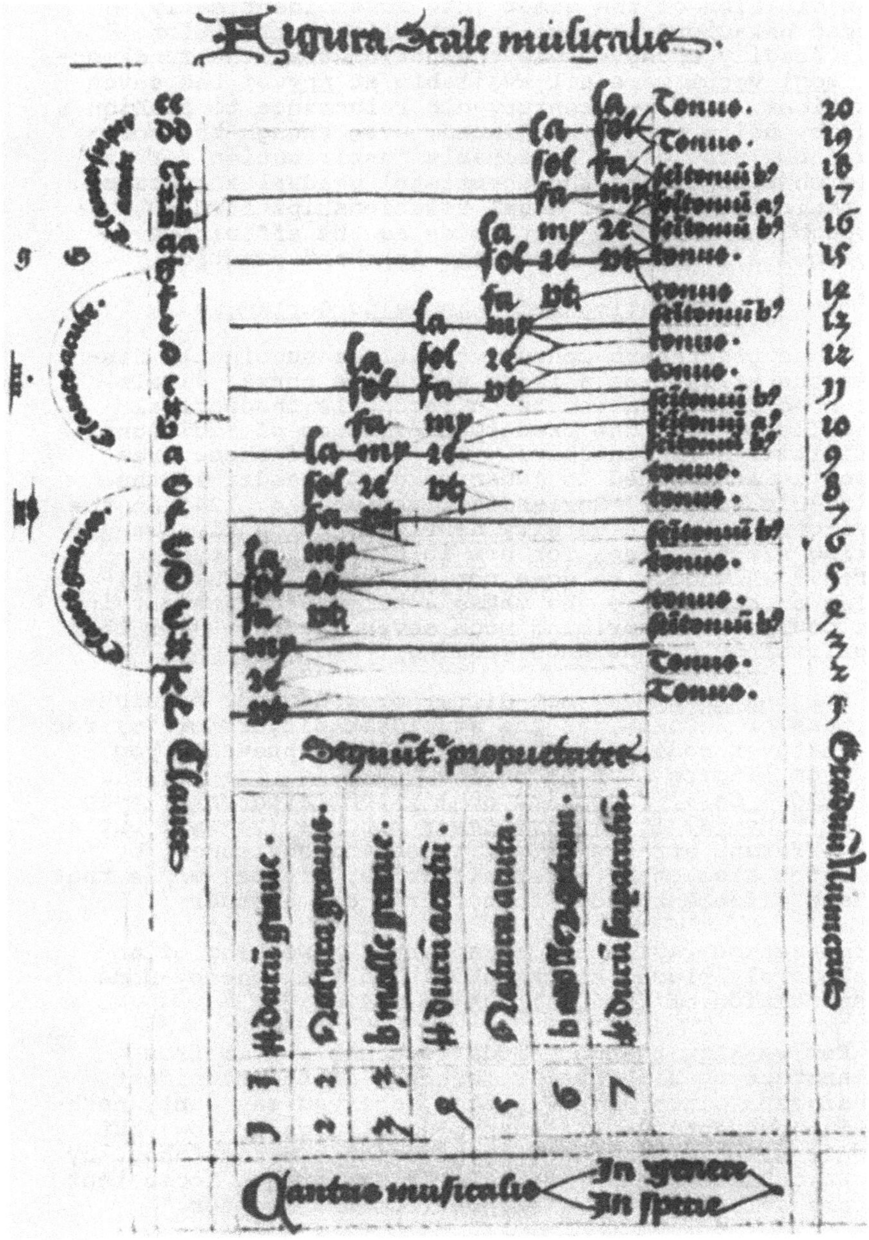

helm of Hirsau (see p. 29), who explicitly recognized a third position, F to d, which he then rejected in practice. But here were the seeds of later hexachord theory.[4]

For thirteenth- and fourteenth-century writers, the neat division of the gamut into seven identically formed hexachords became an established tradition. Less readily accepted was the notion that the fundamental modi vocum were all available at any of the seven positions. The two-century-old reluctance to fashion a mode by using b-flat continued, even though the soft hexachord provided a reasonable justification for it. This chapter traces the theorists' gradual acceptance in their treatises of modal relationships formed through the use of b-flat, even as the affinities remained a fundamental concept in chant practice.

A Treatise by Johannes de Garlandia

Three thirteenth-century treatises succinctly discuss the affinities a fifth above the normal finals, but none of them attempts to reconcile theoretical speculation with the practical evidence of additional affinities a fourth above. The first of these treatises is attributed to Johannes de Garlandia in the Saint-Die MS 42.[5] Garlandia flourished c. 1240 in the environs of the University of Paris, evidently preparing his treatises for use in his university lectures.[6] Although he does not directly discuss affinales or confinales, he makes a relevant statement in the course of describing mode seven (see n. 8 for the significance of the underscoring):

> For one mode does not differ from another by highness or lowness, as the stupidest singers claim; for whatever mode you may want, nothing prevents you from singing it high or low, that is, the first [mode] on a, the third on ♮, the fifth on c, even as they [a, ♮, c] have fewer pitches (voces); but a different arrangement of tones and semitones, by which also other intervals arise, creates modes that are different and distinct from one another.[7]

This passage represents an apparent reworking of an analogously placed statement within the mode-by-mode presentation of the Dialogus de musica:

> For we know that one mode does not differ from another by highness or lowness, as the stupidest singers claim; for whatever mode you may want, nothing prevents you from singing it high or low; but different arrangement[s] of tones and semitones, by which also other intervals arise, create modes that are different and distinct from one another.[8]

Apparently, Garlandia understands the *Dialogus* passage as an explanation of the affinities, and he accordingly adds a specific reference to first, third, and fifth modes on *a*, *♮*, and *c*, respectively. He then recognizes the limited correspondence of interval sets around the final and related position by adding the clause, "even as they [*a*, *♮*, and *c*] have fewer pitches (*voces*)."[9]

In contradistinction, the next sentence of the *Dialogus* implies an exactly corresponding interval arrangement around *D* and *a*:

> Again, if through only one distorted sound it ends on the eighth [step] *a*, it again becomes first [mode] throughout; indeed it will have from the final a tone and a semitone, two tones, and the rest which belong to the first [mode].[10]

An explanation for this difference lies in the *Dialogus*' spelling out of mode one with *b-flat* as the normal sixth degree: D E F G a b c d (see discussion on p. 12 above), an interval arrangement that accords exactly with one reckoned from *a*: a ♮ c d e f g aa.

While the *Dialogus* author values the affinities at the fifth for preserving modal identity,[11] Garlandia accepts that the alternative positions offer the possibility of modal variety. Thus, Garlandia has glossed and edited the *Dialogus* to reflect an attitude that apparently originated in the eleventh century and continued into the thirteenth.

Tractatus de tonis by Petrus de Cruce

The second thirteenth-century treatise was written by Petrus de Cruce, who flourished c. 1290, presumably in or near Amiens in northern France.[12] Petrus presents the essential principles of the church modes in his *Tractatus de tonis*;[13] in reference to the affinities, he says:

> Three letters are *affinales*, namely, *a*, *♮*, and *c*, and they are called *affinales* because they fulfill the roles of the other four [*finales*]. This occurs when some of the modes, since they cannot end on the final letters because of their ascent or because of their beginnings, therefore end on these [*affinales*].[14]

This passage is obscure in two respects. First, it does not relate the three *affinales* to specific modes. Second, the meaning of "because of their ascent or because of their beginnings" is not explained. The question then arises, was Petrus only marginally knowledgeable concerning the concept of *affinales*, or did he consider the concept so basic and well-understood that he did not need to explain further?

In answer, it should be noted that the treatise is merely an introduction to a didactic tonary. Judging from the content and its manner of presentation, one might conclude that Petrus intended his "treatise" only as a reminder of principles already known to his readers. Accordingly, he saw no need for elaborating upon his brief explanation of _affinales_. In the Guidonian tradition, his mention of _a_, _♮_, and _c_ together would suggest related tones a fifth above the finals. On the other hand, Petrus' expressions "because of their ascent" and "because of their beginnings" resemble most closely wording used by Berno in his _Prologus_. One recalls that Berno named several chants ending a fifth above the final because of "extra regulam ultra nonum in decimum sonum ascendens." Later, Berno named chants that "lacked semitones" because their beginnings occurred in inadvisable places. In the latter case, he prescribed transposition to the fourth above, resulting in fourth-mode chants ending on _a_. If Petrus' reasons can be taken to mean the same thing as Berno's, it may be that Petrus' simple naming of _a_, _♮_, and _c_ as _affinales_ was meant to include some alternative finals at the fourth as well as at the fifth above.

The tonary proper also contains material relevant to the present discussion. Under mode four, the incipit to the antiphon "Ex Egypto" and its EVOVAE are given as follows (Example 3):[15]

Ex. 3. Incipit and EVOVAE of the antiphon "Ex Egypto" according to Petrus de Cruce.

The incipit agrees with what is found in extant versions of the entire antiphon that end on _a_. Furthermore, the pitch location of the _differentia_ indicates that the psalm tone was accordingly placed a fourth higher than usual: the recitation would be on _d_ (rather than on _a_) ending with d c d e c c a ♮ . Clearly, through the "Ex Egypto" example, the tonary, if not the treatise, bears witness to the use of _a_ as a fourth-mode final, even though Petrus chose not to address the underlying theoretical issue.

Practica artis musice by Amerus

The third treatise dealing with the standard affinities is that of Amerus, an English theorist active in Italy at the end of the thirteenth century. Amerus was a member of the household of Cardinal Ottobono Fieschi, and it was in Fieschi's house, perhaps in August 1271 at Viterbo where the Cardinal was staying, that Amerus wrote his Practica artis musice.[16]

Amerus defines mode as follows:

> . . . mode indeed [is] a rule which classes every song according to its beginning, middle, and end.[17]

This definition adds new criteria to the Dialogus author's statement on the final as modal determinant. From this time onwards, many writers besides Amerus adopt this broader definition as they attempt to refine modal classification.

Amerus begins his discussion of affinales with this sentence:

> And it should be understood that D, E, F, and G are finales, a, b, c, and d are confinales and affinales or consociales.[18]

The apparent confusion of terminology can be explained by Amerus' familiarity with the anonymous commentary from Liège or perhaps the source upon which it drew, as well as with Berno's Prologus. Thus, affinales derives from the anonymous commentary's usage and (con)sociales from Berno's, while confinales seems to be a thirteenth-century construction.

That Amerus knew the anonymous commentary or its source is confirmed in the paragraph that follows the sentence quoted above. For, with a few differences, Amerus' exposition is modeled after the passage in the anonymous commentary which begins, "Sometimes plagal protus, deuterus, and tritus end by necessity on a, ♭, and c."[19] The first difference is the elimination of the phrase "by necessity." Secondly, Amerus cites three examples for transposition ex toto, namely the gradual "Haec dies," the gradual "Ostende," and the offertory "Dominus dixit," while the anonymous commentary mentions only "Haec dies."[20] Thirdly, Amerus adds to the statement that plagals, and not authentics, use transposition, "but all these end freely, and not regularly." The significance of the qualifier "not regularly" will be examined below.

Amerus next reveals his familiarity with Berno's treatise and his apparent disagreement with some contemporary practice. The section is entitled "Regule Bernonis super mensuram Boecii," and reads as follows:

> There are four pitches called finales, and unless an old melody or a similar new one is ended on these, it is judged without doubt to be irregular and not legitimate. But it ought to be understood that, among the ancients, at the fifth position [above] always there was such condicio of the higher with the lower finals that some viella were found to be ended as if regularly in these [the fifth positions]. But because all musicians assert that there are only four finals by whose rule all songs of the eight modes are governed, it pleased the ingenuity of the moderns that songs distorted as if through negligence be emended and be sung properly with their own finals, for example, "Terribilis est locus," "Cantabo domino qui tribuit," and others of this type.[21]

This passage mentions two of the three chants cited by Berno in his opening statement on the sociales, "Terribilis est" and "Cantabo Domino." Further, beginning at "among the ancients," if viella is a misreading for mela and condicio for concordia, this sentence follows Berno.[22] The excerpt also describes the attitude of some modern musicians who, in contrast to Berno, believe that the type of chant represented by those examples should not be allowed to end on the affinales, but rather should be emended to end on the normal finals.[23] It is difficult to determine what viewpoint Amerus adopted regarding these chants. He mentions "Terribilis est" twice, first in the context of the anonymous commentary gloss as an example of partial transposition, at which point he appends the comment that endings on the affinales are not regular, but free. The second reference focuses on how contemporary musicians alter chants such as "Terribilis est" and "Cantabo Domino." By immediately preceding this with an acknowledgement that earlier musicians had considered chant endings at the fifth above regular, Amerus seems to suggest that his contemporaries went too far in emending the chants. In any case, Amerus uses the expressions "irregular" and "not legitimate" to refer to chants that end on finals other than the usual four, a terminology that becomes pervasive during the next several centuries.

Tractatus de musica by Magister Lambertus

In Magister Lambertus' treatise, dating from the third quarter of the thirteenth century, most probably from the late 1260's or early 1270's,[24] we encounter the first theorist to present his explanation of basic and alternative finals in terms of the hexachord. He begins his discussion of mode as follows:

> Their [the modes] final syllables are _re_, _mi_, _fa_, and _sol_; the final seats are _D_, _E_, _F_, and _G_.[25]

Lambertus places the traditional rule concerning the location of the finals at _D_, _E_, _F_, and _G_ within the hexachord framework. By naming the syllable on which the _maneria_ should end, Lambertus leaves open the possibility that each _maneria_ could find its associated syllable in any of the hexachords, a possibility for which Guido and Hermannus already had laid the groundwork. Whether Lambertus fully realized the implications of his statement is not clear.

In the next paragraph, he seems to turn from the abstractions of modal classification to a description of practice. After relating each modal pair to its normal final (e.g., "Primus finitur in D, pariterque secundus."),[26] Lambertus states:

> But the end of the fourth mode occasionally is found on _a lamire_, to which the rule gives its name, because it appears to end there through _b-flat_. Likewise the end of the sixth [mode] is sometimes _c solfaut_.[27]

Lambertus implies that he has some familiarity with fourth-mode chants ending on _a_, a related tone a fourth above the final,[28] and sixth-mode chants ending on _c_, a related tone a fifth above the final. But his passage lacks the precision of other writings where the authors state that _a_ as _mi_ serves modes three and four, and _c_ as _fa_ serves modes five and six. If Lambertus did understand related pitches at the fifth in reference to the hard hexachord, and related pitches at the fourth in reference to the soft hexachord, he did not so elucidate them in his treatise.

Tractatus de musica by Jerome of Moravia

Jerome's compilation _Tractatus de musica_ was most likely written after 1272, since it cites a commentary by St. Thomas Aquinas completed in that year.[29] Scholars have characterized the _Tractatus_ as a compilation because it includes four treatises on mensural practice by various authors in its last part, while the beginning sections on music as a liberal art and as a mathematical science are also strongly derivative, mainly from Boethius and the monk John. The middle section on chant presents certain ideas peculiar to Jerome, particularly concerning authentic/plagal designations when the range is ambiguous.[30]

In Chapter Twenty "De sedibus tonorum duplicibus" or "Concerning the Double Seats of Modes," Jerome pinpoints the tetrachord of the _finales_ (_D E F G_) and the tetrachord of the _acutae_ (_a ♮ c d_) as modal locations.[31] By utilizing a tetrachord rather than a hexachord framework, Jerome displays a certain conservative bent. Further, he reveals the medieval predilection for symmetry by including d in this context, even though in his summary statement he says that only a, ♮, and c are used as alternative finals.[32]

In the next sentences, Jerome acknowledges not only affinities at the fifth above, but also a deuterus affinity at the fourth above, on a:

> The second seat is, namely, the tetrachord of the acutae in which, just as in the first seat, the named modes end. For the first and second mode end on a with re; the third and fourth in the same place, but on mi; also, the third and fourth [end] on ♮ acuta. The fifth and sixth [end] on c acuta; the seventh and eighth [end] on d acuta.[33]

Instead of the traditional expression that a serves modes three and four through b-flat, he says simply that a functions as mi (implicitly as part of the soft hexachord). This syllabary would have been understood immediately by singers for whom mi-fa signaled a half-step progression, and hence, a to b-flat. It appears that Jerome, perhaps progressing one step beyond Lambertus, recognized how the theoretical construct of the soft hexachord would justify the presence of b-flat within a modal nucleus.

Also of some interest is Jerome's Chapter Twenty-Three, an outline of the principal hexachords used in solmizing each mode.[34] Such a presentation is striking for its completeness, considering the date. Even more unexpected is Jerome's working out of the applicable hexachords for the affinity position as well. Thus, for example, he states that, ". . . a melody of the first mode ending on a acuta yields the second hard [hexachord], second natural [hexachord] and second soft [hexachord] licentialem . . ."[35]

Chapter Twenty-Three ends with a discussion of altered tones. Specifically, Jerome projects synemmenon tetrachords at ten points in the gamut, adopting as his model the synemmenon tetrachord a b-flat c d, which is based on the standard Greek pattern semitone-tone-tone.[36] Through the use of the syllables mi, fa, sol, and la, Jerome transfers this very pattern to other positions in the gamut, and thus generates flats on A, D, E, G, a, d, e, and aa, in addition to those on B and b. By applying the Greek theoretical term synemmenon to each of the new tetrachords, and also to the flat generated, Jerome apparently sought to make acceptable accidentals other than b-flat. However, the final sentence in this section reveals that he is not recommending the application of his synemmena theory in all musical contexts: "Although synemmena are useful in discant, nevertheless ecclesiastical song does not accept them in any way."[37] Thus his apparent effort to add credibility to flats does not apply to chant.

Implicitly, he reveals that a common reason for transposition to the affinities, avoidance of accidentals, is still valid. His treatise also reveals that at least one thirteenth-century theorist made important tonal distinctions between polyphony and chant.

Speculum musicae by Jacques de Liège

Speculum musicae, the longest surviving medieval music treatise, has been attributed to Jacques de Liège only since about 1925.[38] Opinions vary as to precisely where and when he wrote the treatise. Besseler speculated that Jacques, in his old age, wrote the treatise in Liège, not before 1330,[39] and Steglich, Ludwig, and later, Bragard, made observations in support of this hypothesis.[40] Smits van Waesberghe, on the other hand, proposed the identification of Jacques with a Jacobus de Oudenaerde, canon of Liège and professor at the University of Paris in 1313. Accordingly, Smits believed that Jacques would have written the Speculum for use at the University.[41]

Both opinions are not inconsistent with the observation that Jacques knew and referred to theoretical writings associated with Liège. With regard to the affinities, his most significant borrowing comes from the Quaestiones in musica. The first of three discussions about the affinities within book six of the Speculum is based in part upon it. The second discussion presents an elaboration of statements found in the Dialogus and in Guido's Epistola, while the third seems to be Jacques' own explanation grounded in the terminology of solmization.[42]

The first discussion of the affinities occurs in Chapter Forty-One, "Quod sint aliquae voces vel claves affinales."[43] Although a significant part of this chapter relates to the passage on transposition in the Quaestiones, one finds opinions that are apparently Jacques' own. He begins the chapter as follows:

> Besides the four frequently mentioned pitches of the tetrachord of the finals, which are more essentially called finales, there are also others on which some songs end, namely A, B, and C. These, although they are not called finales, by adopting the name of the others, they are nevertheless called affinales or sociales.[44]

Like Amerus, Jacques presents synonyms for naming alternative finals. Throughout most of his three presentations, however, he favors the term affinales, consistent, it would seem, with the Guidonian orientation of his ideas. In the quoted passage, Jacques names A, B, and C graves as affinales, although subsequently his references are to a, ♮, and c acutae. The discrepancy apparently results because Jacques, like Guido, sets out to explore systematically his tonal system before he refers to practice. The three graves demand identification since they are among the seven basic and distinct pitches of the gamut, A B C D E F G: each must have a single modal function. Jacques returns to this argument at the end of the chapter, but now in reference to the upper designates, a ♭ c:

> . . . because there are only seven distinctions between pitches, and four of those are properly and naturally finals, since only three remain, there could only be three affinales, unless they coincided with the finals.[45]

Thus, he offers an explanation for excluding d as an affinalis, the same one that Guido implicitly voiced.

After naming the affinales, Jacques discusses affinitas or the broad concept of relationships of pitches within the gamut, and this discussion represents the first comprehensive treatment of the term since Guido broached it in Chapters Seven and Eight of the Micrologus. Whereas Guido presented affinities at the fifth, followed by "other" affinities, namely at the fourth, Jacques works out a systematic scheme:

> Affinity is a likeness, that is to say a certain association or similarity, of certain pitches to the pitches which are truly, peculiarly, and naturally finals. This likeness, association, or similarity, moreover, arises either by reason of the agreement between dissimilar pitches or by reason of a certain conformity between similar pitches.
>
> First, I say that affinity can be threefold: perfect, more perfect, and most perfect. That is called perfect which exists through the diatessaron, and with respect to this, G is related (affinis) to D, a to E, b to F. For indeed, a diatessaron interval is contained between these named pitches or notes. A more perfect affinity is that which exists through the diapente, and in this way, a and D are related, similarly, ♭ and E, c and F. These mentioned pitches are, moreover, distant from one another through the diapente. That affinity is called most perfect which exists through the octave. In this way, d is related to D, e to E, f to F, g to G.[46]

Jacques thus establishes a hierarchy of pitch relationships, which though expressed in his own peculiar terminology, agrees with what Guido proposed: that an octave relationship is stronger than a fifth relationship, which in turn is stronger than a fourth relationship.

Jacques' definition of _affinitas_ includes an ambiguous reference to "agreement between dissimilar pitches." While he does not explain that phrase further, he does elaborate upon "conformity between similar pitches":

> Affinity . . . is found between those notes that are similar in some syllables. And with respect to this, any note in which _re_ is found is related to _re_ at _D solre_. And in this way, any note containing _mi_ is related to _E lami_; and [any] that contains _fa_ to _F faut_; and [any] that contains _sol_ to _G solre_.[47]

This statement suggests a conceptual linkage of modal identity to hexachord syllable, a construct that allows a mode to end at any point in the gamut where its associated syllable is found. Jacques returns to this concept in Chapter Seventy-Eight, but both there and in the present context, he indicates that in practice he does not accept it entirely. In Chapter Forty-One, he complains about the unnecessary notation of some chants at related positions:

> Already, moreover, in antiphonaries and ecclesiastical books of songs, it is unfortunately observed that, as if indiscriminately, many songs are notated on related notes which could be suitably notated on their proper finals. And thus, a greater confusion and unsuitability arises . . . as would happen in the case of a song which can be notated and ended suitably on _E_, if it were notated and ended on _a_, or if it were notated on _G_ when it could be notated on _D_.[48]

The sentiment behind this statement resembles that expressed by earlier writers when they referred to "unnecessary" transformation. It is significant that Jacques does not use the word transformation in this context. Still, he apparently did not wish to condone without reservation the practice of notating chants at the fourth above the final, even though he seemed to recognize the theoretical justification for it. He ends the chapter with a traditional statement that there are three _affinales_, _a_, _♮_, and _c_, connected respectively with the first and second, third and fourth, and fifth and sixth modes, and as noted above, he justifies the absence of _d_ for the seventh and eighth modes.[49]

Jacques devotes the middle portion of the same chapter to a discussion of the three reasons given by the _Quaestiones_ author (in Jacques' words "secundum Guidonis expositorem") for transposition of a chant from its _finalis_ to _affinalis_.[50]

For the first category, "by will" or _voluntate_, Jacques paraphrases the _Quaestiones_' explanation that such transposition is carried out to avoid _b-flat_.

Jacques adds a clause implying that he also includes under this designation whimsical, unnecessary transposition, which he further characterizes as faulty and irregular.[51]

The discussion of transposition "by necessity" follows the basic outline of the comparable passage in the Quaestiones.[52] Jacques spells out the occasional need for a ditone under D protus, three tones under E deuterus, or one tone under F tritus, none of which can be obtained at the final position. Unlike the author of the Quaestiones, Jacques gives a chant example only for tritus, the responsory "Honor virtus."

Jacques' exposition on transposition "by will and necessity" is taken almost word-for-word from the Quaestiones passage, but Jacques adds a chant example, stating, "as it is seen with regard to secular Liègois churches in the 'Alleluia. Judicabunt Sancti'."[53] Interestingly, both the Alleluia and the responsory "Terribilis est," which Jacques mentions next, were cited in manuscripts of the anonymous commentary from Liège. Smits van Waesberghe has observed that in various places in the Speculum, Jacques extracted passages from the anonymous commentary,[54] which seems to be the case with these examples as well.

With regard to the ending of "Alleluia. Judicabunt" and "Terribilis est" on the affinales, Jacques voices a decidedly negative opinion, for three reasons: "Firstly, because a song and mode indeed should not have two endings."[55] Jacques refers to the fact that the Alleluia and its verse "Judicabunt" would have two different endings, D and a, respectively, and thus unfold on two tonal levels.

"Secondly, because it agrees with no mode to descend below its ending more than a diapente. This is not true of that song ["Judicabunt"], because whereas it ends on a at last, it descends to C."[56] This statement paraphrases the anonymous commentator's disapproval of ending "Judicabunt" on a.[57]

"Thirdly, because from a regular song arises an irregular song . . . Therefore, in many other churches, that song is corrected: indeed, it ends on D, not on a."[58] Jacques expresses the viewpoint that an ending on a makes the chant irregular, and he further reports that some church musicians accordingly emend the chant. After he mentions that "Terribilis est" is treated similarly to "Alleluia. Judicabunt" in some Liègois churches, Jacques offers this last observation:

> It is otherwise, however, regarding certain other songs, which, ascending high, linger there so long, all the way to their ending or almost so, that they are not fitting to return so suddenly and precipitously from a position so high to their proper ending. Therefore, such songs are to be excused more [than others] if they end on the nearest affinalis.[59]

Jacques gives no examples to illustrate such acceptable instances of transposition by will and necessity.

In summary, Jacques' discussion concerning the reasons for transposition of chants to the affinales is derived mainly from the Quaestiones. In one instance, Jacques seems to have stood at odds with the practice at Liège as represented in that treatise, whereby certain chants are transposed "by will and necessity." Jacques favors the "correction" of these chants made in other locales.

In Chapter Fifty-Three, Jacques discusses the use of b-flat in each mode, describing how it changes the proper species of fourth and fifth. He concludes:

> Therefore, b-flat is used most rarely, except in the fifth or sixth mode, . . . Oh that they had heeded this who ruined many songs through b-flat and maintain those songs in their error . . .[60]

Having made this point about the distorting effects of b-flat, Jacques begins his second discussion of the affinities in Chapter Fifty-Four, "De vocum similitudine et clavium diversarium affinitate." In this context, he combines ideas derived from the Dialogus de musica and from Guido's Epistola with his own.

Jacques first paraphrases the passage in the Dialogus that begins with "Unaquaeque vox modorum supradictorum . . ." and ends with a diagram relating the modes to each tone in the gamut.[61] Among Jacques' few interpolations and changes, the most significant is his statement that Γ could be used as final for the seventh mode. Based on his understanding that the hexachord syllable for Γ is ut, he concludes:

> From the given sentence of Guido we hold that the syllable, which is ut, is not in conflict with the final syllable of the seventh mode, which is sol.[62]

This association of seventh-mode final with ut or sol will gain further significance in later passages of the Speculum.

Jacques also interpolates a paragraph following the Dialogus statement that a serves first mode through b-natural, and third mode through b-flat. Jacques adds that the former occurs when a is re and applies to both modes one and two, and the latter occurs when a is mi and applies to both modes three and four.

Interestingly, Jacques' diagram, although clearly modeled after the one in the Dialogus, does not include mode three at a or mode eight at c. Jacques' chart is a straightforward presentation of affinities at the fifth, despite his remarks quoted above that allow for the possibility of affinities at the fourth. Guido's influence apparently prevails, especially since the next section derives from the Epistola.

The discussion turns to the concept of the *modus vocum*, with Jacques quoting part of Guido's explanation from the *Epistola*.[63] Jacques clarifies the statement that modes seven and eight are found only at *G* by spelling out the different ascents from *G* and its defective affinity *D*.

The rest of the section is only loosely derived from the *Epistola*. Guido had noted that the succession of tones and semitones from *D* and *a* does not correspond exactly (outside of the *modus vocum*), and in both the *Epistola* and the *Micrologus*, he recommended choosing one or the other position according to the requirements of a chant. Jacques, too, recognizes the lack of total identity between a final and its *affinalis*. Because of his reliance on species in defining mode, he objects to the changes that occur in those species through unnecessary use of *affinales*:

> . . . it is evident that neither mode one nor two can, with respect to their regular formulas previously mentioned, be ended on the first [note] *A* or the eighth [note] *a*; and therefore, many songs of the first [mode] are in some respect corrupted, in that they are notated not on the proper final, but on the *affinalis*. It is evident in certain books with regard to the responsory "Christi virgo" or the responsory "Circumdederunt me viri mendaces" and many others.[64]

Both chants cited by Jacques end on *a* in the thirteenth-century Worcester antiphoner.[65]

After he cautions against overuse of the *affinales*, Jacques admits that there are chants whose particular arrangements of tones and semitones can best be accommodated at the *affinales*, but, unfortunately, he gives no examples. Finally, in another loose paraphrase of the *Epistola*, he discusses chants of limited range which "can be sung and notated at various positions," and by way of illustration, he includes Guido's example, the antiphon "Spera in Domino":[66]

G	G	a	G	a	♭	G	a	♭	G	a	G
F	F	G	F	G	a	F	G	a	F	G	F
C	C	D	C	D	E	C	D	E	C	D	C
Spe-	ra	in	Do-	mi-	no	et	fac	bo-	ni-	ta-	tem

The ascent from each of the three finals is by tone-tone. Jacques states that an ending on *C* or *F* would be classified as fifth or sixth mode, but preferably sixth, and the ending on *G* as eighth mode.

Jacques devotes the next chapter, Fifty-Five, to an explanation for why *B-flat* should not be placed in the *graves*. He does not consider it advisable for the human voice to attempt this, although *B-flat* is used on certain "artificial" instruments, such as the organ.[67]

The basis for his argument is the passage in the *Epistola* regarding the confusion caused by *b-flat acuta*. His conclusion:

> If, indeed, *b-flat* causes great confusion in many songs, even in the *acutae*, as has been seen above, how much more it would cause if it were placed in the *graves*. Consequently, we ought to use *b-flat* in songs as little as we can . . .[68]

Thus, these middle chapters reveal a conservative attitude toward modal identity, one that combines Guido's concern for diatonic purity with the German emphasis on characteristic species of fourths and fifths.

Jacques' final discussion of the affinities occurs in Chapters Seventy-Six through Seventy-Eight and employs hexachord terminology.[69] Jacques now expounds in detail the principle implied earlier -- a mode may end at any point in the gamut where its associated syllable is found.

Chapter Seventy-Six, entitled "De tono cantuum terminatorum in ut vel in la," or "Concerning the Mode of Songs Ending on *Ut* or on *La*, presents this passage about *ut*:

> It should be said that songs which end on *ut* are of the fifth, sixth, seventh, or eighth mode, and not of the first, second, third, or fourth. I say more particularly that, if they should have an ending on *ut* at *C* or *F graves* and on *c acuta*, they are of the fifth or sixth mode. But if some songs should end on the Greek *Γ*, which is not seen, or on *G gravis* or *g acuta*, they are of the seventh or eighth mode.[70]

Jacques allows both *F* and *G*, respectively *tritus* and *tetrardus* finals, to carry the syllable *ut*, and thereby demonstrates how truly practical he is. The association of *F* and *G* with *fa* and *sol* respectively establishes them within the range of a sixth that represents the identifying *modus vocum*. In practical terms, however, few chants have the limited ascent from the final that is offered by the *tritus* pattern *fa sol la* or the *tetrardus* pattern *sol la*. It seems that Jacques is trying to integrate theoretical and practical concerns by acknowledging that mutations of the syllable associated with a final do occur when a chant is solmized.

In the same passage, Jacques holds that chants ending on *ut* at *C gravis* or *c acuta* belong to the fifth or sixth modes, an opinion in keeping with Guidonian theory. Jacques does, however, explain how *c acuta* could in theory serve modes seven and eight:

> But it is otherwise regarding *c acuta*, because in that *ut* is joined not only with *fa*, but also with *sol*.[71]

Thus, c could be solmized as either fa or sol (within the hard and soft hexachords), and accordingly be a final for either tritus or tetrardus modes. Yet the persistent concern over b-flat surfaces here, too:

> . . . it appears, nevertheless, that such songs should be called preferably of the fifth or sixth mode rather than of the seventh or eighth. Firstly, because c acuta, according to Guido, is called an affinalis, just as [there are affinales] for other modes. Secondly, because sol at c acuta, since it is sung through b-flat, does not belong to that note naturally, as does fa. Thus, in that place, ut has greater affinity to fa than to sol.[72]

In this passage, Jacques alludes to the less natural character of c as sol, through b-flat, than as fa, through b-natural. In support of his preference, he calls upon his concept of comparative degrees of affinity: F faut, located a fifth below, has greater affinity to c solfaut than does G solut, located a fourth below.

Jacques next refers to chants ending on la:

> . . . they are of the first, second, third, or fourth mode and not of the fifth, sixth, seventh, or eighth; they are of the first, second, third, or fourth if they end on a acuta or aa superacuta, because in these notes la is joined to re which is the final of the first and second [modes], and to mi which is the final of the third and fourth [modes].[73]

This assignment of a to two maneriae, protus and deuterus, follows the same rationale according to which c serves tritus and tetrardus. That is, both a and c carry the syllables associated with their respective two maneriae. But in the case of a, Jacques does not inveigh against its identity as deuterus through b-flat. We do not know why, but we can only speculate that the use of a as deuterus final had become more acceptable in practice, as Jacques then understood it, than c as a tetrardus final.

In Chapter Seventy-Seven entitled "De cantuum irregularitate" or "Concerning the Irregularity of Songs," Jacques outlines the reasons why melodies are labeled "irregular" -- because of defects in their beginning, middle, or end. A defect in the beginning occurs when a chant does not utilize one of the notes upon which chants of the given mode usually begin. A defect in the middle refers to range, specifically, an excessive range which cannot easily be assigned to the authentic or plagal form. Finally, a defect in the end refers to the following tonal situation:

> But if songs possess two endings, so that they end first on the proper final and afterwards on the *affinalis*, there is an imperfection and a certain irregularity; thus are certain alleluias and certain responsories in some churches, and those songs are transposed according to the ancients. There was mention of these earlier.[74]

We assume that Jacques refers here to the "Alleluia. Judicabunt" and the responsory "Terribilis est" in their versions ending on *a*, which earlier he had described as irregular.

In Chapter Seventy-Eight "De tono cantuum irregularium" or "Concerning the Mode of Irregular Songs," Jacques states that any song, regular or irregular, can be assigned a mode "if it ends suitably at last" on one of the syllable(s) assigned to that mode.[75] For *protus*, the syllable is *re*, for *deuterus*, *mi*, for *tritus*, *fa* or *ut*, and for *tetrardus*, *sol* or *ut*. Jacques expresses, in the most direct manner yet encountered, the idea that there are multiple final locations associated with a given syllable:

> Therefore, it appears that the naming of modes is made more generally from the mentioned syllables than from the four final notes [*D E F G*], because those syllables look not only to the tetrachord of the finals, but also to others. Indeed, *they are contained seven times in the gamut*, and therefore, songs can be ended elsewhere than exclusively on those four proper final notes. (emphasis added)[76]

Here one sees a theoretical recognition that a modal final can be located in any of the seven hexachords. Thus, *protus*, through its association with *re* can find its final on *D* in the natural, on *a* in the hard, and on *G* in the soft hexachord. Jacques has used the soft hexachord as a means to legitimize a modal position a fourth above the normal one. It is noteworthy that he indirectly informs his readers that he does not consider this location with its integral *b-flat* to be automatically one of "transformation." After his statement regarding the "suitable" ending of a chant, he continues:

> I have said, however, "if suitably," because of certain songs which have an ending on *re* at *G gravis* through *b-flat*, but not suitably. . . . And it is likewise with certain other antiphons and responsories that are distorted in the final pitch through *b-flat*.[77]

In this context, he refers to the antiphon "Magnus sanctus Paulus," also cited by the *Quaestiones* as an example of a *tetrardus* chant on *G* transformed into *protus* through the use of *b-flat*. As Example 4 shows, some scribes added *b-flats* at two points to correct tritones; there is no evidence suggesting that the antiphon was ever classified as *protus* on *D* and later transposed to *G*.[78] Therefore, both authors' reference to transformation in "Magnus sanctus" must mean that the addition of *b-flat* at the chant's normal position on *G* distorts its *tetrardus* modal character.

Ex. 4. Excerpt from the Antiphon "Magnus sanctus Paulus".

Worcester Antiphonale 330

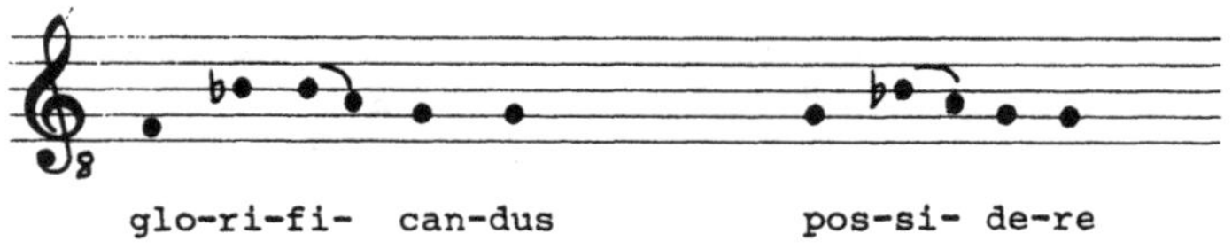

Lucca Antiphonale 423

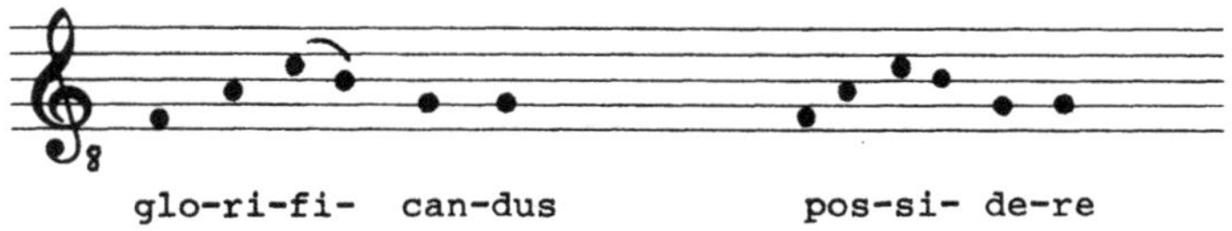

Jacques' solution (Bragard, 223)

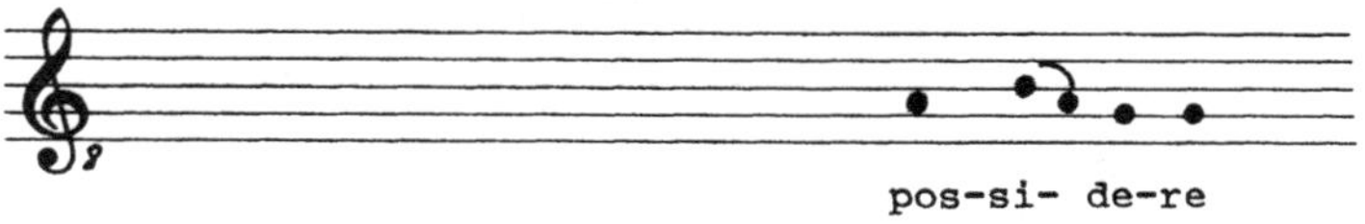

The evidence of this chant example and Jacques' pronouncement on the seven-fold locations of a mode suggest that he had reached a new understanding of Guido's statements on the transforming effects of *b-flat*. *B-flat* added to a chant does transform the mode by distorting its usual arrangement of tones and semitones. However, *b-flat* as the product of transposition does not transform the diatonic tonal sytem, but instead extends it.

In summary, Jacques, the touted conservative of the fourteenth century, makes an important theoretical contribution by explicitly identifying three modal positions within the gamut -- the final (the natural hexachord), the affinity (the hard hexachord), and the fourth above the final (the soft hexachord). There is no denying that he gave preference to the first two in practice, but he had clearly moved to a new understanding of the last, fashioned with its integral *b-flat*.

Lucidarium by Marchetto of Padua

Marchetto's *Lucidarium*, begun at Cesena and completed in Verona, probably between 1309 and 1318, contains a discussion of chant theory with some mention of the affinities.[79] Like Jacques, Marchetto makes a major contribution to the development of the concept of alternative finals.

Marchetto stresses the importance of melodic species for identifying mode:

> There are some who judge, without the rule of species, that songs belong to a mode only on account of the ascent and descent with respect to the final; their judgement is worthless, for many reasons.[80]

Marchetto recognizes that within the diatonic gamut, the modal species cannot be duplicated in their entirety at an alternative location. He notes that when *protus* is placed on *a*, the first species of fifth is present [*a* ♮ *c* *d* *e*], but above that, the second species of fourth occurs [*e* *f* *g* *aa*]. Species theory, however, held that *protus* should consist of the first species of fifth and the first species of fourth. Hence, for Marchetto, a mode positioned at the affinity is "irregular":

> . . . for any mode should be ended properly on its final, and then such mode is called "regular," because it is constructed according to its given rule. If, however, as mentioned, it cannot be ended on the final, it should [be ended] on the cofinal; and then such mode is called "irregular," because on account of the *accidens* which is or can be in it, it does not proceed according to its proper given rule, like the gradual "Nimis honorati sunt" and other similar [chants], . . .[81]

Marchetto refers to *confinales* on *a*, ♮, *c*, and *d*, and links their use to the existence of some *accidens* or altered tone. He then discusses the two problematic spots in "Nimis honorati sunt" (Examples 5 and 6).[82] Both *B-flat* and *E-flat* can be notated acceptably, as *F* and *b-flat*, if the gradual is moved to the *confinalis*. Thus, Marchetto advocates, at least in some instances, the transposition of chants to the fifth above the final to account for tones not found in the normal tone-semitone arrangement of the mode.

Ex. 5. "Tui" from the gradual "Nimis honorati sunt" according to Marchetto.

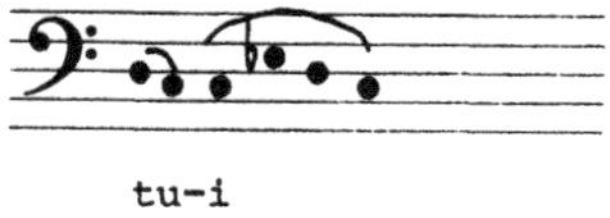

Ex. 6. "Deus" from the gradual "Nimis honorati sunt" according to Marchetto.

Immediately following the discussion of "Nimis honorati sunt," Marchetto states that some melodies terminate on notes other than their finals or cofinals, again because of certain accidentia. By way of illustration, he discusses the by-now familiar communion, "Beatus servus," with its problem spots at both the final and cofinal positions (Example 7).[83]

Ex. 7. Some problematic phrases of the communion "Beatus servus" according to Marchetto.

Final level

Cofinal Level

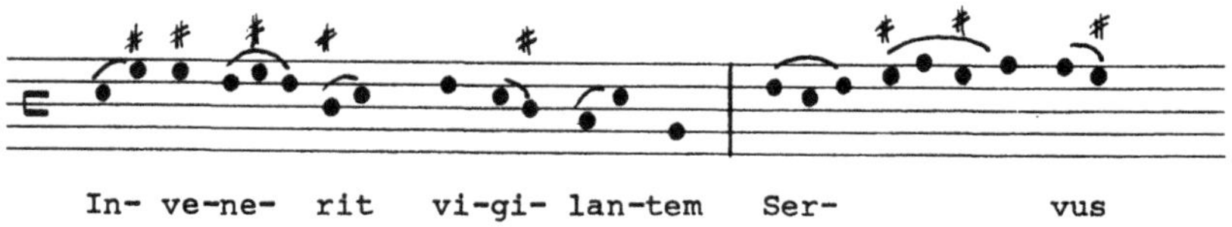

Marchetto's solution to the notational difficulties associated with this chant is the same as that proposed by Berno - a transposition to a. But Marchetto expresses the reasoning behind it in different terms: " . . . we say that any mode may be ended in any position on the hand where its species can be properly obtained."[84] Although Marchetto does not elaborate upon this statement, its significance cannot be overlooked. He indicates that a transposition to the fourth above the final retains the proper modal species. This statement looks forward to a concept of mode as an octave formation, a concept that in turn validated transposition in the modern sense -- transfer of an exact scalar arrangement to multiple locations through the use of chromatic tones. As will became apparent shortly, Marchetto certainly did not carry his theorizing about species beyond the statement quoted above. Yet his thinking, even more than Jacques', represents a turning point in the perennial issue of modal positions formed through b-flat. Jacques' explanation that relied on hexachord theory never caught on, but Marchetto's based on species became the foundation of post-1550 tonal theory.

Let us return to Marchetto's examples. In the quoted passage on "Nimis honorati sunt," Marchetto explicitly designates the ending on the affinity a "irregular," because the proper formation (species) is not present. Although his leanings towards species theory are strong enough to prompt this statement, they are not strong enough to result in rejection of the traditional modal position. His follow-up statements on "Beatus servus" are also noteworthy, because they reveal a need to qualify somewhat his otherwise unhesitating acceptance of the a *deuterus* position:

> . . . and such a mode is called "acquired," because its species are acquired through variation of the signs b and ♮, and because they are terminated in another position improperly.[85]

Marchetto is truly at a midway point in this ongoing theoretical controversy.

With this discussion of "Beatus servus," Marchetto's exposition on the affinities ends, but he does make a few other relevant comments during his description of the modes in ascending diatonic order. His remarks, which include chant citations, are summarized in Appendix C.

In conclusion, Marchetto offers quite a different approach from Jacques to the issue of alternative finals, one in which hexachord terminology does not play a part. Marchetto's designations of modes located a fifth above their finals as "irregular" and a fourth above as "acquired" are in part peculiar to him. But the attitude behind them is essentially that voiced by Berno centuries earlier -- both modal positions are necessary for the notation of a portion of the chant repertory. Most significant in Marchetto's presentation is his justification for finals a fourth above: "Any mode may be ended in any position on the hand where its species can be properly obtained."[86] This statement ultimately becomes the principle underlying the modern concept of transposition, but in the meantime, it provides the tradition-minded and hence diatonic-minded Marchetto with a logical framework for constructing modal positions by means of *b-flat*. Although his thought process is different, Marchetto, like Jacques, recognizes that *b-flat*, nominally a part of the gamut at two points, can play a role in the formulation of modes.

The next three fourteenth-century treatises do not present any significant expansion of the concept of related tones. But two of the authors, Heinrich Eger and Coussemaker's Anonymous I, are particularly noteworthy because of their reliance on grammatical terminology to describe modal constructions at related positions within the gamut. Furthermore, both refine Jacques' explanation of hexachords as modal seats.

Quatuor principalia musicae

The anonymous *Quatuor principalia musicae*, written or compiled in 1351 at Oxford,[87] provides a brief, but startling statement on related tones:

> It should be noted that plagal *protus*, *deuterus*, and *tritus* [modes], because they ascend to the fifth pitches, sometimes end on *a*, *♮*, and *c acutae* against authority, as it will be shown below. But because this happens rarely, it is not a rule, but a false usage (*abusio*). Those three letters are called *collaterales*.[88]

This writer represents the extreme negative position with respect to alternative finals. In place of the traditional statement that plagals sometimes end by necessity on *a*, *♮*, and *c*, he says that they end there "against authority" and designates the practice a false usage.[89] Apparently he objected to an ending at the *affinales* merely because a melody had ascended to that pitch region, an attitude that we have encountered before, but not couched in such negative terms. Another idiosyncracy of his discussion is his designation of endings on *a*, *♮*, and *c* as *collaterales*, a term applied by other theorists to the plagal modes.[90] Inasmuch as no one else I have encountered uses *collaterales* synonymously with *affinales*, it would seem that the author of this section of *Quatuor principalia* misunderstood this term.

In contrast to the quoted passage, a later statement recognizes the occasional need for an alternative final, particularly in mode two:

> And sometimes it ends on a acuta on account of a tone or semitone.[91]

Perhaps the compiler took this statement from another source, since it seems otherwise unlikely that the same author would be so accepting here, but not in the earlier quotation.

Overall, the Quatuor principalia musicae presents some isolated statements concerning related tones, statements that do not appear to represent the consistent views of a single author. Nevertheless, the treatise is the only extant source from mid-fourteenth-century England that transmits information on the affinities.

Cantuagium by Heinrich Eger von Kalkar

Heinrich Eger von Kalkar (1328-1408) was a monk of the Carthusian order who studied in Cologne and Paris. In 1380, during one of his trips to Cologne, he wrote a compendium entitled Cantuagium, which Hüschen characterizes as a schoolbook text for practical use, probably by members of the Carthusian order.[92]

Eger's modal prescriptions deal with chant finals, beginnings, and ranges. He sets forth what constitutes a "regular" chant with regard to mode:

> For let any song whatsoever appear doubtful and roaming according to its beginning or middle [range], yet, if in its ending it is regular, it is accepted and judged certain . . .[93]

Jacques de Liège had explained how a chant might be irregular in its beginning, middle, or end, but he concluded that one could determine the mode of any chant, regular or irregular, if it ended on a syllable associated with that mode. Eger appears to follow similar reasoning, although he expresses it in a much more abbreviated fashion than does Jacques:

> Wherefore, if a song sometimes has its final in other positions, namely at the fourth or fifth, octave, or others above the stated positions [D,E,F,G], which is permitted, because often it is sung higher more appropriately or more sweetly on account of either a semitone or b-flat existing in that place, this nevertheless arises for the reason that the previously stated terminal or final syllables [re,mi,fa,sol] are found proportionally in those notes. And so, from this, the first and second [modes] can have a lamire instead of their final because of the re within it; similarly, both

> the third and fourth [modes can have a lamire] because of the mi within it, and likewise in other instances. And if sometimes a song is ended on ut [recte c solfaut], as often occurs in the eighth mode and sometimes in the fifth, this happens only on account of sol or fa concealed there, by which such song is recognized.[94]

Judging by Eger's reference to alternative finals in the order fourth, fifth, and octave, he may have known Jacques' theory of affinity, but even if he did, he did not write about its implications. He states no preference for c solfaut as tritus (relationship at the fifth) versus tetrardus (relationship at the fourth). Furthermore, the usual qualifying reference to how the latter is formed through b-flat is absent from his discussion.

A final noteworthy point in the passage quoted above is Eger's reason for ending chants on alternative finals. He characterizes singing at the higher location as "often more appropriate or sweeter," the latter description being peculiar to his discussion. His final phrase, "on account of either a semitone or b-flat existing in that place," is ambiguous. Most likely "in that place" means the higher location, and he recognizes that the b-flat within the modus vocum or a semitone outside the modus vocum accommodates the chant's particular melodic character. But "in that place" might refer to the lower position, and possibly he is discussing the avoidance of a semitone or b-flat at that level. There is a clarification of this point later in the treatise.

In a final section,[95] Eger reveals that he, like Jacques, favored systematic classification of chants, and to this end, he adopts certain terms used, as he says, in the discipline of grammar. For instance, didactic speeches are those which have suitable construction, and accordingly, didactic chants "begin, proceed, and end regularly, observing that art or rule which bids to be followed."[96] The chants he labels "permissive" are significant in connection with the affinities:

> They are called permissive which are allowed to deviate from the art in a certain manner; nevertheless, their deviations or failings are excusable. Certain of these are called transposed, namely those which, occurring originally in the graves, were sung there harshly and dissonantly. Afterwards, [they were] transposed by the moderns into the acutae position because of the sweetness either of b-flat or of a tone or of the harmonies of another mode there. And this [occurs] through the diapente as in the antiphon "Germinavit radix" or through the diatessaron as in the antiphon "Oculi mei" and others.[97]

This passage clarifies Eger's earlier statement concerning how the higher position creates a sweeter sound than the original. Here Eger specifically links the sweetness with b-flat or a tone.[98] Once again, he shows no preference for the affinity at the fifth over that at the fourth.

In contrast to his designation of transposed chants as "permissive," Eger uses the term "defective" when he refers to chants on G sounding as protus:

> Certain [songs] are called defective, namely those which . . . do not have the proper final, but a final syllable suitable to its mode, as when a song of the first mode might be ended on G solreut because of re hidden there.[99]

Thus, he implies that the identity of G as the normal tetrardus final should not be changed to protus.

In summary, Eger presents a cohesive, favorable view of the affinities, although he never actually uses the word. In fact, he never discusses the relationship except in terms of syllable correspondence. He is less cautious than Jacques in awarding equal status to alternative finals established at the fourth and fifth above the normal finals. Finally, he confirms the long-standing disapproval of the change of the tetrardus final G into protus. Aside from the latter point, he reveals himself as a thinker not opposed to recording progressive ideas.

Coussemaker's Anonymous I

The anonymous treatise (Coussemaker, Anonymous I) entitled Tractatus de musica plana is attributed by Coussemaker to "Cujusdam Carthusiensis Monachi."[100] Heinrich Hüschen has suggested a date of c. 1380, principally because the treatise draws on Heinrich Eger von Kalkar's Cantuagium and contains a fourteenth-century representation of the monochord.[101]

In his approach to modal classification, Anonymous I emphasizes the importance of the final note, but also calls attention to ambitus, by which he distinguishes authentic from plagal forms, and within each, a regular usage from one "by license."[102] In this context, Anonymous I discusses chants that do not move within their normal ambitus:

> And if any song is found which neither begins nor ends on its regular degrees, but on its related [degrees], which will be discussed below, it should be said that such song is not simply regular, but rather, it is irregular, as in that responsory "Job scio Domine" which is assigned to the sixth mode, as is evident from the melody of the verse; however, the responsory itself neither begins regularly nor ends regularly.[103]

This is an early indication that for Anonymous I, as for a number of other writers so far encountered, all chants ending in the affinities are considered irregular.

Anonymous I's sixth chapter contains his main discussion of alternative finals. It is entitled "De gradibus finalibus octorum tonorum" or "Concerning the Final Degrees of the Eight Modes."[104] Rather than make the usual statement that chants sometimes end by necessity on the _affinales_, Anonymous I poses a question -- why are these related degrees joined to the principal final degrees? He responds that there are two reasons, one of convenience (_commoditatis_) and one of necessity (_necessitatis_). The meaning of "convenience" is vague:

> I say "of convenience" so that singers who might run too freely to all higher degrees in the composition of songs may be held back strictly.[105]

He seems to suggest that a related degree with its nucleus corresponding to that of the final gives a welcome framework to cantors who might be inclined to roam indiscriminately within a composition.

The explanation of "necessity" is the usual one, that certain chants must be notated in the _acutae_ because they have semitones or tones that cannot be realized in the _graves_. Anonymous I gives three examples of chants transferred to the affinities out of necessity: the first-mode antiphon "Magnum hereditatis mysterium," which needs a low _B-flat_, the second-mode antiphon "Tu Domine universorum," which also needs a low _B-flat_, specifically at "Qui nullam habes vides," and the second-mode communion "De fructu," which needs an _E-flat_ at "In oleo."[106]

In accordance with the two reasons "of convenience" and "of necessity," Anonymous I explains why _tetrardus_ does not have a related degree:

> And because the _tetrardus_, that is, the fourth _maneria_, does not permit the above-mentioned _impedimentum_ in its songs, it does not need to be transposed . . .

Further,

> The authentic _tetrardus_, that is, mode seven, although it ends on the last of the principal degrees [_G_], nevertheless it always moves in the _acutae_. Also, the plagal _tetrardus_, that is, mode eight, although it descends to the _graves_ below its final, nevertheless it always revolves in the usual degrees; thus it does not need to be transferred.[107]

Thus, Anonymous I suggests that _tetrardus_ modes do not have occurrences of _B-flat_ and _E-flat_ that might necessitate transposition to a related degree. Also, *tetrardus* chants already move about in the *acutae* as part of their normal range, so any issue of "convenience" is irrelevant. Anonymous I recommends that any *tetrardus* chant which had been transposed through ignorance be reinstated to its proper final position.[108]

There follows a parenthetical comment of great interest:

> . . . all the things which are mentioned above concerning the reason for the need of related notes can be saved by means of *conventae* [*recte* *coniunctae*][109] in the *graves* of a song of this type, as if it were being sung as perfect music. But to this it can be answered that such *conventae* [*recte* *coniunctae*] or such *musica ficta* should not be admitted easily into common songs, since this *musica ficta* derives from the mere curiosity and will of the composer, supported by no divine mystery.[110]

In this passage, the author considers an alternative to transposing chants that contain anomalous tones and semitones. He says they can be "saved in the *graves* through *coniunctae*," a term he seems to equate with *musica ficta*. Thus, the altered tones would be realized at the normal pitch level. He hesitates over the acceptability of this practice in chant, however, referring to the preference for transposition according to "both Saint Gregory and the monk Guido."[111] Both the word "preferably" and some of the subsequent phrases suggest, however, that he knew musicians who did allow altered tones (*coniunctae*) in chant.[112]

Anonymous I then summarizes the final degrees used in each mode, and in this context, he describes the endings on the *affinales* as "by license" (*licentialiter*). More significant, it is here that he makes his sole clear mention of related notes a fourth above the final. Specifically, mode four sometimes ends on *a lamire*, ". . . when the hexachord is of *b-flat* [i.e., the soft hexachord], as is evident in those antiphons 'Rorate caeli' and 'Emitte agnum.'"[113] Both antiphons fit Gevaert's theme 29 model (see p. 17), with its two inflections immediately above the final.[114]

Anonymous I also makes a statement on unusual seventh-mode endings:

> Also it happens that the seventh mode ends on *F faut*, on the line, and this when the hexachord is of *b-flat*. And both arise more by privilege than by right.[115]

Again, he describes an alternative ending effected by means of the soft hexachord. But the association of *tetrardus* with *F* interferes with the neat framework of a modal nucleus that is found in an analogous position within three hexachords. One interpretation of this passage is that Anonymous I, like the author of the Dialogus, recognized the similarity of ascent between tritus and tetrardus modes, and so was not adverse to shifting a chant between their basic positions. Yet in the next passage, he reiterates that F faut serves modes five and six and G solreut modes seven and eight, the former even when F is ut in the soft hexachord. Furthermore, when he spelled out the nucleus identifying each maneria, he assigned to tritus a semitone below, and tetrardus a whole tone, and so the semitone found below F faut would not accommodate tetrardus. Based on these several factors, it is possible, if not likely, that Anonymous I meant c solfaut, not F faut, in the quotation given above.

In the final paragraph of Chapter Six, Anonymous I states that there is one basic syllable associated with the finals of each maneria. He proceeds from the negative, that is, from the premise that a given pair of modes cannot end on every syllable found on their finals. Protus ending on D solre cannot use sol, and protus ending on a lamire cannot use la or mi. Having made the basic connection of protus with re, he proceeds to relate deuterus to mi, tritus to fa, and tetrardus to sol. As mentioned above, he adds that tritus F can be ut when the melody descends to F through b-flat, and tetrardus G can be ut when the melody descends to G through b-natural.

A final passage relevant to the affinities and transposition is found in Chapter Seven, where Anonymous I defines regular and irregular song. Like Eger's, his subcategories rely on grammatical terminology. A regular song is "that which does not exceed its prescribed boundaries with regard to beginning, middle, and end."[116] An irregular song exceeds them with regard to beginning, middle, or end, and further, that irregularity is either of materia, of form, or of both.[117] By irregular materia, Anonymous I means that the mode is not proper to the intended emotional affect. Irregular form is either excusable or inexcusable.

According to Anonymous I, excusable irregular form has, like its analogue in grammar, a reason why it can be made and a reason why it ought to be made. An authentic mode can enter the range peculiar to its plagal and vice versa because of the agreement they have, while the obligation to exceed boundaries is tied to the fulfillment of specific affects. Anonymous I mentions indignation and grief, among others.

Inexcusable irregular form, on the other hand, does not occur for any apparent reason. Here, Anonymous I focuses on chants transposed without cause, distinguished from those transposed by necessity. (Again he cites "Magnum hereditatis mysterium" as an example of the latter.) He finds the transposition of chants inexcusable when "it could be made otherwise pleasantly. . .,"[118] and the alternative he offers is emendation. Both this solution and the example he cites indicate that he knew the work of John, the author of <u>De musica</u>. Like John, he specifically criticizes the transition from <u>D</u> to <u>a</u> at "et porta coeli" in the responsory "Terribilis est locus iste."[119] Anonymous I concludes, however, that emendation would be undesirable in that instance, because "it is difficult to attempt something counter to long-standing usage, however perverse."[120] Thus, contrary to the position of Jacques de Liège, Anonymous I condones the transposition of this chant in spite of his disapproval of it. One cannot help but wonder whether "Terribilis est" might have been the sort of chant he meant to include under the designation "by convenience," since the issue of unfolding on two tonal levels is relevant to both that chant and this kind of transposition.

In summary, Anonymous I offers a discussion of the affinities distinctive in terms of its rhetoric, though its attitudes are closely aligned with those of his contemporaries. He labels all chants that end on the affinities irregular, and those which he admits in practice seem to coincide with the chants traditionally "transposed by necessity."

His understanding of alternative finals viewed through syllable association is complete, although conservative in application. He follows in the tradition of Jacques, rather than of Eger, in that he qualifies his acceptance of related notes a fourth above the final. They arise, he says, "more by privilege than by right." He shows the widespread hesitance towards full acceptance of <u>b-flat</u> and its attendant soft hexachord.

IV. *Coniunctae* or Transposition

Because the concept of the affinities is related to altered tones, discourses on *coniunctae* are germane to this study. Several treatises originating in the late fourteenth and fifteenth centuries contain information relevant to *coniunctae*: the Berkeley Manuscript,[1] the anonymous treatise in Rome, Vatican lat. 5129,[2] Coussemaker's *Anonymous XI*,[3] the Szalkai treatise in Esztergom, Erzbischoefliche Bibliothek, MS II, 395[4] and *Lectura* by Petrus Tallenderius.[5] The first four represent links in a chain of text transmission.

Each of the authors suggests or openly states that the use of *coniunctae* precludes the need for transposition of chants to related tones in the gamut. Oliver Ellsworth has argued that these theorists thus accept *coniunctae* in the chant repertory.[6] It is my contention that the writers or compilers used certain chant examples merely as "school demonstrations," since their readers were familiar with these melodies, and that their ultimate intention was to justify altered tones needed in polyphonic practice. Further, even if these writers in theory admit altered tones into chant by way of the *coniunctae*, their expressed preference for transposition as a means to avoid them remains constant.

The Berkeley Manuscript

The Berkeley Manuscript consists of five treatises, the third of which contains an explicit dating the work to 1375. The question of its authorship has not been resolved. Oliver Ellsworth has suggested two candidates, Jean Vaillant, a composer and singing teacher in Paris, and Gostaltus, a writer presumably of German extraction.[7]

In the explicit, the author calls himself a "compiler," but Ellsworth notes that his borrowings are typically subjected to revision. Therefore, Ellsworth considers him a compiler and editor in the manner of

Jacques de Liège and Jerome of Moravia.[8] It is significant, however, that the first treatise on modes and hexachords, which concerns us here, ". . . does not appear in any form in any source prior to the Berkeley MS . . .," according to Ellsworth,[9] who believes that it may have existed previously in a single prototype or may be a totally original work of the author. In either case, the first treatise or its prototype was known and borrowed from by the writers to be discussed later.

The first treatise of the Berkeley Manuscript begins with an explanation of the Guidonian hand, the gamut division according to _graves_, _acutae_, and _superacutae_ designations, the hexachords and the three _proprietates_ -- natural, hard, and soft, and mutation. The author next discusses _coniunctae_:

> . . . everyone can distinguish the syllables of any song and judge them as bound by reason, unless by chance some unusual song should turn up, which some call--but wrongly--_musica falsa_, others _musica ficta_; still others name it--and rightly--_coniunctae_. It is like a connection by the aforesaid regular properties. And so these _coniunctae_ were invented so that a song formerly called irregular could be brought into regularity by them in some manner. For a _coniuncta_ is the attribute, realized in actual singing, of permitting one to make a semitone out of a tone and conversely. Or rather, a _coniuncta_ is the mental transposition of any property or hexachord from its own location to another location above or below. As evidence of this, it must be noted that every _coniuncta_ is signed by b or #, placed in an unusual location. Also, wherever the sign b is placed, the true sound of that joint ought to be lowered by a major semitone and called fa. And where the sign # is placed, the sound of that joint ought to be raised by a major semitone and called mi.[10]

This author equates _coniuncta_ with _musica ficta_. In fact, his first definition of _coniuncta_ coincides with that given for _musica ficta_ by Johannes de Garlandia: ". . . when we make a tone into a semitone and vice versa."[11] Also, like _ficta_, _coniunctae_ are signed by _b_ and _#_(♮), called respectively _fa_ and _mi_. On the other hand, this author specifically states that the signs call for pitch alteration, a point not made in contemporaneous discussions of _ficta_.[12] _Coniunctae_ are thus clearly associated with the alteration of tones in the gamut. The word _coniuncta_ is, incidentally, the Latin equivalent of the Greek term _synemmenon_, meaning "connected." One recalls that Jerome of Moravia used the term _synemmena_ in referring to the flats useful in polyphony, and hence there is an historical link to the Berkeley author's use of _coniunctae_ for altered tones in general.[13]

The second definition of coniuncta steps beyond the descriptive to create a systematic theoretical framework for altered tones. The hexachord system was conceived with the tonal materials of chant in mind, a diatonic gamut, with the possible addition of b-flat in the acutae and superacutae. Yet the Berkeley author suggests that the hexachord system can be extended to include altered tones through the construct of a coniuncta. A coniuncta is then part of a process that preserves one of the three hexachord proprietates or qualities by means of one or more altered tones. For example, for the tone C-sharp, the author states:

> Its hexachord begins on A gravis, ending on F gravis, and this hexachord is sung by #. This coniuncta is nothing else than the mental transposition to a higher location of the property or hexachord that begins on Γ; . . .[14]

Aside from Berkeley, the other treatises do not give this second definition of the coniuncta as a mental transposition of a hexachord.[15] Since their discussions follow Berkeley's closely in other respects, it is possible that the omission was a conscious one, reflecting a hesitancy to accept the altered tones on the same level as the constituent notes of the gamut.[16]

The Berkeley author says that while others have named seven, eight, or more coniunctae, he accepts ten.[17] They are B-flat, C-sharp, E-flat, F-sharp, a-flat, c-sharp, e-flat, f-sharp, aa-flat, and cc-sharp. This statement confirms that the theory of coniunctae was not first proposed by this author.[18] Figure 5 lists the chants illustrating each coniuncta according to the Berkeley author (and the three related treatises). Except for the obscure "Ave," all the chants named by the Berkeley author are indexed by Bryden and Hughes (see listing of sources in Figure 5). Only one, the second-mode responsory "Emendemus in melius," is listed in a version that actually contains the altered tone described by the Berkeley author, in this instance, B-flat (Example 8).[19] There is evidence, however, that at least five other chants (marked with an asterisk) would have contained an altered tone if notated at the final level. Four of these, the responsory "Sancta et immaculata," the responsory "Gaude Maria," the communion "Beatus servus," and the responsory "Conclusit vias meas," are transposed to related tones in some surviving sources.[20] The fifth, the introit "Adorate Deum," ends on its normal final G in all its available sources. However, SYG shows a transposition up one degree of a brief passage, "Deum omnes angeli," that would contain e-flat if retransposed downward (Example 9).

Fig. 5. Chants cited as illustrations of various coniunctae in four treatises.

	Berkeley MS	Vat. lat. 5129 Anonymous	Anonymous XI	Szalkai MS
B^b	Sancta et immaculata* at "non poterant"	Sancta et immaculata* at "non poterant"	Sancta et immaculata* at "non poterant"	Sancta et immaculata* at "non poterant"
	Emendemus in melius* at "et miserere"	Emendemus in melius* at "miserere"	Emendemus in melius* at "et miserere"	Emendemus in melius* at "et miserere"
		A timore at "eripe Domine animam meam"		
			Fuerunt sine querela* at "calicem Domini"	Fuerunt sine querela* at "calicem Domini"
$C^\#$	Vidimus stellam eius in oriente			
E^b	Gaude Maria* at "interemisti"	no examples	Gaude Maria* at "interemisti"	Gaude Maria* at "interemisti"
			Gloriosa sanctissimi at "et precibus"	Glosiosa sanctissimi at "et precibus"
			O Crux gloriosa* at "et mirabile signum"	O Crux gloriosa* at "et admirable signum"
$F^\#$	Beatus servus* at "invenerit"	no examples	Beatus servus* at "vigilantem"	Beatus servus* at "vigilantem"
			(Gloria in excelsis Deo. Missus est angelus) (musical example)	
				Quae est ista* at "per desertum"

Fig. 5. (continued)

	Berkeley MS	Vat. lat. 5129 Anonymous	Anonymous XI	Szalkai MS
a♭	Conclusit vias meas*	no examples	Conclusit vias meas* at "lapidem contra me"	Conclusit vias meas* at "quid contra me"
			Fidelis servus at "in tempore"	Fidelis servus at "in tempore"
			Jesum tradidit impius*	
c♯	Ave at "triclina"	no examples		
			Assumpta est Maria in caelum*	Assumpta est Maria in caelum*
			Beatus servus* at "invenerit vigilantem"	
e♭	Adorate Deum*	Adorate Deum* (musical ex.)	Adorate Deum* at "Deum"	
	Multipharie at "nobis"			
			Immutemur* at "ieiunemus	Immutemur habitu* at "ieiunemus"
				Ite in orbem at "universum"
f♯	Si consurrexistis at "que sursum sunt"	no examples		
	Liberavit			
	Caro mea			
			Hodie Maria virgo at "Maria"	Hodie Maria virgo at "Maria"

Fig. 5. (continued)

	Berkeley MS	Vat. lat. 5129 Anonymous	Anonymous XI	Szalkai MS
f#				Ingressus Pilatus at "iudeorum"
aa^b	no examples	no examples	no examples	no examples
cc#	no examples			

Sources as Listed in Bryden and Hughes' Index

responsory "Sancta et immaculata"	LR 62, 247, PM 38, AR 130, LU 384, AM 1184, VP 39, LA 34, WA 29
responsory "Emendemus in melius"	GR 86, WA 85, LA 128, LU 524, PM 47
"Alleluia. Vidimus stellam eius in oriente"	GR 58, LU 460, GrS 19, GB 33^v, SYG 31
responsory "Gaude Maria Virgo"	PM 146, AM 1195, VP 130, LA 354, WA 271
communion "Beatus servus"	GR [45], LU 1203, GrS 223, SYG 28, GB 29
responsory "Conclusit vias meas"	LA 176, WA 115
introit "Adorate Deum"	GR 70, LU 488, SYG 42, GB 39, GrS 23
"Alleluia. Multifarie olim Deus loquens"	GR 49, LU 441, GrS H, SYG 19, GB 31^v
commmunion "Si consurrexistis"	GR 249, OHS 787, LU 791, SYG 157, GB 135, GrS 120
antiphon "Liberavit"	OHS 382, LU 638, WA 118, LA 190
antiphon "Caro mea requiescit"	OHS 593, LU 573, WA 125, LA 201
antiphon "A timore inimici"	AR 192, AM 52, 53, WA 67, LA 95
responsory "Fuerunt sine querela"	LR 138, LA 509, WA 413

Fig. 5 (continued)

Sources as Listed in Bryden and Hughes' Index

antiphon "O Crux gloriosa"	WA 370 (inc illeg)
communion "Fidelis servus"	GR 570, LU 1185, GB 52^v, SYG 56, GrS 224
responsory "Jesum tradidit impius"	OHS 507, LU 711, LA 199
"Alleluia. Assumpta est Maria in caelum"	GR 591, LU 1603
antiphon "Immutemur habitu in cinere"	GR 85, LU 523, GrS 30
antiphon "Hodie Maria virgo"	WA 272
responsory "Quae est ista"	PM 261, LR 253, LA 443, WA 355
responsory "Ite in orbem"	LR 114, LA 258, WA 148

Ex. 8. Excerpt from the responsory "Emendemus in melius."

(GR 86)

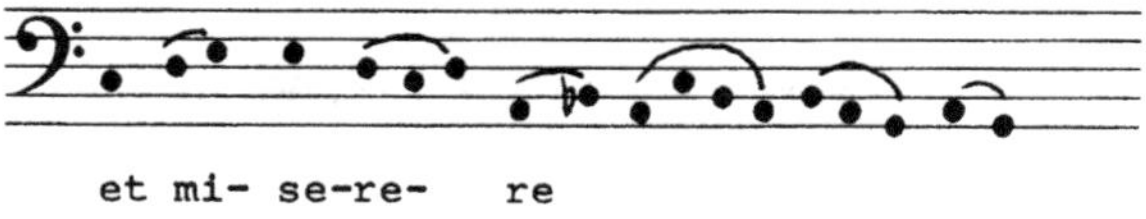

Ex. 9. Excerpt from the introit "Adorate Deum."

(GR 70) (SYG 42) transposed down

As for the six remaining chants named by the Berkeley author,[21] there is no surviving indication, or, at most, only the barest of hints, that a version existed with the altered tones he mentions. In the case of the antiphons "Liberavit" and "Caro mea," which begin alike, the only apparent reason for the addition of *f-sharp* at the particular point indicated by the Berkeley author would be to perfect the diminished fifth (Example 10).[22] For the "Alleluia. Vidimus stellam," the communion "Si consurrexistis," and the passage of "Ave" illustrated by the author, the altered tones appear to result from applying the raised-leading-tone principle (Example 11).[23] This superimposition of a contrapuntal principle onto chant lends support to a theory that the Berkeley author was using chant melodies merely as illustrations in a presumed defense of polyphonic practice.

Ex. 10. Incipit for the antiphons "Liberavit" and "Caro mea" according to the Berkeley author.

Ex. 11. Excerpts from three chants according to the Berkeley author.

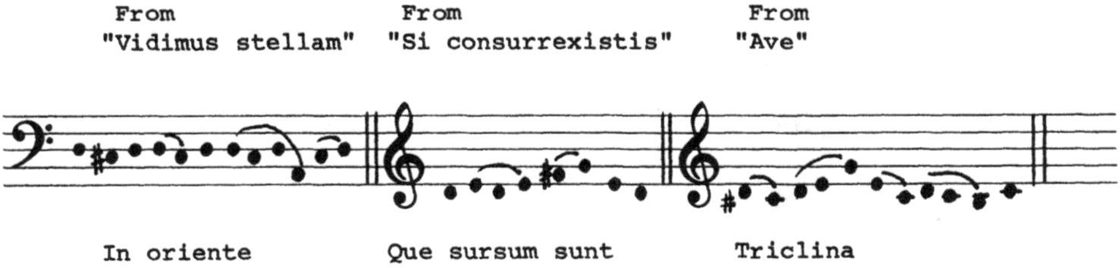

In any case, when the Berkeley author treats the subject of mode in his first treatise, he reveals an awareness of alternative finals:

> Therefore, every ecclesiastical song of the first or second tone ought regularly to end on D *gravis*; it can, nevertheless, end more freely on A *acuta*. All ecclesiastical song of the third or fourth tone ought to end on E *gravis*; the third can end more freely on B *acuta* and the fourth on A *acuta* (provided that mi is sung there by b). Therefore, all ecclesiastical song of the fifth or sixth tone ought regularly to end on F *gravis*; nevertheless, it can end more freely on C *acuta*. Likewise, all ecclesiastical song of the seventh or eighth tone ought regularly to end on G *gravis*; nevertheless, it can end more freely on D *acuta*.[24]

This brief statement provides no indication as to whether the author understood the application of the principle of the affinities in the same sense that, for instance, Jacques de Liège did. The inclusion of *d acuta* for *tetrardus* suggests that the author may not have been thoroughly familiar with practice regarding alternative finals, since *tetrardus* had traditionally been denied one at the fifth above.

At the conclusion of this presentation of chant theory, the Berkeley author devotes a paragraph to mode of other songs -- "motets, ballades, rondeaux, virelais, and the like."[25] As Richard Crocker has stated, this is the earliest reference to mode in polyphony.[26] Significantly, this discussion, in contrast to the one on chant, is presented in terms of hexachord syllables, a difference in treatment that again emphasizes the polyphonic bent of the Berkeley author -- he applies practical terminology to finals in polyphony, but not in chant. Figure 6 shows the appropriate finals for each modal pair as stated by the Berkeley author.[27]

Fig. 6. Modal finals in polyphony according to the Berkeley author.

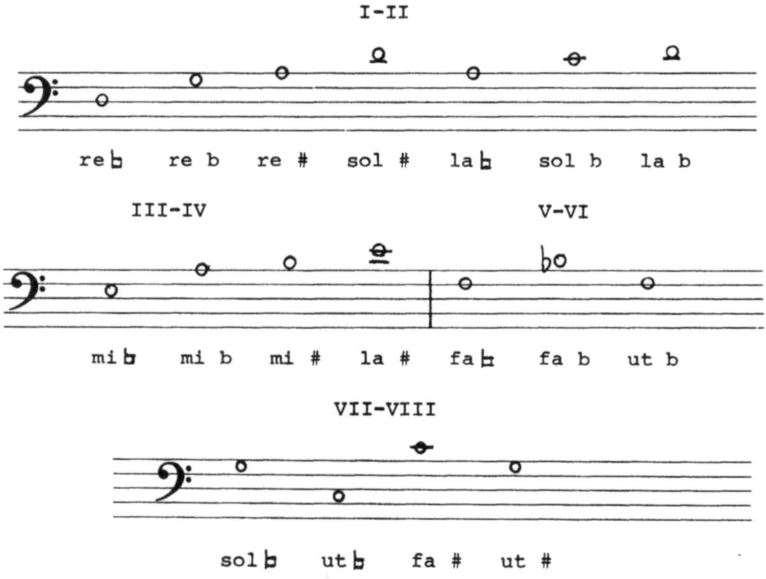

Three points are revealed in this exposition. First, each of the basic finals, *D*, *E*, *F*, and *G*, receives an additional syllable besides the one usually associated with it. Jacques had in a more limited fashion proposed an additional syllable for *F* and *G*, *ut*, apparently in recognition of hexachord mutations that occur with frequency. In the Berkeley author's presentation, *d* (*protus* up an octave) can be *sol* in the hard hexachord or *la* in the soft, while similarly *e* (*deuterus* up an octave) can be *la* in the hard. Further, *F* can be *ut* in the soft hexachord and *G* can be *ut* in the hard.

Second, all four *maneriae* have a modal final at the fourth above the normal final: *protus* on *G*, *deuterus* on *a*, *tritus* on *b-flat*, and *tetrardus* on *c*. Interestingly, the last, *c*, is not placed within the soft, but rather within the hard hexachord. In order to explain this anomaly, a third point seems relevant: *tritus* has lost *c* as an alternative final. Ellsworth believes that the takeover of *c* in the hard hexachord by *tetrardus* is related to the use of leading tones in polyphonic cadences. Specifically, in both *tritus* and *tetrardus* modes, a semitone would now occur under the final, whereas in chant, *tritus* has a semitone below, distinguished from the whole tone of *tetrardus*. Without the latter distinction, the tone-semitone arrangement *above* the final acquired a new significance. Since the ascent by tone-tone-semitone from *c* agrees best with *tetrardus*, *c* took on that association as opposed to *tritus*.[28]

This discussion of mode in polyphony is significant because it reveals the author's forward-looking understanding of the tonal system. Further, it contributes to an impression that his musical insights were the result of his consideration of polyphony rather than of chant. This latter point is worth emphasizing because it supports a contention that the Berkeley author did not understand, or understood but chose not to discuss, the connection between *affinales* and altered tones in chant theory. Instead, he viewed altered tones in terms of the *coniuncta*, a concept better suited to the exigencies of polyphonic practice.

Anonymous, Rome, Vatican lat. 5129

The anonymous treatise found in Rome, Vatican lat. 5129, dates from around 1400.[29] Its first mention of *coniunctae* occurs early in the treatise following brief discussions of the hand, hexachords, and psalm tones. Under the rubric "Sequitur de coniunctis" appears:

> The first is signed with *b-flat* on *B gravis*, as is evident in the responsory "Sancta et immaculata," in the place where one says "non poterant," and in the responsory "Emendemus in melius," in the place where one says "miserere," and in the antiphon "A timore," in the place where one says "eripe Domine animam meam."[30]

What is striking about this passage is its naming of the same two chant examples given by the Berkeley author for the first *coniuncta* (see Figure 5). The anonymous author adds a third example, the antiphon "A timore."[31] Although no further enumeration of *coniunctae* occurs, there are two indications that the author intended to continue. One is the obvious plural reference in the rubric. The other is the inclusion of musical notation for the responsory "Sancta et immaculata" and then unexpectedly for the introit "Adorate

Deum," a chant that was one of Berkeley's examples for the coniuncta e-flat. The coincidence of these examples suggests that the anonymous author may have known the first Berkeley treatise, or else the prototype of it.[32]

The second and third mentions of the coniuncta both occur during discussions about polyphony. Specifically, in his explanation of intervals, the author refers to the change of a minor third into a major one by means of a coniuncta. He continues:

> What is a coniuncta? It is to make a semitone out of a tone, or a tone out of a semitone, or a tone and a semitone out of two tones, or two tones out of a tone and a semitone.[33]

The third reference appears in the last section of the treatise, which Albert Seay believes may represent the beginning of another source copied by the scribe in error.[34] In verse form, the author enumerates eight coniunctae: B-flat, E-flat, F-sharp, a-flat, c-sharp, e-flat, f-sharp, and aa-flat. Then:

> And so one asks: what is coniuncta in music? A coniuncta in music is a sign or figure by which (according to the voice) in a hexachord a semitone is made from a tone and a tone from a semitone.
>
> Why was the coniuncta invented? It was invented for two reasons; the first reason was a reason of necessity, the second for making it from the reversal, or the second reason was in order to have a more beautiful sound or a sweeter semitone.[35]

The second and third mentions of coniuncta define it respectively as a pitch alteration and the sign that represents it. The reasons given for inventing coinunctae (presented nowhere else that I have discovered) are necessity and beauty. These are the same two reasons given by some theorists for the existence of musica ficta,[36] a correspondence that again suggests the relationship of coniunctae to polyphony, rather than to chant.

Anonymous XI

As it is presented in Coussemaker's edition, the treatise by the unidentified author known as Anonymous XI appears to be a unified work. Study of its one surviving source, British Library, Add. MS 34200, has led Richard Wingell to conclude, however, that it consists of a number of treatises, which may or may not be related.[37] They were copied into the manuscript during the second half of the fifteenth century by several scribes of uncertain nationality.

Sections or treatises one, two, and three, as designated by Wingell, are relevant to the present study. The first, which is about music in general, mentions _affinales_ in the context of naming the tetrachords of the gamut:

> . . . _D E F G_ are called _finales_, because every song regularly composed and not transposed ends on them. After these follow four, namely _a b c d_ which can be called _affinales_, as it were, "like finals," since just as a song can be ended principally on the four preceding notes, so it can be ended less directly on these four.[38]

The second treatise begins "Sequitur de naturis coniunctarum" and is an exposition on _coniunctae_ related to that found in the Berkeley manuscript. As Figure 5 indicates, the chants cited in association with each _coniuncta_ coincide for the most part with those cited by Berkeley, although Anonymous XI adds a few more. The basic wording and ordering of their respective explanations also agree.[39] However, in both the introductory paragraph and in the individual discussions that follow, Anonymous XI offers a way to avoid each _coniuncta_ by means of transposition. For example, he refers to three chants that contain _B-flat_:

> But if someone wished to avoid the aforementioned _coniunctae_, then this responsory, namely, "Sancta et immaculata" should be begun on _a acuta_, that is, on _a lamire_; but the following two responsories, namely "Fuerunt sine querela" and "Emendemus" should be begun on _E finalis_, that is, on _E lami_.[40]

In all three instances, these recommended positionings are at a pitch level a fifth above that usually associated with the given mode.[41]

Referring again to Figure 5, a high percentage of the chants cited by Anonymous XI apparently called for some altered tones at the final level (see asterisks). The chants he related to _B-flat_, _E-flat_, and _F-sharp_ would need those exact tones.[42] However, those cited for _a-flat_, _c-sharp_, _e-flat_, and _f-sharp_ would not necessarily have the altered tones that Anonymous XI implied they would. It may be that he engaged in a bit of hypothetical positioning of some of the chants so that he could illustrate higher altered tones. This conjecture is supported by the fact that he cites "Beatus servus" under _c-sharp_, after having already cited it under _F-sharp_.[43]

In spite of the repositioning that Anonymous XI carried out for purposes of demonstration, it is clear that he was trying to address the problem of altered tones actually found in some chants. After he defines _coniuncta_ as making a semitone out of a tone and vice versa, he says, ". . . the knowledge of such coniunctae is necessary in plainchant and also in polyphony . . ."[44] Unlike the Berkeley author, he does not attempt to legitimize the tones by embedding them in a hexachordal framework. In fact, he cautions against equating the named positions with the mi-fa semitones inherent in the gamut.[45] Most revealing of his attitude towards coniunctae is his suggestion that they can be avoided in notation through transposition. Thus, the concept of the affinities continues to serve the theorist confronted with altered tones in chant, even as he espouses a new concept, the coniuncta, to account for them in polyphonic practice.

The third treatise is a tonary, which Wingell believes may have been written along with the first in the thirteenth century, primarily because the language of these two sections draws occasionally on thirteenth-century usage.[46] Wingell failed to note, however, that the tonary contains the word coniuncta several times, a clear indication of origin later than the thirteenth century.

In the introductory passages to the tonary, the author makes a rather lucid statement concerning chants that end on alternative finals:

> . . . but [they] also [end] on others, namely, on a, b, c, or d acutae, that is, on a lamire, b fabmi, c solfaut, or d lasolre, which are referred to by another name, affinales. And therefore, because just as it [a song] can be ended primarily on the four notes previously enumerated, so it can be ended incidentally on these four. And so, in this art simple songs of this type are accustomed to cause doubt, because they are not regularly ended on their final notes. For this reason, some are asserted to be irregular, when nevertheless, very many songs of diverse modes are not able to rest on the proper final seat, sometimes because of a b-flat or because of the effect of a tone or semitone. Therefore, we should not consider antiphons that transfer to [other] positions irregular, but call them transposed songs.[47]

Anonymous XI obviously disagrees with those theorists who consider all chants ending on the affinales "irregular." He recognizes the necessity for their transposition in order to avoid b-flat or some altered tone.

When the author summarizes the finals for each maneria, he includes a lamire for mode four, specifically for theme 29 antiphons such as "Stetit Angelus," "Benedicta tu in mulieribus," and "Exaltata est."[48] Later, in the tonary proper, he cites these chants and others which must be transposed, along with their differentiae, to the fourth above the normal final. For example:

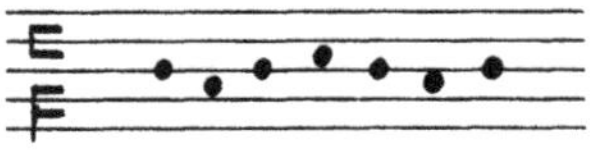

EVOVAE

This differentia however has one initial letter, namely G finalis, that is G solreut; but because an antiphon with this differentia beginning on G solreut proceeds less perfectly by coniunctae, thus for the integrity of solfami, and to avoid coniunctae, it takes its beginning on c acuta, that is, on c solfaut, and then the EVOVAE of this differentia should place its tenor on d lasolre . . .

EVOVAE 49

The author stresses that this class of fourth-mode antiphons, if begun on G, will contain coniunctae (presumably F-sharps) and cannot be solmized. To avoid the problem, the author recommends transposition of the antiphons (from a beginning on G to one on c) and of their reciting tones (from a to d). Thus, the author links his earlier discussion of coniunctae to chant theory and practice.

In summary, the first three treatises of Anonymous XI present a traditional understanding of affinales that has been integrated and reconciled with the newer concept of the coniuncta. This was not the case with the Berkeley treatise, in which the need to systematize a theory of altered tones occupied a major part of the author's attention.

The Szalkai Treatise

The Szalkai treatise, Esztergom, Erzbischoefliche Bibliothek, MS II, 395, is part of a diary kept by the fifteen-year-old Laszlo Szalkai (1475-1526) while he was studying in the cloister school at Sarospatak in 1490-91. Folios 30a-63b preserve Szalkai's music notes and represent the only extant music schoolbook from medieval Hungary.[50] Unlike many other music compendia of the fourteenth and fifteenth centuries, Szalkai's deals only with chant theory. Dénes Bartha has estimated that one-fourth of the text is actually based on school lectures, while the rest is derived from previous writers. Foremost among these is Anonymous XI.

Whether Szalkai knew the source upon which Coussemaker based his edition of Anonymous XI, Regensburg, Bischoefliche Zentralbibliothek 98 (formerly owned by the Abbey of St. Maximinus, Trier), or some other source of it remains an open question.[51] Whatever the case, Szalkai interpolates new material into the portions of Anonymous XI he reproduces. These include a few noteworthy changes in the section, "Sequitur de naturis coniunctarum," which otherwise closely agrees with Anonymous XI's passage of the same title. The latter begins, "Now follows a discussion of the nature of coniunctae. About the subject we must note: one might ask, what is a coniuncta?"[52] Szalkai interpolates between these two sentences a parenthetical statement:

> The reason, however, for the invention of coniunctae is the transposition or non-transposition of songs, whence if sometimes a certain song were transposed, it would not require a coniuncta of this kind, and conversely, if it were not transposed, it would require [a coniuncta] . . .[53]

Thus, from the outset, Szalkai asserts that the use of coniunctae is an alternative to the transposition of chant.

Szalkai's musical examples agree for the most part with those of Anonymous XI (see Figure 5). For F-sharp, Szalkai mentions the communion "Beatus servus" plus the responsory "Quae est ista."[54] For both a-flat and c-sharp, Szalkai omits the chant named last by Anonymous XI. He also omits the introit "Adorate Deum" for e-flat, but adds the responsory "Ite in orbem."[55] Finally, he gives a second example for f-sharp, the responsory "Ingressus Pilatus."[56]

The Szalkai treatise differs somewhat from Anonymous XI in its exposition of the affinales. When Szalkai first employs the term to designate the tetrachord above the finals, the wording is only slightly changed.[57] However, in the tonary, where Anonymous XI holds forth on the subject of alternative finals and the reasons for them, Szalkai offers rules for regular ascent and descent of authentics and plagals.[58] Nevertheless, he eventually does communicate the essence of Anonymous XI's view that endings in the affinales are not irregular.[59]

A further apparent difference between the treatises concerns the use of a as an alternative final for mode four. Szalkai presents the same differentiae cited by Anonymous XI (see above, p. 93), but he does not recommend their transposition, nor does he mention relevant coniunctae.[60] Still, since in the section on coniunctae Szalkai recommends a transposition of the third-mode communion "Beatus servus" to a, it seems unlikely that he would reject the transposition of similar fourth-mode chants.

Lectura by Petrus Tallanderius

Lectura by Petrus Tallanderius does not appear to represent a link in the chain of text transmission to which the four previously discussed treatises evidently belong. But because Tallanderius discusses transposition as an alternative to *coniunctae*, the treatise is relevant to the present study.

Lectura, apparently written in the mid-fifteenth century,[61] is found in Rome, Vatican lat. 5129, the source of an anonymous treatise discussed earlier. According to its implicit, it was Tallanderius' intention to discuss both rules of chant and of measured music.[62] The section in Vatican lat. 5129 is devoted almost exclusively to chant, however, ending with the explicit "Finis Cantus Planus, Deo Laus." Albert Seay considers it likely that there was once a second section on measured music.[63]

The treatise is amazingly concise, even though it covers numerous topics, including music and its effects, the hand, hexachords, mutations, modal classification, psalm tones, composition according to modal affect, and basic notation. Many subjects are presented solely in the form of a chart, a verse, or a musical example. In comparison to the compact treatment given these topics, the generous amount of space allotted to *coniunctae* by Tallanderius is striking.[64]

Tallanderius' definition of *coniuncta* introduces a slight twist on the prevailing one: he defines it not as making a semitone out of a tone, and vice versa, but rather as the change of any *mi* to *fa* or of any *fa* to *mi*. Although he does not spell out the possible *coniunctae*, his musical examples contain a total of ten, including every point in the gamut where *mi* or *fa* occurs, except *♮ mibfa* and the same an octave higher (see Figure 7). Thus, like the Berkeley author, Tallanderius allows *B-flat*, *C-sharp*, *E-flat*, *F-sharp*, *a-flat*, *c-sharp*, *e-flat*, *f-sharp*, *aa-flat*, and *cc-sharp*. It is significant that he illustrates each *coniuncta* as part of a three- or four-note scalar figure. Example 12 shows his representation of *B-flat*:

Ex. 12. Tallanderius' representation of the *coniuncta B-flat*.

Although Tallanderius makes no mention of the *coniunctae* in relation to transposed hexachords, these musical segments do suggest that he thought of the *coniunctae* as part of transposed tetrachords, if not full hexachords. In each instance, he starts the figure on what would be *ut* in order to yield the *coniuncta* as *mi* or *fa*, the note on which he generally stops.

Lectura contains a full paragraph on alternative finals:

> Further, modes can end anywhere provided that they do not let go the armonia of their songs. Albeit many assert that songs are irregular which end anywhere except in the mentioned four letters. It should be noticed that if any song ends on a lamire, there it can be of the first, second, third, or fourth [mode]; example[s] of this: concerning the first, "Cunctipotens," etc.; concerning the second, "Requiem aeternam," etc.; concerning the third, "Beatus servus"; concerning the fourth, [blank].[65]

Tallanderius recognizes that there is a school of thought which calls chants irregular when they end on alternative finals. That he is in disagreement with such an opinion is confirmed shortly after the quotation given above. He reiterates what others say, and then adds, "But that should be called simply 'to change species.'"[66] Thus, Tallanderius, like Marchetto before him, openly acknowledges that alternative modal positions in the gamut do not necessarily preserve modal species. Additionally, by allowing a lamire to serve as the final of modes one, two, three, and four, he indicates that he sanctions the use of alternative finals at both the fourth and fifth above.[67]

Tallanderius follows the above remarks with a brief aside that begins, "It follows that it is not proper to assign coniunctae everywhere . . ."[68] Here he implies that he recognizes a danger in notating chants with coniunctae, even though it might be more desirable to keep the chants at their original and proper position. The danger apparently is that someone might take it upon himself to cancel the coniunctae, "for ignorance of coniunctae destroys the armoni(c)ae of a song and makes regular [songs] irregular."[69] It appears that, for Tallanderius, emendation, rather than transposition, is what makes chants "irregular."

Finally, Tallanderius treats the subjects of finals, intonation formulas, etc., in verse. The verse on alternative finals is conservative, referring only to those a fifth above, and including the G-d pair for the sake of symmetry:

> Est in D vel in A primus atque secundus,
> Ternum cum quarto in B vel in E reperimus.
> Quintum cum sexto C vel F tu semper habeto.
> Septimus, octavus in G vel in D requiescent.[70]

Fig. 7. Positions in the gamut where coniunctae occur according to Petrus Tallanderius.

Γ	A	B	C	D	E	F	G	a	b	♮	c	d	e	f	g	aa	bb	♮♮	cc	dd	ee
ut	re	mi	fa	sol	la	fa	sol	la	fa	mi	sol	la	la	fa	sol	la	fa	mi	sol	la	la
			ut	re	mi	ut	re	mi			fa	sol	mi	ut	re	mi			fa	sol	
							ut	re			ut	re			ut	re					
		↓	↓		↓	↓		↓			↓		↓	↓		↓			↓		
		fa	mi		fa	mi		fa			mi		fa	mi		fa			mi		
		B^b	$C^\#$		E^b	$F^\#$		a^b			$c^\#$		e^b	$f^\#$		aa^b			$cc^\#$		

V. The Rise of Octave Species Theory

The fifteenth-century treatises discussed in the previous chapter focus on mode as it relates to the chant repertory. In the 1470s and '80s, Johannes Tinctoris uniquely turned to the issue of mode in polyphony. Perhaps in reaction to the practice of using texted flats and flat signatures in polyphonic compositions, Tinctoris expressly accepted transpositions to related notes a fourth above the usual finals. His contemporaries are conservative by comparison as they continue to make only passing reference to transpositions to the upper fourth while they describe in detail transpositions to the affinities.

In the first two decades of the sixteenth century, consideration of polyphonic practice seems to affect theorists' statements on mode rather more consistently. Those two decades constitute a period during which transpositions to the affinities and to notes a fourth above the usual finals are described and accepted on an equal basis. The 1520's, however, witnessed the rise of species theory, in which a mode is equated primarily to an octave species -- a particular arrangement of tones and semitones as defined within a diatonic octave, and this development was to effect the traditional view of the affinities. Although there had been theorists from the late ninth century onward who had used species terminology in discussing mode, they did not consider species fundamental to modal recognition. Instead, the concept of a recognizable modal nucleus, which underlies the concept of the affinities, had prevailed.

The rise of species theory coincides with outspoken criticism of the affinities by some eminent theorists of the 1520's and 1530's, the foremost being Pietro Aaron and Martin Agricola. Side by side with them are theorists who espouse the new species theory, but who are still willing to allow the validity of the affinities concept. The culminating criticism of the affinities occurs in Glareanus' Dodecachordon of 1547.

Glareanus rejects the affinities because of their irregular species content and creates new modes in their stead. This chapter traces the fifteenth- and sixteenth-century developments leading to this milestone in the history of music theory.

Declaratio musicae disciplinae by Ugolino of Orvieto

Albert Seay characterizes Ugolino's Declaratio musicae disciplinae of 1430 as one of the last speculative treatises of music.[1] Ugolino's approach to chant theory is not that of a practicing musician, but of a university-trained scholar presenting a rational explanation of a system. At least with regard to the issue of affinities, however, he reveals a knowledge of practice and a willingness to adapt his theory to the deamnds of that practice.

Ugolino's exposition on modes is grounded in the principle of constituent species -- each mode has a perfect formation that consists of a diapente and a diatessaron species joined to form an octave species. Unlike his predecessors who also utilized species theory to define mode, Ugolino uniquely incorporates some hexachord theory into his explanations.

Chapter Six is entitled "De troporum fine seu terminatione" or "Concerning the End or Termination of Modes."[2] Following the practice of his thirteenth- and fourteenth-century forebears, he identifies the primary finals by letter and syllable, namely, D, E, F, and G, respectively re, mi, fa, and sol. He continues:

> But these syllables and letters are graves and in them the ends of modes are established so that there is fulfillment through the perfection and formation of the authentics and their plagals. . . . If they [modes] were located in the higher [notes], the order of species, on which the formation of modes depends, is lost entirely, as is evident to the intelligent. Accordingly, modes are established in these seats by necessity. But because of certain [things] which sometimes happen which are to be stated below, the three acutae syllables and the three letters, corresponding to the first three graves syllables and letters, have been added, so that the end and termination of the modes may also be there, namely, re, mi, and fa, joined to a, ♮, and c, . . .[3]

Ugolino refers to related tones on a, ♮, and c, and like Marchetto, remarks that the proper modal species are lost at this higher position. But his follow-up statements differ. Whereas Marchetto merely labeled the alternative position "irregular," Ugolino draws upon the hexachord framework to justify its use -- a, ♮, and c do possess an identifying modal nucleus, as their syllables re, mi, and fa reveal.

The brief passage quoted above is the only one devoted to the affinities until near the end of Book One. At the end of his tonary, Ugolino discusses chants that are difficult to classify, particularly the graduals of the "Justus ut palma" type and the communion "Beatus servus." In both instances, chant sources preserve them with a finals. Although Ugolino's predecessors frequently discussed the reasons for notating "Beatus servus" in this way, they gave less attention to the "Justus ut palma" graduals.[4]

Ugolino introduces his discussion of the "Justus ut palma" graduals in Chapter One Hundred and Fifty, "De troporum terminatione prima et secunda" or "Concerning the Primary and Secondary Ending of Modes":[5]

> For example, in the primary and secondary ending places, authentic and plagal modes can establish their end, but in the primary [ones], these modes, those which retain the suitability of their form, place their seat. However, those which undergo unsuitability (inconvenientia) when placed in these primary endings are established in the secondary ending places, because they are not able to have the series of neumes or form and order of tones, ditones, and other intervals in the primary ending places which they have in the secondary [ones].[6]

By stating that some chants are "unsuitable" at the finales location,[7] Ugolino suggests that these graduals were transposed because their particular pitch content could not be notated at the lower level. Among the "Justus ut palma" graduals, he first discusses "Haec dies," which was mentioned by several eleventh-century writers as well. Like them, he describes certain of its intervals that are formed with B-flat.[8]

Ugolino's explanation for the location of the gradual "Justus ut palma" in the acutae is somewhat more circuitous. His description can be judged against the version found in the Graduale Romanum (Example 13).[9] He refers to the words "caedrus Libani" as they appear in the transposed position with b-natural on "-drus" and F on "-ba-", and says that the tritone between them should be altered by adding b-flat, and thus the third species of diatessaron is created (F‿G‿a‿b). That species cannot be formed in the primary position a fifth lower, because there one finds B-natural and E, and they form a second species diatessaron (B‿C‿D‿E), which "is not according to the order of neumes of the gradual."[10]

Ex. 13. Excerpt from the gradual "Justus ut palma" (GR 42).

On first reading, it appears that Ugolino is choosing the higher position because the tritone can be corrected there. In reference to the unaltered interval, however, he indicates that it cannot occur at the lower level -- F to b-natural does not find its equivalent in B-flat to E. Thus, he again indirectly remarks on the failure of the gamut to provide the low B-flat needed in certain chants. The issue of correcting the tritone is a concealment for this more fundamental problem.[11]

Ugolino closes Chapter One Hundred and Fifty with a remark that the same explanations can be applied to three other "Justus ut palma" graduals that are established in the higher position.[12]

The premise of Chapter One Hundred and Fifty-One, entitled "De graduali, Beatus servus" or "Concerning the Gradual Beatus servus"[13] (Ugolino's designation of this communion as a gradual is an error), is similar to Marchetto's in the Lucidarium -- the chant cannot be established in either the primary or secondary positions, but only at a third location a fourth above the final. Using a very closely reasoned argument, Ugolino dismisses the first two positions because they cannot accommodate the chant's inherent interval structure. He adds here, however, as he did not do for the second-mode graduals, an explanation couched in hexachord terminology. Specifically, he states that there should be conformity between the figures and sounds of a chant: the figures are its neumes as realized on the staff, and its sounds are the uttered solmization syllables. He then gives both for "Beatus servus" at its location in the finales to demonstrate that instead of conformity between the two, there is inconvenientia, or unsuitability.[14] Similarly, inconvenientia exists at the secondary position, as this quotation indicates:

> . . . at d, ut would be said where there is no ut, re at e where there is no re, mi at f where there is no mi, . . .[15]

Finally, Ugolino reaches the acceptable solution:

> Certain people, wanting to avoid the unsuitable things already mentioned, have placed the named gradual in another position so that a conformity of figures or notes and of syllables might be maintained, as well as the perfect form of the mode itself. They place the beginning of this gradual on *a*, . . .[16]

Ugolino thus notes that the *a* position preserves not only the chant's inherent melodic structure, but also the perfect form of the mode. This latter recognition comes as something of a shock after all the previous discussion which has emphasized a diatonic approach to the gamut and *not* the correct form of a mode. In spite of his opening definition of mode according to species theory, Ugolino does not make it an overriding concern of his treatise. Instead, he places greatest importance on preserving the chant repertory and notating it acceptably. In the immediate context, it is noteworthy that Ugolino does not label the *a* *deuterus* position "acquired" in the manner of Marchetto, but only refers to the "mediation of *b-flat*."[17]

In summary, Ugolino's treatment of alternative finals is distinctive by virtue of its omission of certain negative qualifiers typical of similar discussion since the eleventh century: "irregular," "transformed," and "acquired" are notably absent. Ugolino, like Marchetto, recognizes that a position a fourth above the final preserves a mode's characteristic species, which is not true of a position a fifth above. Both are needed to notate the chant repertory, however, and so Ugolino turns back to hexachord theory to explain the traditional *affinales* -- they are *re mi fa*. Hence, we observe Ugolino relying upon both the concepts of species and modal nuclei in his eminently practical approach to modal classification.

Liber de natura et proprietate tonorum by Johannes Tinctoris

Johannes Tinctoris (1435-c.1511) completed twelve music treatises between the years 1474 and 1484, so comprehensive in scope that he has rightfully earned the title of "musical encyclopedist."[18] Although many theorists tend to be retrospective in their outlook, Tinctoris reflects a preoccupation with practices of his day, particularly those related to polyphony. Accordingly, it is not surprising to find that he puts great emphasis upon modal locations a fourth above the finals, since their use was reflected in the presence of texted flats and one-flat signatures within polyphonic compositions. It is surprising that he fails to mention the traditional affinities in any of his treatises that deal with modes or the tonal system, namely, *Terminorum musicae diffinitorium* (1472?), *Expositio manus* (after 1477?), and *Liber de natura et* proprietate tonorum (1476).[19] Their omission from the last is particularly striking since in it Tinctoris claims that he intends to treat the principles of modes used in plainsong and in polyphony. But, in the main, Liber de natura discusses modal concepts as they apply to polyphony.[20]

Tinctoris begins his discussion of alternative finals in Chapter Forty-Five, "Concerning Irregular Finals of Tones":

> . . . four places, mentioned earlier, are regularly attributed to our four tones, hence, when they finish on these they are called regular. However, these tones can finish in all places by other rules, coming about through true or ficta music, either within or without the hand, and then they have been called irregular.[21]

In the four succeeding chapters, Tinctoris spells out the alternative finals for each maneria, in each instance setting out the coniunctae and hexachords that would accompany the new final (Figure 8).[22]

Fig. 8. Alternative finals for each maneria according to Tinctoris.

maneria	final	coniunctae	hexachords
protus	G solreut		soft and natural
	C faut	E lami, ♭mi	soft
	C outside hand	♭mi, 2 others (Eb & Bb outside hand)	
deuterus	a lamire		soft and natural
	D solre	E lami, ♭mi	soft
	D outside hand	♭mi, 2 others (Eb & Bb outside hand)	
tritus	C faut		natural and hard
	b fami	e lami (if necessary)	soft and natural
	F outside hand	♭mi (if necessary)	hard and natural
tetrardus	F faut	e lami, E lami	soft
	c solfaut		natural and soft
	F outside hand	♭mi, E lami	

For protus, deuterus, and tetrardus, Tinctoris presents both a transposition to the fourth above the normal final, which uses b-flat of the soft hexachord, and a second-level flat transposition, which uses b-flat and E-flat.

Tritus has an alternative final at the fourth above, on *b-flat*, where the same species of diapente and diatessaron common to *F* can be formed (third species diapente T-T-T-S; third species diatessaron T-T-S). By his inclusion of *C faut*, Tinctoris recognizes a second *tritus* formation with the fourth species of diapente (T-T-S-T). In medieval discussions of the affinities, theorists had stated that *tritus F* has an affinity with *c*, and the latter was used at times because it could express diatonically a necessary *b-flat* above *F*. In effect, Tinctoris adopts this affinity, but for a different reason: he is not interested in eliminating *b-flats*, but rather in finding alternative positions for the exact melodic species of each mode. *C* serves this function for one form of *tritus*.[23]

At the conclusion of this presentation, Tinctoris states that there are other "irregular places" where the modes can end, for which he gives an example of mode six on high *ff* and of mode eight on high *gg*. His naming the higher positions is somewhat troublesome, since, in the polyphonic context, he attributes mode to the tenor voice, which does not move in that range. In any event, Tinctoris accepts only those positions that preserve the modal octave exactly. He represents a musical purist of a different sort than Guido and some of his followers, who made efforts to preserve the diatonic purity of the gamut and certainly gave it preference over any abstract modal formula. Tinctoris, on the other hand, stresses that a mode must possess a given octave structure. Because of this attitude, he bypasses the traditional hesitancy to use *b-flat* in a modal construction, and acknowledges instead that it can help him find alternative modal positions. What is startling is the absence of any comment on the second-level flat transpositions achieved through *E-flat*, which, unlike *b-flat*, was not a part of the traditional gamut. Tinctoris matter of factly presents what is, in essence, the modern concept of transposition.[24]

The next three treastises, dating from the 1480s and 1490's, stand together in the sense that all three concentrate on mode as it relates to chant. Guilielmus basically summarizes *affinales* according to traditional usage. Burtius concentrates on the *a deuterus* modes, offering a defense based on species theory. And Gaffurius, like Ugolino before him, accepts both the traditional *affinales* and related tones a fourth removed from the normal finals, without attempting to reconcile the varied arguments offered on their behalf.

De preceptis artis musicae by Guilielmus Monachus

The monk Guilielmus, who was probably an Italian, wrote his *De preceptis artis musicae* in the 1480s.[25] In this treatise devoted to plainchant, Guilelmus organizes his discussion of mode according to the various features by which it is recognized: by ascent and descent, by beginnings, by mediants, by endings, and by *differentiae*. This list shows how the traditional modal indicators, final, beginning configuration, and ambitus, have now become mixed with functional features of psalmody, namely mediants and *differentiae* of the psalm tones.

In his discussion of modal endings, Guilielmus makes a distinction between regular or natural endings and irregular ones. He offers this didactic verse on irregular endings:

> Sit in A primi pariter finisve secundi,
> Tertios B iunges quartumque non excludes,
> Sub C fundat quintus iunctoque sibi sexto,
> D subdit septimum addensque sibi octavum.[26]

This verse presents the traditional statement on alternative finals at the fifth above the normal finals, including one for modes seven and eight. In accordance with his tendency to present several opinions on a given topic, Guilielmus offers a second verse on irregular finals:

> Sunt in D vel in A primus tonus atque secundus;
> Tertius et quartus in E vel in B reperiuntur;
> Sed quandoque per A quartum finiri vidimus,
> Tunc per B molle locatus;
> Quintus cum sexto in F vel C locantur,
> Septimus et octavus in G vel in D requiescunt.[27]

This verse says that the fourth mode may also end on *a* using *b-flat*. In his commentary, Guilielmus adds, ". . . the mentioned fourth mode [ending on *a*] should have its proper mediant, namely, on *d lasolre*, saying *re ut re mi re*."[28] By describing a mediant that begins on *d* (*re*), when it usually begins on *a*, he informs the reader that the reciting tone, like the final, is transposed to the fourth above its normal position.

Guilielmus offers no further comments on irregular endings in this or any other section of the treastise. Based on the two verses that are quoted above, one may conclude that he was concentrating on modal endings encountered in chant, his apparent concern for mode in polyphony notwithstanding: "Mode . . . is distinguished in all song, and well I say in all song, whether plainchant or figured music."[29]

Musices opusculum by Nicolaus Burtius

Musices opusculum[30] was printed in Bologna in 1487. Burtius's primary reason for writing the treatise was to defend the hexachord system from the attack on it launched by Ramos de Pareja,[31] a stance that is indicative of his generally conservative attitudes.

Burtius does not discuss alternative finals exhaustively, but rather devotes several paragraphs to the issue of fourth-mode chants ending on a. He questions (rhetorically) why anyone should call them irregular when their mode can be determined by an examination of their species. Referring to four antiphons, "Dominus regit me," "Sicut myrrha electa," "Factus sum," and "Benedicta tu," he states:

> For while those antiphons . . . are plagals, yet with respect to the diatessaron which they have, they are reckoned sequentially from the fourth [mode] rather than from another mode . . .[32]

All four antiphons belong to Gevaert's theme 29, the melodic prototype that contains both b-flat and b-natural.[33] Accordingly, their diapente, formed from a, is not modally conclusive, yet Burtius concludes that the diatessaron E F G a and the reciting tone on d (regular fourth tone transposed up a fourth) warrant their classification as mode four. He states that, although most musicians agree with his conclusion, another viewpoint exists:

> . . . nevertheless, a few ventured to call these [modes] "commixed," that is, put together as much out of their proper species of diatessaron and diapente as out of ones belonging to others . . .[34]

Earlier, Marchetto had defined tonus commixtus as a mode that uses its normal diatessaron and diapente, but also mixes them with species from other modes. Marchetto's descriptive term does indeed fit these fourth-mode chants, although there is no evidence that Marchetto himself applied it to them.

At the end of this discussion, Burtius advises his reader to make a modal judgement about endings on ♮ and c according to the species that surround them. Because of his emphasis on species, one wonders whether or not he accepted transpositions to the fourth above for the other maneriae besides deuterus.

Practica musicae by Franchinus Gaffurius

Franchinus Gaffurius (1451-1522) described his Practica musicae (1st ed., Milan, 1496)[35] as a summary of earlier writings on music, and thus one finds that he presents a traditional view of affinities along with a discussion of other related tones where species are intact. Practica also provides a glimpse of the Ambrosian usage of affinales, since Gaffurius was working in Milan and in contact with Ambrosian practices during at least part of the time the Practica was being written.[36]

Gaffurius calls alternative finals at the fifth above the normal finals *confinales*, and he allows that all four *maneriae* may end irregularly on them:

> There are four confinals in the series of eight Tones. . . . The seventh and eighth Tones end regularly on low *G sol re ut*, and irregularly on high *D la sol re*. Although Gregorian antiphons, graduals, and other plainsongs have rarely been allowed a confinal since it is maintained that they always end regularly, Ambrosians frequently end the seventh Tone on its confinal, but rarely the eighth Tone.[37]

Gaffurius reports on an Ambrosian practice in which *d* is used in an affinity relationship to *G*.[38] He concludes with a paraphrase of Marchetto's statement on how modes may be located at any position where their proper species can be found:

> Moreover, any Tone in the *Introductorium* can be formed wherever its lateral parts or interval species can be extended; when it goes beyond its natural and primary arrangement, we call it *fictum* or acquired.[39]

Marchetto had referred to the alternative positions that offer the proper species as "acquired," to which Gaffurius adds a second designation *fictum*, apparently because he includes *b-flat* as a *ficta* tone.[40] In any event, he understands a theory of alternative modal positions based on species.

There is one other noteworthy mention of traditional affinities in Book One during Gaffurius' discussion of mode seven. He refers to the antiphon "Nos qui vivimus," for which he says the Gregorians have provided a special psalm tone. Today that psalm tone is commonly known as the *tonus peregrinus* (Example 14).[41]

Ex. 14. Antiphon "Nos qui vivimus" with *tonus peregrinus* (*AM* 132).

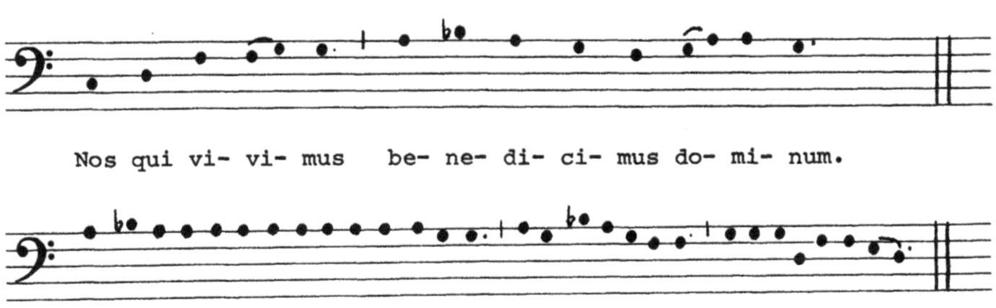
Nos qui vi- vi- mus be- ne- di- ci- mus do- mi- num.

Although the *tonus peregrinus* was generally adopted in Gregorian practice in connection with these antiphons, it remained a source of consternation throughout the Middle Ages for theorists and other musicians who were trying to refine modal classification. This becomes apparent from the conflicting modal designations applied to these antiphons in various chant books.[42] Gaffurius, writing at the end of the fifteenth century, tells his reader that the Ambrosians do not use the *tonus peregrinus*, but instead use a reciting tone on *G* to complement the seventh-mode character of the antiphon, as shown in Example 15.[43] He then provides an interesting account of earlier practice:

> A very old antiphonary I have seen contains this antiphon by St. Ambrose notated on the untransposed pitches of the seventh Tone. It belongs to the seventh octave-species and the Mixolydian on low *G sol re ut*. It ends on its untransposed *confinalis*, *d la sol re*, (which frequently happens in authentic Tones), . . .[44]

Gaffurius' subsequent example (Example 16) does indeed show the antiphon notated in the seventh-mode range *G* to *f*, ending on the *confinalis d*; and since the *d* ending was a legitimate one for *tetrardus*, according to Ambrosian practice, it is simply accompanied by the seventh-mode reciting tone (Ambrosian version) on *d*.

Ex. 15. "Nos qui vivimus" with Ambrosian seventh psalm tone according to Gaffurius.

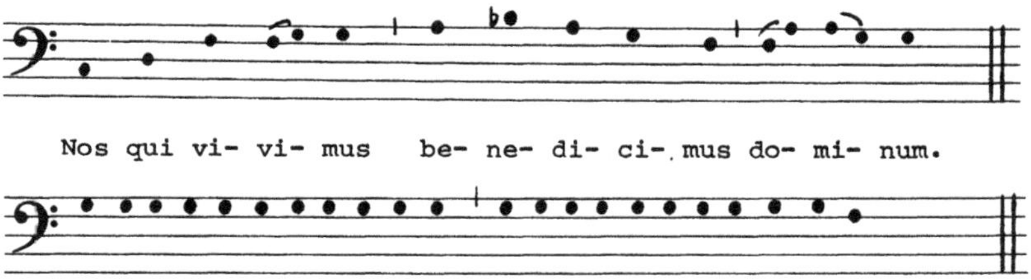
Nos qui vi- vi- mus be- ne- di- ci- mus do- mi- num.

Ex. 16. Untransposed version of "Nos qui vivimus" according to Gaffurius.

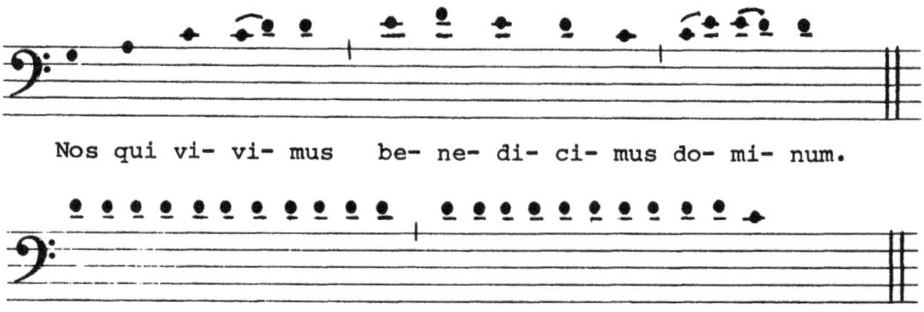
Nos qui vi- vi- mus be- ne- di- ci- mus do- mi- num.

A modern chantbook based on the earliest Ambrosian sources, *Liber vesperalis*, contains this version of

"Nos qui vivimus" with only a slight variant in the psalm-tone formula (LV 7). Both this version and Gaffurius' statement are evidence that the Ambrosians found a solution to the problems associated with "Nos qui vivimus," a solution based on the acceptance of d as an alternative final to G.[45] Such evidence is important to this study because it shows another purpose served by the affinities.

The next two theorists, Wollick and Ornithoparchus, published their writings in Germany between 1500 and 1520. Their treatises share a common vocabulary when they refer to the issue at hand -- for them, it is one of "transposed song," a phenomenon of both chant and polyphony. In the main, the authors report upon, rather than explain, the alternative finals in usage, but in so doing, certainly give a greater credibility to related tones at the fourth than had any previous generation.[46]

Opus aureum musicae and Enchiridion musices by Nicolaus Wollick

Nicolaus Wollick (c. 1480-1541) was one of several theorists working in Cologne during the first quarter of the sixteenth century who proposed a humanist approach to music theory.[47] Wollick's two music treatises are Opus aureum musicae, published in 1501, and its revised and expanded version, Enchiridion musices, published in 1509.[48] In compiling the Opus aureum, Wollick drew upon treatises by Adam of Fulda, Hugo Spechtshart [of Reutlingen], and Michael Keinspeck. Hugo Spechtshart's Flores musicae omnis cantus Gregoriani, written in 1332, served as the basis for passages in the Opus aureum concerning related finals.[49]

Wollick titles Chapter Eight of the Opus aureum "De tonorum notitia" or "Concerning the Knowledge of Modes." It begins with a verse describing regular and alternative finals that is identical to the one in Spechtshart's Flores.[50] The verse conservatively describes alternative finals only at the fifth above the regular finals for the first three maneriae. However, Wollick appends three rules (presented below in his ordering), which augment the contents of the verse considerably. According to Wollick, rules two and three apply to any transposed song, and rule one to any song ending regularly:

Rule 3	c solfaut		7		8	and this oc-
	b fa♮mi	belongs	5	or	6	curs if fa
	a lamire	to	3		4	is said on
	G solreut	modes	1		2	b fa♮mi.

C faut belongs to modes 7 and 8 and this occurs if fa is said on ♮mi, but if mi is said, it belongs to modes 5 and 6.

Rule 2	c solfaut		5		6	if mi is
	b fa♮mi	belongs	3	or	4	said on
	a lamire	to modes	1		2	b fa♮mi.
Rule 1	G solreut		7		8	
	F faut	belongs	5	or	6	
	E lami	to	3		4	
	D solre	modes	1		2	51

In rules two and three, Wollick presents the concepts of transposition to the fifth and to the fourth above, the first utilizing b-natural, and the second b-flat. Also, he recognizes both tritus and tetrardus maneriae on the pitch C faut.

In his Enchiridion, Wollick again presents his three rules for final notes, varied only in that C faut has been left out and d lasolre added to rule two to complete the symmetry. He then summarizes the alternative finals for the first three maneriae as follows:

protus	A gravis, G capitalis, a confinalis
deuterus	B gravis, a lamire, b fa♮ mi acuta
tritus	C faut, b fa♮ mi, c solfaut[52]

He adds that since the same intervals rarely occur in such positions, most songs have been notated at the final level. Of course, this leaves one wondering whether he recognized that the proper species of fourth and fifth occur a fourth above the final, a question to be discussed further below. In any event, he concludes the exposition on alternative finals in this way:

> . . . and when a song was not able to be notated in these [the finals] suitably, it was changed to the confinales . . .[53]

He thus endorses the usefulness of the traditional affinales for notating chants that could not be notated at the final position.[54]

Mention of tetrardus finals is conspicuously absent from Wollick's summary of alternative finals, in spite of his inclusion of d lasolre under rule two and c solfaut under rule three. An explanation is found earlier in this same chapter (Book Three, Chapter Two) when he remarks that among those who follow Gregorian usage, tetrardus rarely has a confinalis. He further reports that the Ambrosians often transpose mode seven, but eight only rarely.[55] According to Wollick, the Gregorian avoidance of d tetrardus results because seventh-mode songs sometimes reach a tenth above their final, an ascent which, reckoned from d, would place part of a melody outside the upper limit of the gamut. A similar consideration leads him to dismiss C faut as an alternative position. To his way of thinking, eighth-mode melodies frequently descend a fifth below their final, a descent which, reckoned from C, would place part of a melody outside the lower limit of the gamut.

Finally, Wollick informs his reader that certain irregular endings are excusable, others inexcusable. We recall that Coussemaker's Anonymous I had applied "inexcusable" to cases where emendation could have been carried out to avoid the need for transposition. Wollick pointedly refers to the "ignorance of singers" and directs our attention to a chant inexcusably transposed, the responsory "Sancta et immaculata virginitas." He describes its use of B-flat at "poterant" and recommends that this coniuncta be removed. His unwillingness to notate this chant at the cofinal position is puzzling in view of his statement above (p. 110).[56]

After his discussion of the confinales, Wollick devotes a paragraph to modal positions at the fourth above the normal finals, positions that are the result of transmutatio and transpositio.[57] The attitude conveyed by this discussion is a neutral one: he neither condemns the finals at the fourth for "transforming" the modal identity of G, a, ♭, and c -- although he acknowledges that others do -- nor does he applaud these finals for preserving the proper modal species. Instead, he pragmatically accepts their serviceability. He does, incidentally, name two chants as examples of transposition to the fourth above, the fourth-mode antiphons "Paradisi porta" and "Dominus veniet."[58]

The next paragraph is noteworthy:

> But transformation of this sort was invented only on account of irregular solmization of songs which arose perhaps at finals through coniunctae or fictae, likewise because of conflicting parts of counterpoint to be placed on the hand (which pleases me more). A tenor, therefore, that sets up the bass under itself is raised higher . . .[59]

In this reference to transformation, he gives two reasons for the transposition of a melody a fourth higher. The first involves the avoidance of altered tones, while the second, to which he explicitly gives preference, states that the tenor should be moved to a higher position so that the contrapuntal bass will not interfere with it. This seems to be the earliest mention of setting up convenient ranges in polyphony as a reason for transposition.

In conclusion, Wollick's two treatises, Opus aureum and Enchiridion musices, reveal that he, unlike Tinctoris, does not justify transpositions to the fourth above the final by means of species theory. Instead he emphasizes the practical necessity for them, both in chant and in polyphony, and thereby places them on equal terms with transpositions to the fifth above.

Musicae activae micrologus by Andreas Ornithoparchus

This practical treatise by Andreas Ornithoparchus was published in Leipzig in 1517.[60] Ornithoparchus followed the lifestyle of a travelling humanist scholar, pursuing his studies at universities in Wittenberg, Leipzig, and Greifswald, as well as in Austria, Bohemia, and Hungary. As he travelled, he gave public lectures based on his treatise, a factor which may have contributed to its popularity. In 1609 John Dowland translated it into English.

Ornithoparchus follows the humanist predilection for citing the authority of past writers. Not only does he name sources intermittently throughout the treatise, but he also puts into the preface a list of twelve authors upon whom he draws. For his discussion of the affinities, he alludes to the writings of Guido, Berno, and St. Gregory as sources of information, but the most direct borrowing comes from the treatise he attributes to "Joannes Pontifex," his name for the elusive John, sometimes called "Cotton" in the literature.[61]

Ornithoparchus begins his exposition with a sentence on transposition that is related to the ideas expressed by the writers treated in Chapter Four:

> [Transposition of song] is the avoidance of *coniunctae*. For while we strive to avoid *coniunctae* (because they ruin a song), we raise a song from the proper location of its ending to the fifth above, as is clearly evident in the responsory "Ite in orbem."

The regular way The irregular way

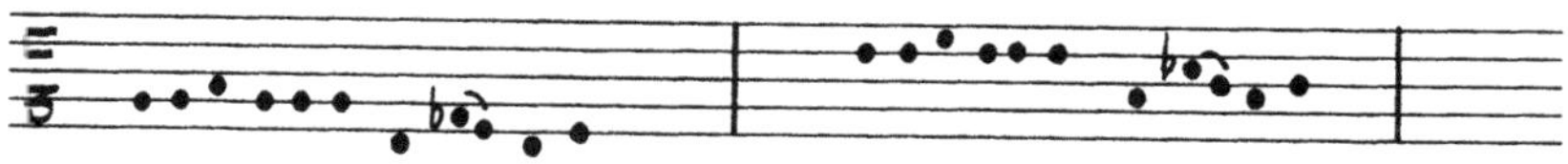

I- te in or- bem I- te in or- bem [62]

The example of the responsory "Ite in orbem" illustrates a transposition to avoid *E-flat*. It is noteworthy that the Szalkai treatise cited the *coniuncta e-flat* in this same responsory.[63]

Ornithoparchus next presents the usual final notes of irregualr songs, that is, the *affinales* according to Guido, Berno, and, as he would have it, St. Gregory: *a lamire* for modes one and two, *b fa♮ mi* for modes three and four, and *c solfaut* for modes five and six. He notes that the Ambrosians allow more. The reasons he gives for the existence of irregularity of endings derive from John:

> That irregularity of songs arises, however, as Pontifex writes [in] Chapter 14 of his *Musica*, sometimes by license, sometimes by the idleness of singers, sometimes by irrefutable antiquity, very often also by reason of counterpoint, so that the bass may find a place to descend below the tenor *choralis*.[64]

The last reason was of course not cited by John, but it was mentioned by several writers in the decade before Ornithoparchus' treatise.

Ornithoparchus presents ten points on transposition, all of them practical considerations. Numbers one and two concentrate on the reason why *tetrardus* modes are not and should not be transposed; Ornithoparchus adopts Wollick's argument that a seventh-mode ascent of a tenth would not be possible at *d lasolre*, while an eighth-mode descent of a fifth would not be possible at *C faut*. Numbers three and four recommend transposition as a means to avoid *coniunctae*. Number five states that transposition to the fifth above should be given priority, and transposition to the fourth used only when the other does not solve the notational problem of a *coniuncta*. He accompanies this point with an example from the chant repertory (Example 17).[65]

Ex. 17. The responsory "Quae est ista" at three positions according to Ornithoparchus.

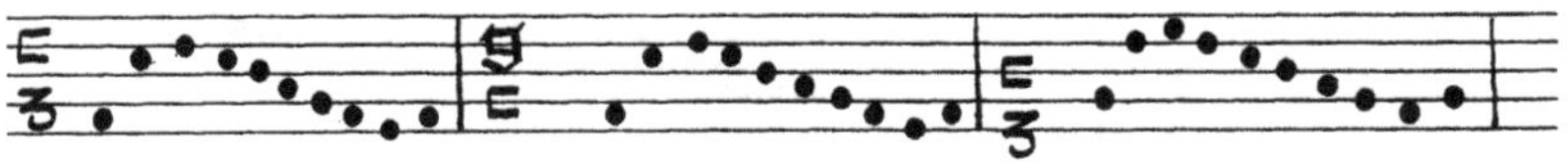

regular — fifth transposition not valid — fourth transposition thorougly valid

Number six concerns the syllabary that accompanies a transposition: "The same syllables should be sung after transposition which were sung before."[66] Numbers seven and eight specify the use of *b-natural* and *b-flat* in transpositions to the fifth and fourth, respectively. Number nine quotes Bernard of Clairvaux on the confusion caused by transposition to the fourth. Although Ornithoparchus presents this viewpoint, he does not appear to follow it, since number ten summarizes transpositions to the fourth that do occur in music:

> A song ending on *G solreut* signed by *fa* on *b fa♮mi* is of the first or second mode transposed to the fourth. And that which [ends] on *a lamire* is of the third or fourth, as "Quae est ista," and likewise regarding others.[67]

Ornithoparchus' ten rules do not provide a systematic approach towards understanding how and to what degree related notes at the fifth and fourth preserve modal identity. The underlying theoretical conflict is not even broached in the general way that it was in Wollick's writings. Yet Ornithoparcus' presentation bears witness to the importance of the principle of affinities in a sixteenth-century textbook on music fundamentals. Just as important, it reveals one more theorist's acceptance of transposition to the fourth on an essentially equal basis with transposition to the fifth.

The Writings of Pietro Aaron

Born in Florence c. 1480, Aaron, a practicing musician as well as a theorist, held the position of cantor at the cathedral of Imola from c. 1515 to 1522, and that of maestro di casa in a religious house in Venice beginning c. 1525. In general, Aaron falls among the more progressive thinkers of his time; he is often cited as the first theorist to favor written indications of accidentals at all times and also uniform rather than conflicting signatures. In the controversy over octave versus hexachord division, he championed Ramos' viewpoint. Not surprisingly, his questioning attitudes towards traditional theory also affected his viewpoint on the affinities. Aaron's most controversial statements in this respect appear in his treatise on modes, Trattato della natura et cognitione di tutti gli tuoni di canto figurato (1525),[68] but the roots of his attitude may be found in Libri tres de institutione harmonica (1516)[69] and in Il Toscanello in musica (1523).[70]

Chapter Thirty-Two of Libri tres is entitled "De terminatione troporum irregularium," or "Concerning the Ending of Irregular Modes."[71] Here Aaron elaborates upon a point that others have only fleetingly mentioned, that a mode's regular species of fifth and fourth are not duplicated in their entirety at the cofinal position a fifth above. He describes which species do occur when modes end on a, ♮, c, and d:

> . . . so that the first and second modes end on high a lamire in which we have one species of the first and one of the third; in b fa♮mi we have third and fourth [modes] and species of the fifth and sixth; in c solfaut [we have] fifth and sixth [modes] and a species of the seventh and eighth; in d lasolre we have seventh and eighth [modes] and species of the first and eighth.[72]

Figure 9 summarizes Aaron's findings.[73]

Fig. 9. Species of fifth and fourth available at the final and affinity positions for each *maneria*, according to Aaron.

Species of 5th / 4th	Species of 5th / 4th
D E F G a ♮ c d modes 1 & 2 / 1 & 2	a ♮ c d e f g aa 1 & 2 / 3 & 4
E F G a ♮ c d e modes 3 & 4 / 3 & 4	♮ c d e f g aa ♮♮ ? / ? or b c d e f g aa bb 5 & 6 / 5 & 6
F G a ♮ c d e f modes 5 & 6 / 5 & 6	c d e f g aa ♮♮ cc 7 & 8 / 5 & 6
G a ♮ c d e f g modes 7 & 8 / 1 & 2 or 7 & 8	d e f g aa ♮♮ cc dd 1 & 2 / 7 & 8

This crucial statement follows:

> Because of this, indeed, as it appears to me, a great confusion arises so that modes do not have the correct formation and are judged more from their species than from [their] ending.[74]

Aaron provides us with the most direct evaluation to date of the changing approach to modal classification. He, in effect, says that the principle of the affinities, which links a mode to a specific nucleus of melodic movement, is being ousted by species theory, which links a mode to a particular species of fifth and fourth.

In the following sentence, Aaron specifically advocates irregular endings at the fourth above the finals, since they preserve the modal species *in toto*: he recommends modes three and four on *a*, five and six on *b*, and seven and eight on *c*. Without any explanation, he offers *d lasolre*, and not *G solreut*, for modes one and two. Might the traditional concern over retaining the *tetrardus* character of *G* have been surfacing here?

With an expressed recognition that he is denying tradition by speaking out against the affinities, Aaron offers a conciliatory passage near the end of this chapter. He says that, although there are more suitable locations (presumably at the final or fourth above), any mode can end on its *confinis*. His final sentence is noteworthy: "Truly, I claim that irregular form of this sort [is] necessary more to measured songs than to unmeasured."[75]

Turning now to Il Toscanello, we see Aaron carrying out a rather peculiar exercise in modal classification.[76] He refers to various parts of the Mass Ordinary and not only assigns a mode to a given section, but also offers a modal explanation for why internal divisions end on the notes they do -- they are equal to a beginning note in that mode, to the last note of a differentia in that mode, or to the cofinal of that mode. This is a forced categorization in comparison to the statements of most earlier theorists, who had said that phrases should end on a note consonant to the final. In many cases, the beginning notes and differentiae endings are consonant to the final, and the confinalis is always so. Aaron, however, refers to the functional connecting note of a differentia as though it had an inherent modal property. This particular approach takes on greater significance in his Trattato.

In the Trattato, Aaron turns to the question of mode in polyphony with an assertion that theorists before him have not confronted the issue fully. He attempts to assign a mode to polyphonic pieces composed one or more generations before his time, and in doing so, imposes a classification scheme onto music that had not necessarily been composed with such a scheme in mind.[77] As will become evident below, he faced considerable difficulties in reconciling the polyphonic repertory with the system.

Like Tinctoris, Aaron states that the mode of a polyphonic work should be judged from its tenor. He also tells us the specific approach he is to take to modal analysis: ". . . at one time the final governs and at another time the species."[78] Aaron holds with tradition as long as he is dealing with finals on D, E, F, and G: when a composition ends on any of these notes, that note determines the mode, even when, in the case of D or F, there is a flat in the signature.[79] But this point of view is somewhat inconsistent, inasmuch as his complaint about the change of species that occurs on irregular finals could also be applied to mode on D and F that use b-flat. However, Aaron apparently believes that the traditional association of these two finals with protus and tritus maneriae overrides any concern for purity of species. On the other hand, G with a flat signature assumes the character of a protus final, while the three other maneriae respectively may adopt a, b, and c with a flat signature as finals. In these four instances, the finals alone tell little, but the species of fifth and fourth definitively identify the maneria.

It is in connection with an irregular final on a without b-flat that we encounter Aaron's idiosyncratic approach to modal identity. He explains his understanding of a as follows:

> . . . if a composition ends in the position called A la mi re and there is no flat in the signature, the

> final will be common to the first and second tones with respect to confinality and also to the third with respect to difference, provided--as you will understand from what follows--that the procedure in the composition be suited and appropriate to confinality or difference.[80]

Aaron implies that an a final does not automatically signify an *affinalis* to modes one and two. Just as he had done in *Il Toscanello*, he also gauges a against the ending note of a *differentia* (in Strunk's translation, "difference") in mode three (or four, as he later states). The artificiality of attributing modal properties to a *differentia* has already been mentioned above. It may be that Aaron himself recognized how precarious a concept this was, for nowhere in his detailed discussion of a finals does he in fact rely on this aspect of his argument. He does, however, return to the last feature mentioned in the quotation above, "procedure" or what he defines as the choice of internal cadences. In Chapters Nine through Twelve, he outlines the most serviceable cadence points for each mode. For the modes relevant to a, modes one through four, he gives these cadence points: mode one, D, F, G, and a; mode two, A, C, D, F, G, and a; mode three, E, F, G, a, ♮, and c; mode four, C, D, E, F, G, and a. Although there is overlap among the choices available to each *maneria*, one point becomes evident: a composition that has a high percentage of cadences on D and a (*protus*) would be distinguishable from one with a high percentage on E and a (*deuterus*).[81]

In the midst of Aaron's emphasis on cadences in this discussion, one is struck by his failure to confront the issue to which he had lent such importance earlier, species. Suppose a tenor has the range E to e, ends on a, and has most of its cadences on E and a -- was it *deuterus* in terms of species? In one example given by Aaron, the structure of the work offers an affirmative answer. The tenor of Josquin's "Miserere mei Deus," which has a range of E to f, consists of an ostinato on e-f that moves stepwise down to E-F, stepwise back up to e-f, and then descends again, coming to rest on a.[82] The functional outline of the work is E to e, and thus the entire *deuterus* octave species is emphasized.

In the other two *deuterus* examples, Eustachio's "Benedic anima mea" and Isaac's "La mi la sol,"[83] the octave species is not brought into play directly. In the former, the tenor range is C to g, while in the latter it occupies the narrow span of a to e. In neither case does the entire range reflect a *deuterus* outline. The a to e segment could be viewed as a species of fifth that connects two important *deuterus* cadence points as defined by Aaron.[84] However, Aaron was careful to spell out the species of fourth and fifth proper to each *maneria* at the beginning of the *Trattato*; the *deuterus* species of fifth is semitone-tone-tone-tone, which fits E to ♮, not a to e. Aaron, in fact, attributes *a* to *e* to modes one and two when he discusses the species available from an *a* final in *Tres libri* (see p. 114).

Is there then a contradiction in his assigning "La mi la sol" to mode three? I think not. Returning to the beginning of his discussion in the *Trattato*, one recalls his statement that at times species govern. Presumably he meant that mode was indicated by whatever melodic fourths and/or fifths were emphasized as the tenor line unfolded. Thus we find an explanation for the modal assignment of "La mi la sol": the tenor ostinato, *e ƀ e d*, *e d e ƀ*, outlines a second species fourth (ascending semitone-tone-tone) throughout the entire piece, until it cadences on *a* in measure 31 of the *secunda pars* (Wolf's ed.; see n. 83). After a four-measure soprano-alto duo, the ostinato moves to the bass (and remains there until the end, measure 51) on the pitches *a E a G*, *a G a E*, again a second species fourth. It seems that Aaron attributed the ending on *a* to *deuterus*, not only because his system allowed it through the somewhat artificial explanation of cadences and *differentia* ending, but also because a *deuterus* species (S-T-T) prevailed. The same may be said of Eustachio's "Benedic anima mea," where the most frequently outlined interval is the fourth *E* to *a*.

In accordance with this version of species theory, whereby a prevailing species of fourth *or* fifth can identify a mode, Aaron's assignment of examples to *protus* also becomes intelligible. He cites Compere's "Se mieulx ne vient" and Josquin's "La plus des plus," both of which have a range of *C* to *f* and end on *a*.[85] The first emphasizes *a* to *e*, while the second emphasizes *D* to *a* and *a* to *e*, and thus, the primary interval set is a first species diapente (tone-semitone-tone-tone). Just as with the *deuterus* species of fourth in the pieces discussed earlier, the relative pitch position of the *protus* species of fifth in these two chansons does not seem to be of consequence with regard to the modal identity.[86]

The foregoing analysis is based on the theory and approach Aaron espoused in the *Trattato* of 1525. Is his approach to irregular finals consistent with the comments he made nine years earlier in the *Libri tres*? There he had said that first and second modes ending on *a* have "one species of the first and one species of the third." Taken as an isolated statement, this might suggest that Aaron, like his predecessors of the previous two centuries, viewed the mode on *a* as an irregular *protus* formation. Since he identified the mode three component, he might even have called this mode "commixed" *protus*, thereby acknowledging the *deuterus* aspect while emphasizing the *protus* foundation. Instead, he simply said "[such] modes . . . are judged more from their species than from [their] ending," thereby paving the way for the approach he takes in the *Trattato*, where an ending on *a* does not necessarily suggest a *protus* classification.

In essence, Aaron discards the concept of a modal nucleus, by which *a*, without *b-flat*, was a related note to *protus*. Yet, according to octave-species theory, he could not explain away the mixture of *protus* and *deuterus* in the *a* to *aa* octave. So, after he had rejected the affinity concept and had found the octave-species theory deficient, he devised a distinctive means by which to assign mode. His system derives from the conflict inherent in the *a* to *aa* octave: since it contains components of both *protus* and *deuterus*, he judged which is predominant and assigned the mode accordingly. If a *protus* component prevails, he designates the ending on *a* "by confinality," and if the *deuterus* prevails, "by difference." This means of expression is, at least in part, a concealment of his distinctive method.

The other irregular final frequently encountered by Aaron was *c*, and his treatment of it appears to be consistent with that of *a* outlined above. In *Libri tres*, he said that *c solfaut* has "a species of modes seven and eight." The diapente c d e f g fits that description, although it could also belong to modes five and six. Here arises one of the inconsistencies of Aaron's system. He accepts either a *b-flat* or *b-natural* in *tritus* modes on *F*, but he does not concede that two species of *tritus* fifths are formed as a result. The tone-tone-semitone-tone arrangement on *c* is peculiar to *tetrardus*, according to Aaron. Therefore, when a tenor has the range *G* to *g*, ends on *c*, and emphasizes the fifth *c* to *g*, Aaron designates it *tetrardus*.[87]

He does not provide an opportunity to test whether a prevailing *tritus* species of fourth would result in a *tritus* designation. In fact, his discussion of modes five and six on *c* is unusually brief and somewhat problematic, particularly when he says:

> The sixth tone is lacking on this step, even though it is the confinal of the fifth and sixth tones regularly ended, for the step can bear no form or difference appropriate to it.[88]

This passage uses the term "confinal" to mean simply the note a fifth above the final, with no functional implication. When Aaron says that *c* is incapable of having a form appropriate to mode six, his reasoning seems false since *c* can yield the proper descending species of fourth, c‿♮‿a‿G. Moreover, in the previous sentence he allowed that mode five could end there, although "solely in view of the difference which the plainsong sometimes exhibits here."[89] The lack of "form" is ultimately no more acute at *c* for mode six than for mode five. The fact that Aaron resorts to the *differentia* explanation in order to justify some compositions as belonging to *tritus* suggests that he felt constrained by his own species theory. After all, it stood at odds with the traditional viewpoint, which had accepted a modal relationship between *F* and *c*.

One last treatise by Aaron confirms his rejection of the affinities as they were traditionally formulated -- the Lucidario in musica, published in 1545, twenty years after the Trattato.[90] In Book One, Oppenione Five,[91] Aaron repeats the argument he presented in Libri tres concerning the failure of the confinales to produce the species of fourth and fifth proper to their associated maneriae. Now he offers a "resolution" to this problem, a solution that appears to be merely theoretical. He proposes that protus, deuterus, tritus, and tetrardus species can be correctly realized at their respective confinalis by adding f-sharps.[92] Hence, the following forms would result:

protus	a	♮	c	d	e	f#	g	aa
deuterus	♮	c	d	e	f#	g	aa	♮♮
tritus	c	d	e	f#	g	aa	♮♮	cc
tetrardus	d	e	f#	g	aa	♮♮	cc	dd

Chant did not use these forms, and the vocal polyphony of the time did not incorporate sharp signatures. Sharps could be designated within the musical text, however, and Peter Bergquist further speculates that improvised transposition by instrumentalists may have resulted in the scales indicated.[93] These possibilities notwithstanding, it is evident that Aaron was proposing a scheme that could compensate for the failure in theory of the affinales.

In conclusion, the writings of Aaron reveal a theorist who felt compelled to view mode in terms of a rigid system. The eightfold system, when grounded in octave species theory, did not suit him since it could not absorb formations on a and c. Further, he rejected the concept of a modal nucleus, and hence the affinities, because inherently they allowed variations in a mode's identity. He adopted instead an approach to modal classification that centered on modally recognizable units abstracted from their relationship to the final note. As mentioned above, this approach engendered difficulties when applied to diatonic segments around c. Aaron called them tetrardus in bold opposition to affinity theory which had considered them tritus. His discomfort with the conflict was reflected in his turning to a somewhat spurious modal characteristic, the differentia ending, as a justification for calling some c endings tritus. Aaron's approach is distinctive, to be sure, yet his writings did not enjoy wide transmission, in spite of his high level of activity as a music theorist, and his direct followers are few in number.[94]

The Writings of Martin Agricola

Martin Agricola (1486-1556) was a German theorist, teacher, and composer. Of his numerous treatises, the earliest were written in the vernacular and addressed to pupils and amateur musicians. His later treatises retain the nature of practical compendia, but they are in Latin, perhaps in answer to the dictates of humanism. Three of his treatises, published over a span of ten years, delineate a gradually changing attitude on his part towards transposition: _Musica choralis deudsch_ (1533), _Rudimenta musices_ (1539), and _Quaestiones vulgatiores in musicam_ (1543).[95]

Musica choralis deudsch was originally published in 1528 as _Ein kurtz Deudsche Musica_. Although the revised title suggests that Agricola was to treat only plainsong (_Musica choralis_), he makes references to principles of contrapuntal music (_Musica figuralis_) as well. Such is the case in his discussion of transposed songs, where he supplies polyphonic examples. I have indicated where such examples occur in the following excerpt:

> Any song that ends on another key, outside of the four named, is called a transposed song. Therefore, a song which has _fa_ on _b fa♮ mi_ and ends on _G_ is of the first or second mode; on _A_, of the third or fourth; on _b fa♮ mi_, of the fifth or sixth; on _C_, of the seventh or eighth mode.
>
> [Example]
>
> A song which has _mi_ on _b fa♮ mi_ and ends on _A_ is of the first or second mode; on _C_, of the fifth or sixth.
>
> [Example]
>
> But when a song comes to an end on _A_ and has _fa_ on _b fa♮ mi_, it then belongs to the third or fourth mode, as follows in the example.
>
> [Example][96]

This presentation is reminiscent of ones that appeared in several German compendia already discussed, and like them, it simply reports on alternative endings rather than provide a theoretical explanation for them. It is noteworthy that Agricola lists finals at the fourth above the normal finals before he lists those at the fifth above, a fact that can be explained by his inclusion of only polyphonic examples throughout this section of the _Musica_. Unlike Aaron, Agricola considers the affinities to be useful in polyphony as well as in chant, so he presents _a_ as a _protus_ final in one of his polyphonic examples. That the tone _a_ is difficult to classify, however, is emphasized by his appending a reminder that its use in connection with _b-flat_ changes the mode to three or four. Of the other two traditional affinities, _♮_ and _c_, he only mentions _c_, which he associates with _tritus_ modes.

The second treatise that sheds light on the issue of alternative finals is the _Ruidmenta musices_ (1539). Whereas in the _Musica_ Agricola referred to songs with alternative endings as "transposed," in the _Ruidmenta_ he adds the expression "or irregular." He then defines transposition:

> There is transposition here, however, that is, the shifting of some song from its proper seat to a foreign one, which is given consideration rarely in plainsong (where the harmonies of individual modes are sung most properly in their own particular places), but in figured music, in which melodies frequently are raised and lowered from their own seats out of necessity to the fourth, fifth, and octave, it is given special consideration.[97]

He next links the possible final notes with the syllable(s) they would carry in a given *maneria* (see Figure 10).[98] One new feature of this exposition is the association of each note with one of two "systems," *cantus-durus* or *cantus mollis*. The *cantus durus*, or "*b-natural* system," places *mi* at every *b* position within the gamut, while the *cantus mollis*, or "*b-flat* system," places *fa* at each *b* position. As the sixteenth century progressed, reference to these two systems prevailed in tonal/modal discussions. As far as Agricola's figure is concerned, it is clear that endings a fourth above the final are *cantus mollis*, and those at the fifth and octave are *cantus durus*.

In apparently mistaken fashion, Agricola omits from the figure a *D* final for *protus*. Every *maneria* has endings at the fourth and fifth above the normal final, except *tetrardus*, which lacks an affinity on *d*. It is also noteworthy that Agricola includes some of the finals in several octave positions, thereby suggesting that he is assigning mode to voices other than the tenor. One last notable feature of the figure is its inclusion of the normal *tritus* final *F* under *cantus mollis*. Although other theorists allowed *b-flat* freely in *tritus*, Agricola implies that it is integral. He reflects further on this point in the *Quaestiones*.

To a large extent, the *Quaestiones vulgatiores* is an elaboration of the materials presented in the *Rudimenta*, and thus Agricola adds a few refinements to his earlier presentation on alternative finals. For example, he gives the reason for the invention of transposition:

> The transposition of song was invented for the sake of figured song in which the first and second modes especially are raised again and again from their seat *D* to the fourth *G* in the scale of *b-flat*, evidently so that the mutual hindrance of tenor and bass might be removed in a composition.[99]

The wording suggests that he might have read Wollick's explanation in the *Enchiridion*. In any event, he remarks that transposition can be made to the fourth, fifth, or octave, above or below. There follows a passage in which transposition to the affinities is relegated to a secondary status:

> In the first, second, third, fourth, seventh, and eighth modes, a fourth transposition of songs (when the system is changed from *b-natural* into *b-flat*), is more fitting than a fifth transposition. For the same arrangement of tones and semitones exists altogether equally in only the octave and fourth [positions]. But yet the fifth and sixth modes require a fifth transposition subject to the scale of *b-natural*.[100]

Fig. 10 Summary of modal finals, linked with syllable and "system," from Martin Agricola's *Rudimenta musices*.

Any melody ending on the key where one sings

sol descending *ut* ascending	cantus	♮ durus b mollis	on	Γ G.g. C.c.cc.		7 or 8
fa	cantus	♮ durus b mollis	on	C.c.cc. F.F.b.bb.	belongs to modes	5 or 6
mi	cantus	♮ durus b mollis	on	E.e.ee.♮. A.a.aa.		3 or 4
re	cantus	♮ durus b mollis	on	A.a.aa. Γ.G.g.		1 or 2

Agricola recognizes that *protus*, *deuterus*, and *tetrardus* modes can preserve their species only at the fourth (with the aid of *b-flat*) and octave above, not at the fifth. *Tritus*, on the other hand, with *b-flat* as an integral note, finds its exact interval arrangement at the fifth above, on *c*: F G a b c d e f = c d e f g aa ♮♮ cc.[101]

Thus, because of Agricola'a concern for exact octave species, only the affinity *c*, judged in relation to *F* (with *b-flat*), remains serviceable. Yet, ten years earlier, he had proposed a *protus* ending on *a*. It seems that, to some degree, other theorists' emphasis on species may have affected his thinking too.

Scintille di Musica by Giovanni Maria Lanfranco

Scintille di Musica or "Sparks of Music" by Giovanni Maria Lanfranco (c. 1490-1545) was published in Brescia in 1533.[102] Of its four distinct sections, the third treats the topic of mode, and within it, there is a rather traditional statement on finals and cofinals.[103] Lanfranco says that the *confinales* are placed a fifth distant from the finals, and that modes ending on the *confinales* are irregular. He then integrates this traditional viewpoint with more current thinking. Among the features by which mode can be recognized, he says, are transpositions, "because each mode can be transposed by a fifth and, with greater suitability, to the fourth with the authority of *b-flat*."[104] The linking of "greater suitability" with transpositions to the fourth suggests an awareness of species theory, which is confirmed shortly after when Lanfranco is discussing reasons for transposition:

> Transposition of a song is made by a fifth when the song is formed of few notes, that is, when it passes little higher than the fourth of the mode. But one can transpose each song by a fourth with the help of *b-flat*, and similarly, where one wants, provided that after the transposition the minor semitone is not removed from the place where it first was . . .[105]

In the second sentence, Lanfranco echoes Marchetto's sentiment of two centuries earlier, that one may locate a mode anywhere that its species can be formed. Furthermore, in the first sentence, he recognizes that the affinities retain only a limited portion of a modal ascent. Finally, Lanfranco acknowledges that transposition to the affinities serves a purpose in chant -- it is used in plainsong to avoid "false notes," but in figured music, "in order to have more space for consonance or by the will of the composer."[106]

Recanetum de musica aurea *by Stefano Vanneo*

In the same year that Lanfranco's treatise appeared, Stefano Vanneo's *Recanetum* was published in Rome.[107] He had completed the treatise in Italian in 1531, but its publication was delayed two years until it had been translated into Latin by the humanist scholar Vincenzo Rosetti. Like Lanfranco's work, *Recanetum* is devoted to basic music principles.

Vanneo discusses alternative finals in Chapter Sixty Eight, "De clavibus seu litteris tonorum finalibus et confinalibus" or "Concerning Final and Cofinal Notes or Letters of Modes."[108] His exposition presents nothing startlingly new, but is worthy of consideration as one more theorist's slightly divergent way of viewing the affinities.

Vanneo states quite directly that modes are judged as regular or irregular according to whether their proper species are present. Although for centuries theorists had been saying that there are irregular modes on a, b♭, and c, Vanneo is really the first to state so unequivocally his rationale for the designation. He next identifies the final letters of irregular modes as affinales or confinales, and he numbers d among them. He is somewhat vague as to why d should be included, saying that men "who are especially experienced in figured songs" resist the logic that excludes d."[109]

It becomes clear in what follows that Vanneo considers irregular form of modes, and hence, modes formed at the affinities, to be more necessary in measured music than in plainsong. One recalls that Aaron made a similar statement in his Libri tres.[110] It seems evident that both theorists had in mind the numerous pieces in the polyphonic repertory ending on a and c, which cannot be classified modally by means of octave-species theory. Vanneo's solution for the a and c endings is more traditional than Aaron's, for while he admits that their species arrangement is irregular, he considers their centuries-old connection with protus and tritus, respectively, intact. It may be supposed that he accepts the concept of a shared modal nucleus, a concept fundamental to a theory of the affinities.

The Writings of Henricus Glareanus

The final writer to be considered in this study is the Swiss music theorist, geographer, poet, and humanist, Henricus Glareanus (1488-1563). Glareanus began his study of music while at the University of Cologne from 1506 to 1510; he studied there under Cochlaeus who, both in his teaching and writings, approached music as a humanistic endeavor. In 1514, Glareanus travelled to Basel and met Erasmus, and in 1517 he went to Paris and joined a circle of humanists that included Heinrich Faber (c. 1500-1552), Guillaume Budé (1467-1540), and Jacques Lefévre d'Etaples (1455-1536).

In 1529, Glareanus became professor of poetry (later also of theology) in Freiburg im Breisgau. This position was significant for his interest in music, for in the nearby Benedictine monastery of St. George, an extensive collection of early writings on music was at his disposal. From 1530 to 1536, he studied the works of numerous Greek and Roman writers, one result of which was his preparation of a new edition of Boethius' De musica (Basel, 1546). His exposure to early writers also provided the stimulus for his theory of twelve modes, which he published in the Dodecachordon (1547).[111] As might be expected of a humanist, Glareanus found the basis for a solution to his dissatisfaction with the existing theory of eight modes in the writings of antiquity.

What was Glareanus' fundamental complaint about modal theory? He thought that theorists had erred when they allowed b-flat within protus and tritus modes. According to strict species theory, D and F are no longer <u>protus</u> and <u>tritus</u>, respectively, when <u>b-flat</u> is integrally associated with them. In the course of his exposition, he connects the altered <u>D</u> species with the diatonic octave on <u>a</u> and the altered <u>F</u> species with the diatonic octave on <u>c</u>. For Glareanus, the peculiar species arrangements on these two notes, <u>a</u> and <u>c</u>, warrant the status of new modes, entities distinct from the traditional eight modes. This viewpoint carries with it the rejection of the concept of the affinities. In Glareanus' four new modes rested a logical solution to over two centuries of uneasiness concerning the "irregular" modes on <u>a</u> and <u>c</u>.

Glareanus' dissatisfaction with the prevalent view of mode was not pronounced in his first music treatise, the <u>Isagoge in musicen</u> (1516).[112] However, two features presage the distinctive theory that was to evolve: his self-conscious outlining of Greek modes, and his directive to concentrate on octave species, not on final notes.

As to the first, Glareanus presents in Chapter Seven the names of the Greek "modes" (more correctly, "tonoi") according to Boethius: from low <u>A</u> as <u>Hypodorian</u> through <u>G</u> as <u>Mixolydian</u>, with <u>a</u> added as <u>Hypermixolydian</u>.[113] Glareanus readily admitted that he did not totally understand how these modes functioned in Greek music and that there was not necessarily a connection between them and medieval modes:

> But even as I wrote these names, and realized that we are not now entirely agreed as to how the Ancients used them and that many of the things that are current in our day not only fail to accord with the ancient practice but sometimes are quite remote from them, it is not easy for me to put into words with what reluctance I have wielded my pen.[114]

In his discussion of modal identity, Glareanus recommends that attention be given first of all to octave species, but this recommendation is not yet accompanied by the clarity of reasoning that is to surface in the <u>Dodecachordon</u>. Here in Chapter Ten he simply states that endings alone cannot determine a mode, since chants are varied with respect to their position:

> For not every chant of the first and second mode ends on D, but sometimes on a or on the d above. Very frequently, in the polyphonic composers, the cadence falls on G with B^b, using the <u>synemmenon</u> tetrachord.[115]

He also states that the third and fourth modes can end either on <u>E</u> or <u>a</u>, but he reacts critically to those who end them on <u>♮</u>, "[f]or the scale-degrees above and below are inconsistent with the systems . . ."[116] For the fifth and sixth modes he accepts endings on <u>F</u>, <u>C</u>, and c, but he makes no mention of alternative finals for the seventh and eighth modes. Except for the comment concerning deuterus endings on ♮, Glareanus does not expressly differentiate the endings on finals, at the fifth above, and at the fourth above, in terms of their species content. In this treatise, he is concerned only with species in a general sense.

A few other details of Glareanus' discussion in the Isagoge are noteworthy. When he states that protus modes frequently end on G in polyphony, he adds that this occurs because of the desire to keep voices restricted within the range of the Guidonian gamut. That Glareanus is willing to overturn tradition in this respect is revealed in his statement:

> However, this advice is more a matter of prudence than of necessity, since they might also extend beyond the scale.[117]

Not only does he allow notes to occur outside the limits of the gamut, but he also accepts the occasional use of chromatic notes within it. In this connection, he reflects on the earlier practice of transposition in chant:

> In the church melodies, indeed, it is not necessary to transpose the chant because of one or another "ficted," i.e. chromatically altered note, which may be introduced by custom rather than by reason.[118]

In the Dodecachordon, when he repeats his disapproval of transposition for the purpose of avoiding chromatic tones, he states the basis of his objection:

> Sometimes also the first two modes end on a la mi re, but only in songs which do not exceed the fifth, otherwise neither the first mode above nor the second mode below will have kept the fourth, and then la mi will result instead of sol re, which is contrary to the nature of these modes.[119]

Here Glareanus tells us that the positioning of protus modes on a can be valid only if a melody's ascent from the final does not exceed a fifth, in other words, if it does not exceed the ascent common to D and its affinity a. He indicates that the species of fourth at the two positions are different by naming their respective solmization syllables.[120] In spite of his expressed awareness of how this difference in species of fourth allowed his predecessors to preserve certain chants in a given mode, he is unwilling to concede the validity of the concept; hence, his rejection of the affinities:

> . . . some writers have transmitted the general rule, that every song can have, on the fifth above the final key, a *confinalis*, which they call *finalis*. But certainly this is not true in any mode, for everywhere the fourth opposes it.[121]

Following this statement, Glareanus proceeds to sanction transposition to the fourth above the final, achieved through *b-flat*. He recognizes *protus* on *G*, *deuterus* on *a*, *tritus* on *b*, and *tetrardus* on *c*.

Glareanus' announcement of four new modes, two on *a* and two on *c*, does not follow immediately from his rejection of the affinities. In fact, he only indirectly acknowledges a connection between the two. His rationale for the creation of four new modes is an independent line of thought that has as its basis his study and adoption of ancient theory. In Book Two of the *Dodecachordon*, counter to his statement in the *Isagoge*, he turns to the Greek modes and seeks some correspondence between them and his own modal system. The ancient writings served two purposes: they provided him with the names for his new modes,[122] and they offered a systematic method for deriving them. The second contribution is relevant to this study, since it elucidates how Glareanus came to his view of the octave segments on *a* and *c*.

The theoretical principle that Glareanus found useful concerns multiple divisions of an octave species. The ancients had spoken of a harmonic division and of an arithmetic division. In a harmonic division, the interval of a fourth is placed above the interval of a fifth, while in an arithemtic division, it is placed below the fifth. In the *Isagoge*, Glareanus had noted that the eight-mode system includes a dual division of one octave species, *D* to *d*. Mode one comes about by the positioning of the fourth above the fifth, while mode eight results from the fourth being placed below the fifth: mode one D E F G a ♭ c d versus mode eight D E F G a ♭ c d.[123] In the *Dodecachordon*, he extends the possibility for harmonic/arithmetic divisions to all seven octave species; theoretically, twenty-four scale patterns emerge as he considers all the possible connections of fourths and fifths, of which twelve must be rejected because of their improper interval progressions.[124] But among the twelve accepted are the species arrangements belonging to his two *Aeolian* modes on *a* and his two *Ionian* modes on *c*. These four modes rely on a new division of four octaves that already have a modal association: *Aeolian* results from a harmonic division of the *Hypodorian* (plagal *protus*) octave; *Hypoaeolian*, from an arithmetic division of the *Phrygian* (authentic *deuterus*) octave; *Ionian*, from a harmonic division of the *Hypolydian* (plagal *tritus*) octave; and *Hypoionian*, from an arithmetic division of the *Mixolydian* (authentic *tetrardus*) octave.

Glareanus anticipates that some musicians will view his twelve-mode system with skepticism, so he counters with this argument:

> Thus, if the common eighth mode is different from the other seven true and incontestable modes only on account of the inversion of a system, then it is necessary that the four remaining modes, the ninth, tenth, eleventh and twelfth, as we call them, also be admitted into the list of modes.[125]

He thus underscores the fact that a harmonic/arithmetic division (the "inversion of a system") is fundamental to the eight-mode system, and hence, that it would be inconsistent to reject it as the basis for a twelve-mode system. Having arrived at a theoretical justification for his new modes, Glareanus makes a few remarks to remind his reader why he thinks they are essential to the music of his time, and it is here that his disapproval of *protus* and *tritus* modes formed with *b-flat* is brought into focus. Referring to those who allow this to occur, he says:

> They contend that the entire system is in nowise changed because of altering one or another of the semitones. For they say that this song is *synemmenon* and foreign, as it were, changing nothing in the substance of the mode. . . . And so our eleventh and twelfth modes are not to be separated in any way from the old fifth and sixth modes because of changing a single semitone in the fifth. And they do not hesitate to include the ninth and tenth modes, which we formed, with the first and second modes.[126]

Glareanus admits that an occasional altered tone does not change the mode, but he insists that an integral *b-flat* does: *protus* with *b-flat* (D E F G a b c d) no longer has the species proper to that *maneria* (D E F G a ♮ c d). However, the new arrangement of species corresponds exactly to that on *a* (a ♮ c d e f g aa), his *Aeolian* mode. Likewise, the arrangement on *F* with *b-flat* (F G a b c d e f) corresponds to that on *c* (c d e f g aa ♮♮ cc), his *Ionian* mode.

Glareanus has come full circle. In Book One, he rejects the premise that a mode can end on its *cofinalis*, because the *confinalis* does not preserve the exact species proper to that mode. Here, in Book Two, he calls the two most common affinity positions new modes, yet he admits that they serve the same purpose they did as *confinales* or *affinales*: they absorb the variant forms of *protus* and *tritus* modes. This is the subtle irony inherent in Glareanus' rejection of the affinities.

Did the concept of the affinities disappear as a result of Glareanus' statements? The simple answer to this question is no. The concept was kept alive through the continued reading of earlier writings on music. In addition, there were sixteenth-century theorists after Glareanus who expressed the concept in more or less traditional terms in their treatises.[127] Some composers of polyphony acknowledged it within their modally ordered collections by designating as mode one a piece ending on a. In this last regard, Harold Powers has noted that when major composers of the last half of the sixteenth century organized a group of compositions according to the system of modes, they employed an eight-mode design, rather than a twelve-mode plan.[128]

To leave the question posed above so answered, however, would distort the historical picture of the influence exerted by Glareanus' Dodecachordon. Clement Miller mentions several German polyphonic collections organized according to Glareanus' principles, among them Homer Herpol's Novum et insigne opum musicum (1565) and Eucharius Hoffmann's 24 Cantiones 4, 5, et 6 vocum, accommodate ad 12 tonos (1577); he also remarks on canzoni, ricercari, toccate, and fantasie by the Gabrielis, Merulo, and Padovana that incorporate the twelve modes.[129] In addition, there is a long list of theorists of not only German origin, but of Italian and English nationality as well, who adopt Glareanus' theories.[130]

Conclusion

It is not an aim of this study to determine when mention of the affinities ceased in music theory texts, nor to document the contribution that Glareanus' statements made to that end. The decision to conclude with the publication of the Dodecachordon in 1547 results from a recognition that, in Glareanus' writing, the culmination of questioning attitudes towards the affinities had been reached. Even in the eleventh century when Guido first praised them for allowing modal variety, he implied that they should be used with discretion. Fourteenth-century writers attached the label "irregular" to pieces ending on the affinities, even as they exploited the principle behind them, a shared modal nucleus, in order to refine the hexachord system.

From the end of the fourteenth century through the beginning of the sixteenth, the increasing use of one-flat signatures in polyphony resulted in more intense scrutiny of what the affinities had to offer: theorists gradually came to realize that flat transpositions made it possible to retain the exact interval arrangement found at a mode's normal position, whereas the affinities preserved only the modal nucleus.

It was the sixteenth century's infatuation with octave species theory that ultimately stimulated outspoken criticism of the affinities. Theorists pursued their criticisms in various ways. Aaron conceived his own method for analyzing melodies ending on a and c, while Agricola, in his last treatise, essentially ignored endings on a and recommended that protus modes be ended on G. Finally, Glareanus created new modes to explain the distinctive modal formulations that may be constructed on a and c. Glareanus provided the ultimate rejection in theory of the concept of a related note as one that can identify a mode because it shares a nucleus of melodic movement with its final.

One last reflection seems appropriate. We must recognize in the concept of affinitas the medieval predilection for finding relationships within the cosmos.

Once a tonal system, the "sounding-board" of man's experience, was formulated, theorists naturally speculated on the harmonious relationships it embodied. We recall that some of our theorists, the _Enchiriadis_ author, Guido, and Jacques de Liège, actually presented the concept as encompassing a hierarchy of pitch relationships -- at the octave, fifth, and fourth.

But Guido and Jacques turned to a practical matter -- the notation of the chant repertory -- and to that end they found the _affinitas_ at the fifth most serviceable. Whatever speculative motives may have spawned it, the concept of _affinitas_ played an integral role in the medieval theorist's task of notating and classifying according to mode the chant repertory he had inherited. It allowed him to adopt a flexible concept of mode that was not constrained by rigid scalar constructs. We have seen how the tension between these two approaches to mode, one scalar, one nuclear, resulted in centuries of discussion as to what kind of transposition was acceptable. Significantly, the rise of transposition in the modern sense goes hand-in-hand with the gradual rejection of the modal concept known as _affinitas_.

Appendix A

Discussion of Principal *Sedes* According to Wilhelm (Harbinson, *Willehelmi*, p. 60)

Wilhelm's discussion provides a hierarchical ordering among the four principal modal positions. Unfortunately, his language is somewhat vague in this context and the reason for his preferences remains unclear. Beginning with the *sedes* *Γ* to *E*, he remarks:

> . . . because it begins in a regular tone, but ends less perfectly in a semitone, the modes assume no seat in it, and thus, it is not legitimate.

> . . . quia in regulari tono orditur, et minus perfecte in semitonio terminatur, nullam tropi sedem ex illa percipiunt, ideoque legitima non est.

For *C* to *a*, he states:

> . . . it begins in a regular tone and ends in a regular tone, that is, *mese* *a*, and thus it is most noble and perfect, and modes come to rest in its beginning and its end as if in certain seats.

> . . . in regulari tono incipit et in regulari tono id est mese a finitur, ideoque nobilissima et perfecta est, et in initio eius et in fine tropi quasi in quibusdam sedibus requiescunt.

The rejection of the *graves* *sedes* is based on ending "in a semitone," perhaps because only a semitone is available in the gamut above the boundary of the sixth *Γ* to *E*. For the *finales* location *C* to *a*, a tone and a semitone are both possible. It may be that Wilhelm views as most serviceable the positions that allow a mode freedom of movement (to a tone or semitone) beyond the limiting sixth. He similarly qualifies the *superiores* *sedes* *G* to *e*: ". . . and thus, it is legitimate in its beginning, but the end is not accepted." (". . . ideoque legitima est in initio suo, finis vero non recipitur.") Comparing this description to that of Γ to E, it becomes obvious that Γ to E was rejected completely because of the impossibility of movement below Γ as well as only semitone movement above E. Finally, c to aa, although "beginning in a regular tone," has a limitation, since Wilhelm apparently considers his gamut to extend only to aa: "Quarta a regulari tono id est in c. incipiens, terminatur in aa. sed quia synemmenon in monochordo sedes troporum ibidem esse non poterit."

In sum, in spite of its occasional vagueness, this passage suggests that the finales and superiores are the particular locations where modal movement is best accommodated.

Appendix B

Passages on "Transposition by Necessity"

1. The anonymous commentary from Liège

Smits van Waesberghe, Expositiones, pp. 144-45: ". . . necessario finiuntur in .a.♮.c., ascendentes illuc gemina transpositione, scilicet vel ex toto transposita a legitima finali in affinem, ut 'Haec dies quam fecit Dominus' a .D. in .a. ex toto transponitur, ut in .a. tota cantetur, vel transpositione in parte, ut cum cantus in legitimam finalem finire deberet et circa eam aliquamdiu versatus fuisset, ad affinem se transfert per lasciviam et ibi finitur, ut 'Alleluia Iudicabunt.' Notandum quod liber plagis dat transpositionem per diapente super finalem propriam, et non authentis."

2. The Leipzig treatise

Sowa, Quellen, p. 160: "Duobus itaque modis fit transpositio. In aliquibus quippe cantibus necessario plage prothi deuteri triti finiuntur in a ♮ c, ascendentes illuc gemina transpositione: vel ex toto transposita a finali legitima in affinem ut Hec dies quam fecit dominus, in a ex toto transponitur, ut in a toto canitur. Vel transpostione in parte, ut cum cantus finalem in legitimam finiri deberet et circa eam aliquamdiu versatus fuisset, et ad finem [sic] se transferret per lasciviam et ibi finiatur, ut Terribilis est locus iste." "Finem" should read "affinem."

This passage follows the anonymous commentator's almost word-for-word; a notable difference is the chant example for partial transposition: "Alleluia. Judicabunt" in the Liège, and "Terribilis est" in the Leipzig. However, one source of the Liège commentary, Firenze, Biblioteca Medicea Laurenziana, acq. e doni 33, fols. 2v-51r, presents "Terribilis est" as the chant example.

3. Quaestiones in musica

Steglich, Quaestiones, pp. 54-55: "At vero necessitate transponitur primus tonus et ex toto, ut: 'Haec dies' a D in a compare sua, sub hac habentes duos tonos, quibus caret finalis ipsa. Ex parte transfertur ut responsorium 'Factum est.' Tonus secundus eadem causa ex toto ut: 'Te unum' ibi: 'trinitatem.' Ex parte ut: 'Terribilis.' Quartus ex toto transponitur ab E finali in ♮ sotiali propter tres tonos, quos ista habet, illa non habet, ut offertorium: 'Domine fac mecum.' . . . Sextus ex toto cantatur in c per b molle, qui eo tono caret F sub se, ut: 'Honor virtus.'"

4. Practica artis musice by Amerus

Ruini, Ameri, p. 94: "Hec omnia sunt de cantibus in legitima finali concurrentibus, sed plage primi, tercii, quinti aliquando finiuntur in a,b,c ascendentes illuc gemina transpositione, scilicet ex toto transposita a legitima finali in affinalem, ut graduale Ostende, ut graduale Hec dies quam fecit, ut offertorium Dominus dixit; a d in a ex toto transponitur ut in a toto cantetur et finiatur, vel transpositione ex parte ut, dum cantus in legitima finali finiri debet et circa eam aliquam diu versatur, ad finem [sic] se transfert per lasciviam et ibi finitur, ut Terribilis est locus. Nota quod plagis datur transpositio propria et non autentis, sed hec omnia licenter finiunt, non regulariter. Cantus qui supra finalem octavo loco finiunt adulterini cantus vocantur."

Note that the same faulty construction "finem" for "affinem" appears here and in the Leipzig treatise.

5. Speculum musicae by Jacques de Liège

Bragard, Speculum, p. 101: "Necessitate autem fit translatio alicuius cantus a propria finali ad aliquam affinalem, quando cantus aliam requirit tonorum et semitoniorum dispositionem quam in propria finali reperiat, ut fit in proto quando sub fine requirit duos tonos; tunc enim a propria finali .D. transfertur ad affinalem .a. In deutero, quando, sub fine, tres requirit tonos, transfertur tunc ad affinalem .♮., quia, sub propria finali, quae est .E., tantum sunt duo toni continui. In trito similiter fit translatio, quando cantus sub fine tonum requirit; hunc cum non habeat in propria finali .F., quaerit eum in affinali .c. per .b. molle, ut patet in responsorio illo Honor, virtus. Et in multis aliis cantibus de ista translatione et de praecedentibus exempla reperiuntur."

Appendix C

Chant Citations in Marchetto's Discussion of the Eight Modes

Marchetto's discussion of mode one includes two noteworthy passages. The first concerns the gradual "Salvum fac servum":

> The first mode is begun on _B grave_, again, in mixed form, as the gradual "Salvum fac servum," whose verse is "Auribus percipe." But there are some who begin this gradual on _F grave_ and then it is ended on the cofinal of the first [mode] . . .[1]

In his subsequent discussion, Marchetto recognizes two versions of this chant, one ending on the normal final but including _B-flat_, the other ending on the cofinal. Although he had advocated the alternative final to avoid _B-flat_ in "Nimis honorati sunt," here he seems to prefer the normal final with _B-flat_. His reasoning is clear-cut -- at the higher level, an unacceptable _f-sharp_ would appear several times in the verse. As to the _B-flat_, he comments, ". . . such an addition is not there naturally, but for the sake of a better sound."[2] By "better sound," he means that the use of _B-flat_ avoids the formation of a tritone in the opening distinction (Example 18).[3] Even as he recommends the acceptance of this _B-flat_, he acknowledges its anomalous character:

> . . . and such a mode is called "artificial," because a tone is artificially placed where it does not naturally occur.[4]

Citing the first-mode introit "Statuit ei Dominus," Marchetto again touches on the issue of the affinities.[5] He recommends beginning on _D_, but notes that the chant also could start on _G_, where the same species of fourth and fifth arise through the use of _b-flat_:

> We answer that such a mode will be called "proper in the matter of composition," because it is formed out of its proper species, but "improper in the matter of location," because it is placed in a position other than the proper one.[6]

Ex. 18. Beginning of the gradual "Salvum fac servum" according to Marchetto.

Thus, Marchetto alludes to his earlier statement on how melodic species are properly formed at the fourth above the final, but he qualifies the acceptability of such a practice for _protus_. Although he had accepted it for _deuterus_, he apparently retains something of the traditional attitude towards the single modal identity of the four finals: _G_ ought to serve _tetrardus_, and _tetrardus_ only.

Within his description of mode four, there is an apparent inconsistency in his treatment of the antiphon "Sion noli timere," which, like "Beatus servus," usually ends on _a_. Berno advocated beginning "Sion" on _c_ rather than _G_ to accommodate its arrangement of whole tones and semitones. Marchetto, however, prescribes a beginning on _G_.[7] Since he transposed "Beatus servus" to account for the presence of _F-sharp_, which apparently occurred in "Sion" as well, his failure to call for the latter's transposition is puzzling. Did he know another version without an _F-sharp_?[8]

Finally, Marchetto mentions two sixth-mode chants relevant to the present discussion. He states that the responsory "Tradiderunt me in manus" may begin on _C_, and the responsory "Aspiciebam in visu" on _F_.[9] In the available sources, "Tradiderunt" begins a fifth higher on _G_, and in the only source of it listed in Bryden and Hughes' _Index_, "Aspiciebam" begins a fifth higher on _c_. Both of these chants end on the _affinalis_ _c_. As in the case of "Sion," it may be that Marchetto knew a version of "Tradiderunt" that did not have altered tones and thus did not require transposition.[10] The only obvious reason for transposition of "Aspiciebam" would be to avoid low _B-flat_. If this is indeed the reason for the transposed version of the chant that occurs in the _Lucca_ antiphoner, it is not one given by Marchetto.

Appendix D

Treatises by Johannes Cochlaeus, Venceslaus Philomathes and Georg Rhau

Musica and Tetrachordum musices by Johannes Cochlaeus

Seven editions of Cochlaeus' treatise *Tetrachordum musices* appeared from 1511 to 1526.[1] Clement Miller describes it as an elaboration of Cochlaeus' earlier treatise, *Musica*, which was written before 1502.[2]

In the third edition of *Musica* (1507), Cochlaeus includes two rules for transposed song, the wording and format of which derive from Wollick's exposition:

Two Rules Concerning the Transposition of Song

First	a lamire b fa♮mi c solfaut		1 or 2 3 or 4 5 or 6	b fa♮mi mi
Division of transposed song ending on	C faut	belongs to modes	7 or 8	if fa is sung on ♮mi. But if mi, it belongs to mode 5 or 6.
Second	G solreut a lamire b fa♮mi c solfaut		1 or 2 3 or 4 5 or 6 7 or 8	b fa♮mi fa. This rarely occurs, however, in gregorian song, but now and then in figured song.[3]

The rules concern transposition to the fifth by means of *b-natural*, and transposition to the fourth by means of *b-flat*. Cochlaeus adds that the latter rarely occurs in chant, and surprisingly, only now and then in polyphony.

Earlier, Cochlaeus gives the reasons for using alternative finals at the fifth above the normal finals:

> Sometimes, however, to avoid musica ficta or downward movement of a song in its notes, [entering] excessively into gloominess, a song is transposed from its final to confinalis removed by a fifth (as is commonly permitted, but not always).[4]

The idea of transposing a song to avoid chromatic tones surfaces once again, but Cochlaeus also mentions the avoidance of excessive downward movement, by which he apparently means a range that is too low.

The 1507 edition contains a section, "De tonorum finalibus," which is found as well in the second edition printed between 1505 and 1507. This section spells out the content of the figure and comments on it briefly. After Cochlaeus emphasizes that there are three familiar confinales, a, b, and c, which "songs deficient in their proper range use,"[5] he adds:

> But let those who copy mensural songs appropriate confinales to them at will, provided that the same intervals of a song will be able to persist.[6]

In this context, he names related notes at the fourth, G, a, b, and c, and continues:

> . . . they have rarely admitted these four confinales to ecclesiastical notations. For they say that any confinalis whatsoever should be distant from its final pitch by the interval of a fifth.[7]

Thus, indirectly, he associates related notes at the upper fourth with polyphony, not chant. It is also noteworthy that Cochlaeus has borrowed Wollick's clause "provided that the same intervals of a song . . ." and has linked it to a position a fourth above the final. By doing so, he suggests that he recognizes how a transposition at the fourth retains the proper interval arrangement.

The presentation on related notes in the Tetrachordum musices is very similar to the "De tonorum finalibus" section of the Musica, but one small change occurs in connection with tetrardus alternative finals. After Cochlaeus stresses that a confinalis should be a fifth from its final, he remarks that G cannot have a confinalis above "because of the excessive highness of the keys."[8] He accepts the tradition of excluding d as confinalis, but feels compelled to explain why the system he espouses lacks symmetry. Earlier, Wollick had added d to his figure to achieve this symmetry, although he was aware that tradition excluded it.

In general, Cochlaeus, like Wollick, does not explain the principles behind transposed song, either at the interval of a fifth or fourth. He simply reports on practices without trying to reconcile the theoretical inconsistencies that underlie them, and thus reveals himself as more of a practitioner than a speculative theorist.

Musicorum libri quatuor by Venceslaus Philomathes

Venceslaus Philomathes, whose dates of birth and death are unknown, was a native of Bohemia. He studied in Vienna in 1510, and his Musicorum libri quatuor was published there in 1512.[9] The treatise went through five subsequent editions.

Philomathes founded his music theory on the hexachord system. In Chapter Four on modes, he emphasizes the importance of a composition's final syllable for modal recognition:

> A mode should be distinguished by its beginning, middle and ending.
> By its ending, through the last syllables, for the first together with the second finishes on re,
> The third together with the fourth on mi,
> The fifth together with the sixth on fa,
> The seventh together with the eighth on sol.
> The ending is the same, the beginning of the modes is varied.[10]

After he presents D, E, F, and G as the normal finals, he allows that modes may be transposed to the fourth or fifth above when they cannot be sung in those proper seats. Like Wollick and Cochlaeus, he unhesitatingly offers both transpositions as possibilities.

Earlier, in Chapter Three, "De natura trium cantuum" or "Concerning the Nature of the Three Hexachords," he states that a mode does not change when a melody is transposed, and again he points to the final syllable as the modal indicator. In conjunction with these statements, he presents several melodies in their normal and transposed positions. Example 19 shows a protus melody in three positions: at the final, transposed to the fourth above, and transposed to the fifth above.[11]

While Philomathes offers the same three positions for a deuterus melody, his treatment of a tritus example is different. He presents a fifth-mode chant with a normal range of F to d and a one-flat signature, which he then transposes to the fourth below (range C to a) and fifth above (range c to aa). Why did he not transpose it to the fourth above as he did protus and deuterus?

The tritus example includes b-flat, and therefore requires the tones b-flat and e-flat if transposed to the fourth above. Since Philomathes relied on hexachord theory, we would expect him to postulate a hexachord on *b-flat* to make this *e-flat* theoretically possible. Indeed, he does so in Chapter Five when he presents a *musica ficta* scale that contains transposed hexachords on *b-flats* (three locations), and thus yields *e-flats* (Figure 11).[12] However, Philomathes specifically attributes these *ficta* or *coniuncta* tones to organum and to instrumental music, not to chant. Thus, according to his theory, a transposition to the fourth above is not possible for the *tritus* chant.

Ex. 19. The antiphon "Jesus autem transiens" in normal and transposed positions according to Philomathes.

First mode placed in its proper seat

Je-sus au-tem tran-si-ens per me-di-um il-lo-rum i-bat. EVOVAE

First mode transposed through the fourth

Je-sus au-tem tran-si-ens per me-di-um il-lo-rum i-bat. EVOVAE

First mode transposed through the fifth

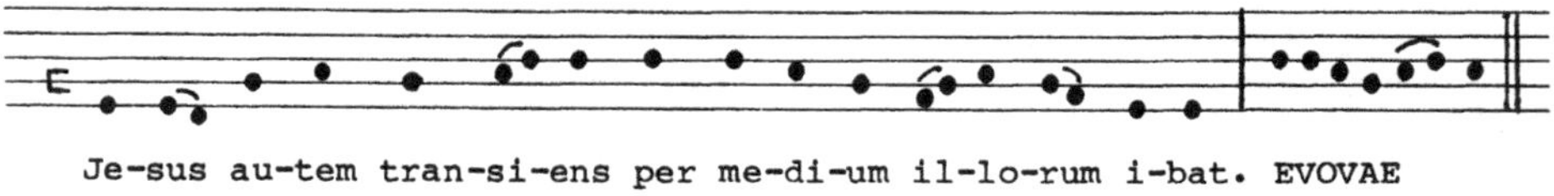
Je-sus au-tem tran-si-ens per me-di-um il-lo-rum i-bat. EVOVAE

Enchiridion utriusque musicae practicae by Georg Rhau

Georg Rhau (1488-1548) was an active publisher in Wittenberg throughout the first half of the sixteenth century. His initial publishing efforts consisted of writings on music theory, and his own interest in the subject led him to write and publish the treatise *Enchiridion utriusque musicae practicae* in 1517, the second part of which he completed in 1520.[13] Although not innovative, the work was well-received and appeared in new editions until 1553.

Fig. 11. *Musica ficta* scale from Venceslaus Philomathes' *Musicorum libri quatuor*.

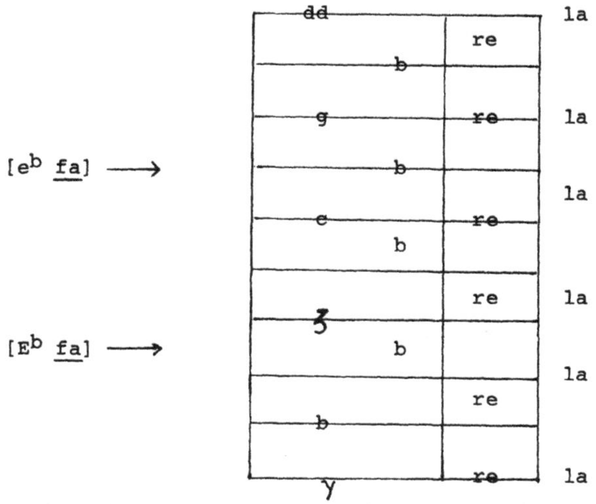

Rhau bases parts of his treatise on Philomathes', and in fact uses Philomathes' exact wording when he refers to transposed modes:

> We transpose those [modes] nevertheless by a fourth or fifth, if they cannot be sung at their proper seats.[14]

He also presents Philomathes' verse on modal recognition through final syllable. However, he then appends a section on transposition that begins:

> Transposition of song is the avoidance of *coniunctae*. For while we strive to avoid *coniunctae*, we raise a song from the proper location of its ending to the fifth above, occasionally to the fourth. Not every melody of the first and second modes ends on *D*, but sometimes also on *a* and *d*; in mensural song, most frequently on *G*, not however, without *fa* on the note *b*; composers do this preferably for this reason, so that pitches will not appear to extend outside of Guido's scale.[15]

Rhau defines transposition as the avoidance of *coniunctae*. By so expressing the traditional concern over altered tones, he reflects the influence that the group of treatises discussed in Chapter Four must have exerted on subsequent writers. Rhau mentions another reason for transposition, specifically to the fourth above, a reason related to Wollick's comment on conflicting parts of counterpoint: one voice is transposed so that a lower voice will not be set down beyond the permissible limit of the gamut.

Rhau presents the most common related endings for each *maneria*. In connection with transpositions using *b-natural*, *protus* modes end on *a* and *tritus* modes on *c*, but *deuterus* modes never end on ♮, because their "systems" are opposed by the pitches surrounding ♮. In his vague way, Rhau is commenting that the fundamental species of fifth formed at *E* is not available at ♮. He allows that irregular *deuterus* modes end most aptly on *a* through *b-flat*. Finally, modes seven and eight are not transposed, "for learned musicians state that melodies which are ending on *d* or on *C* are corrupted by the ignorance of singers."[16]

Thus, Rhau reaffirms the historical importance of *a* and *c* as alternative finals. In saying that mensural songs may use *G* as a *protus* final, he reveals his awareness of current practice, even if he did not attempt a theoretical explanation of it.

Notes

INTRODUCTION

1. See, for example, Lawrence A. Gushee, ed., Aureliani Reomensis Musica Disciplina, Corpus Scriptorum de Musica 21 (Rome: American Institute of Musicology, 1975), p. 78: ". . . tonus est totius constitutionis armonice differentia, et quantitas quae in vocis accentu sive tenore consistit."

2. See Eric Werner, "The Psalmodic Formula Neannoe and its Origins," The Musical Quarterly 28 (1942), pp. 93-99; and Clyde W. Brockett, "Noeane and Neuma. A Theoretical and Musical Equation," Report of the Eleventh Congress of the International Musicological Society, Copenhagen, 1972, ed. Henrik Glahn, Soren Sorensen, and Peter Ryom (Copenhagen: Edition Wilhelm Hansen, 1974), pp. 301-8.

3. The fact that the final is not mentioned earlier has disturbed some modern scholars to the extent that they question whether it was considered at all in the earliest attempts at modal classification. Willi Apel has pointed out that Carolingian writers such as Aurelian and Regino of Prüm devote considerable attention to the way an antiphon begins, which suggests that a chant's incipit, not its ending, was of primary importance. Willi Apel, Gregorian Chant, 3rd ed. (Indiana: Indiana University Press, 1966), pp. 173-78. Both Aurelian's and Regino's remarks must be placed in their proper perspective. They were made in prefaces to tonaries in which chants were grouped according to the eight modes and further subdivided according to psalm-tone endings, or *differentiae*. The theorist's task was to explain how to choose a *differentia* that would complement the opening of the antiphon or responsory -- hence, the emphasis on chant beginnings.

While Regino and Aurelian apparently made their initial modal designations based on the antiphon or responsory ending, it is evident from their tonaries that they sometimes relied on chant beginnings when chants lacked modal unity; in chants of this kind, the beginning suggests a different mode from the ending. Both Regino and Aurelian commented on such chants in their introductions, and classified them according to the mode of their opening. See Gushee, *Aureliani*, pp. 83ff. For discussion of Regino's attitude, see further Chapter One, p. 18.

4. The designation of the modes according to the Greek ordinal numbers *protus*, *deuterus*, *tritus*, and *tetrardus* was the prevailing usage throughout the Middle Ages. Each of the four categories was subdivided into authentic and plagal forms, thus making a total of eight modes within four *maneriae*. See further n. 27 in Chapter One.

Letter designations used throughout this study are in accordance with general medieval usage of a somewhat later time: Γ A B C D E F G a b ♮ c d e f g aa bb ♮♮ cc dd. These letter designations were formulated by the author of the *Dialogus de musica* c.1000. Beginning in the eleventh century, the notes *A* to *G* were referred to as *graves*, the notes *a* to *g* as *acutae*, and *aa* to *dd* as *superacutae*. By the end of the eleventh century, *ee* has been added to the *superacutae*. In the *graves*, the note *B* occurs only in the natural form, so capital *B* has this sole meaning. In the *acutae* and *superacutae*, both the natural and flat form of *b* are used, indicated by the respective symbols *♮* and *b*. Since *b* is the only note in the medieval gamut that is inflected, the symbols given alone always refer to it.

5. See, for example, my reference to Guido in Chapter One, n. 55.

6. The first significant examination of this issue was by Gustav Jacobsthal, *Die chromatische Alteration im liturgischen Gesang der abendländischen Kirche*. (Berlin, 1897; reprint ed., Hildesheim: Georg Olms, 1970). For more recent discussions, see Willi Apel, *Gregorian Chant* (Bloomington: Indiana University Press, 1958), pp. 157-65; and Richard Hoppin, *Medieval Music* (New York: W. W. Norton, 1978), pp. 70-72.

7. *An Index of Gregorian Chant*, 2 vols., compiled by John R. Bryden and David G. Hughes (Cambridge, Mass.: Harvard University Press, 1969).

CHAPTER 1: FROM HUCBALD TO GUIDO: ORIGINS OF THE CONCEPT

1. Published in *GS* I, pp. 103-21. For an English translation see Hucbald, *Melodic Instruction (De harmonica institutione)* in *Hucbald, Guido, and John on Music: Three Medieval Treatises*, trans. Warren Babb, ed. Claude V. Palisca (New Haven: Yale University Press, 1978), pp. 13-44.

2. Yves Chartier, "La Musica d'Hucbald de Saint-Amand (traité de musique du IXe siècle). Introduction, établissement du texte, traduction et commentaire" (Ph.D. diss., Sorbonne, 1973).

3. Translation Babb, *Hucbald*, p. 39. *GS* I, p. 119: ". . . quod finem in ipsis cuncta, quae canuntur, accipiant."

4. Hucbald uses the terms *lichanos hypaton*, *hypate meson*, *parhypate meson*, and *lichanos meson*. I will adopt a letter notation in accordance with general medieval usage described in n. 4 of the Introduction.

5. This again shows his indebtedness to the Greek Greater Perfect System, which also contained a *synemmenon* tetrachord spelled *d c b-flat a*.

6. Translation Babb, *Hucbald*, p. 31. *GS* I, p. 114: "Cuius tetrachordi exempla cum per omnes modos vel tonos se frequentius offerant, tamen praecipue in autento triti vel plagis eius ita ubique perspici possunt, ut vix aliquod melum in eis absque horum permixtione tetrachordum, synemmenon scilicet (et) diezeugmenon reperiatur." *Diezeugmenon* refers to the tetrachord *a ♮ c d*.

7. Translation Babb, *Hucbald*, p. 39. *GS* I, p. 119: ". . . quinta semper loca his quatuor superiora quadam sibi connexionis unione iunguntur, adeo, ut pleraque etiam in eis quasi regulariter mela inveniantur desinere, nec rationi ob hoc vel sensui quid contraire, et sub eodem modo vel tropo recte decurrere. Hac ergo socilitate continentur lichanos hypaton cum mese; hypate meson cum paramese; parhypatemeson cum trite diezeugmenon, quae quinto scilicet loco singulae a se disparantur."

Babb corrected the Gerbert edition based on a reading of the eleventh-century MS Bruxelles B.R. 10078/95, fols. 84v-92r. In that MS, the *G-d* pair is put into the last sentence quoted above, while in Gerbert, the *G-d* pair is placed at the beginning of the next sentence about similarity of chant beginnings (see n. 9).

Babb's translation "notes a fifth above" is somewhat misleading in view of Hucbald's language, which reads "fifth higher positions." Hucbald does not actually use a word like "note," but instead refers to the pitches of the gamut by the Greek designates, *lichanos hypaton*, *mese*, etc.

8. Specifically, Hucbald uses the ablative form *hac socialitate*, which one may translate "by or through this relationship."

9. Translation Babb, *Hucbald*, p. 39. *GS* I, p. 119: "Lichanos meson cum paranete diezeugmenon cum inferioribus quoque quartis, et in quibusdam quintis, parem quodammodo obtinent habitudinem, quamvis non fini, sed initiis deputentur. Usque ad has enim metam inchoandi declinant: hae sunt Proslambanomenos ad lichanos hypaton, hypate hypaton ad hypate meson, sed id raro; parypate hypaton ad parypate meson; lichanos hypatos ad lichanos meson: sed in hoc aliquando usque ad parypate hypaton descenditur, id est, usque ad quintum locum; in caeteris rarissime." See n. 7 above for an explanation of Babb's changes to this reading.

10. This observation is made by Lawrence Gushee in "Questions of Genre in Medieval Treatises on Music," _Gattungen der Musik in Einzeldarstellungen: Gedenkschrift Leo Schrade_, ed. Wulf Arlt et al. (Bern: Francke Verlag, 1973), p. 391.

11. Harold Powers, following Gerbert's reading in which the _G-d_ pair is set apart, believes that Hucbald did recognize the limited agreement of ascending motion from these notes. Powers suggests that Hucbald saw a relationship between _G_ and _d_ in downward-tending lines at the beginnings of chants. See Powers' article "Mode" in _The New Grove Dictionary of Music and Musicians_, 20 vols., ed. Stanley Sadie (London: Macmillan Publishers, Ltd., 1980), vol. 12, p. 381.

12. The most recent editions of the treatises are by Hans Schmid, _Musica et Scolica Enchiriadis una cum aliquibus tractatulis adiunctis_, _Bayerische Akademie der Wissenschaften Veroeffentlichungen der Musikhistorischen Kommission_, Band 3 (Munich, 1981). These editions supercede those found in _GS_ I, pp. 152-73 and 173-212. There are two English translations of the _Musica enchiriadis_: _Music Handbook (Musica enchiriadis)_, trans. Léonie Rosenstiel, _Colorado College Music Press Translations_, no. 7 (Colorado Springs: Colorado College Music Press, 1976); Richard Lee Holladay, "The 'Musica Enchiriadis' and 'Scholia Enchiriadis': A Translation and Commentary" (Ph.D. diss., Ohio State University, 1977). In addition to Holladay's translation of the _Scolica_, there is a translation of part two of the treatise, "De Symphoniis," by Oliver Strunk in _Source Readings in Music History_ (New York: W.W. Norton & Co., 1950), pp. 126-38.

A dating of c. 900 has been offered for the treatises. A summary of the arguments supporting this conclusion is found in Lawrence Gushee's article "Musica enchiriadis" in _The New Grove_, vol. 12, pp. 800-801.

13. Otto Gombosi, "Studien zur Tonartenlehre des frühen Mittelalters III," _Acta Musicologica_ 12 (1940), p. 25.

14. Lincoln B. Spiess, "The Diatonic 'Chromaticism' of the _Enchiriadis_ Treatises," _JAMS_ 12 (1959), pp. 1-6.

15. Schmid, _Musica_, p. 37: "Si tribus, modus nascitur quartus. Si adhuc uno altius spacio efferatur, erit quinta denuo regione primus." _Spacio_ literally means "space" here, since the syllables of the melody are placed on a staff-like graph in spaces that represent tones and semitones.

16. In a later passage, he emphasizes this point in reference to organum at the fourth: "Since, as was said, the same tropes are not found at the fourth positions and the modes of different tropes cannot be maintained throughout at the same time, for this reason in the consonance of the diatessaron the principal and organal voices do not agree throughout at the fourth position." Schmid, p. 105: "Quoniam, ut dictum est,

per quartanas regiones non idem tropi reperiuntur diversorumque troporum modi per totum simul ire nequeunt, idcirco in diatessaron symphonia non per totum vox principalis voxque organalis quartana regione consentiunt."

17. Gustave Reese interpreted this example to mean that some chants could be sung in any of the modes. Gustave Reese, Music in the Middle Ages (New York: W.W. Norton & Co., 1940), p. 159. This interpretation seems to be erroneous. The melody "Tu patris sempiternus es filius" is verse fifteen of the hymn "Te Deum." It is likely that this chant was known by the author's readers and had a clear modal association for them; as a result, they would easily recognize how its mode changed at a new position in the gamut. See LU 1832-34 for the entire hymn. Ruth Steiner lists various functions served by "Te Deum" in both liturgical and non-liturgical contexts. Cf. "Te Deum," The New Grove, vol. 18, p. 641.

18. Schmid, Musica, p. 82: "Praecipue quidem videtur vis cuiuslibet tropi ob id in quolibet finali sono consistere, quod in eo tropus finiendo constiterit. Additur hoc tamen, quod sonus idem finalis et sociales sui frequentiores in commatum vel colarum fine versantur. Sociales autem suos quisque sonus non solum quintis habet regionibus, sed et quartis locis alios sibi quaerit compares, qui tertiae simphoniae locus est. Itaque in particulis, quae membra sunt cantionis, pene semper cola vel commata has in levando aut in ponendo sonorum socialitates petunt, et in eas vel arsis quaerit attingere vel thesis."

The meaning of tropus in this context is different from its more prevalent one, a category of plainchant comprising textual and musical additions to Mass and Office chants. From the sixth century onward, tropus could refer in general to sounding music; in the eighth and ninth centuries, it was interpreted as cantus or sonus. See Bruno Stäblein's article "Tropus" in MGG, vol. 13, col. 798. From the ninth century onward, tropus was also frequently used as a synonym for modus, both at first referring to species of melody associated with each of the four finals. Some later writers distinguish between the two, applying tropus to the consecutive arrangement of tones within an octave species, and modus to the melodic patterns characterizing the octave species. See, for example, Hermannus Contractus in his treatise Musica, Leonard Ellinwood, ed., Musica Hermanni Contracti (Rochester: Eastman School of Music, 1936), pp. 57-59. In general, however, there was no consistent approach among theorists in applying these words. Otto Gombosi attempts to sort out the various usages in his three-part article, "Studien zur Tonartenlehre des frühen Mittelalters," Acta Musicologica 10 (1938), pp. 149-74; 11 (1939), pp. 28-39, 128-35; 12 (1940), pp. 21-52. As to the Enchiriadis author, he generally uses *tropus* as a synonym for *modus* throughout his discussion. In both this passage and the one quoted in n. 20, however, *tropus* may more appropriately be translated "song."

19. The *colon* and *comma* were internal pauses in the reading of prose. The final pause ending a sentence was called a *clausula* or "period." For a discussion of the usage of these terms, see Babb, *Hucbald*, p. 116, n. 9.

20. Schmid, *Musica*, pp. 75-76: "Sciendum tamen, quod prima concordatio haec est, quae fit praefato modo ad meli ductum. Altera est concordatio paulo minor, dum vel elationis difficultatem mitigare volentes vel submissiorem gravitatem erigere aut in sursum aut in iusum quintana transpositione subiungimus. Est et tertia concordatio, quae fit octava sonorum regione, id est dum in novam vocem vel acutiorem melos mutamus. Atque his collationibus cantionum quaedam unanimitas servari potest. Aliter autem non potest, nisi forte ex integro melum quodlibet in modum alium transponendo mutetur. Si melum quodlibet in eadem sonorum serie unius aut duorum seu trium tonorum spacio acutius aut gravius transposueris, simul etiam tropi modus in aliam speciem migrat."

21. Since the *Enchiriadis* gamut has a structure based on perfect fifths, the author could shift a melody to either a fifth above or below and find the identical pattern of intervals.

22. Schmid, *Musica*, pp. 70-73. The author explains how the daseian symbols for the pitches in his gamut can be rearranged to reflect altered tones. For example, the pitches *C D E F G* represented by ʇ Ⱡ ₤ / Ɨ can become *C D E* *F*$^{\#}$ *G* represented by Ɨ Ⱡ ₤ ƒ /; this would occur because ƒ signals a whole tone progression from the previous note.

23. Published in *GS* I, pp. 251-64. Stunk translates a significant portion of the treatise into English in *Source Readings*, pp. 103-16. See Michel Huglo's article "Odo" in *The New Grove*, vol. 13, p. 504 for discussion of its authorship.

24. *GS* I, p. 257: "Tonus vel modus est regula, quae de omni cantu in fine diiudicat." This definition brings to light the fact that yet another word, *tonus*, was frequently used as a synonym for *modus*. *Tonus* also referred to the recitation formula associated with each mode.

25. *Ibid*., pp. 259-63.

26. The association of the modes with octave species began with the treatise *Alia musica* and returned as a major emphasis in the writings of Hermannus Contractus and his followers.

27. My reference is to *b* in the small octave, since the lower octave clearly contains only *B-natural*. The *Dialogus* author refers to the modes in two ways: as the *maneriae* - *protus*, *deuterus*, *tritus*, and *tetrardus*, subdivided into authentic and plagal; and as eight

modes numbered by authentic/plagal pair. Thus authentic *protus* is mode one, plagal *protus* mode two, authentic *deuterus* mode three, and so on.

28. Babb, *Hucbald*, p. 30.

29. The diagrams allow us to speculate that the author permitted either inflection, since all but that for plagal *protus* and authentic *deuterus* show both signs. The absence of *b-natural* in plagal *protus* would be understandable, since *b-flat* is the highest note in the plagal form. The absence of *b-flat* in authentic *deuterus* is explained by the author's statement on *b-natural*: "Indeed, it [the third mode] loves the second ninth [step] *b-natural*, because it forms a diapente with its final, most of all, however, because it forms a diatessaron with its highest [note], that is *e*." (The author sometimes refers to notes by their numerical position in the gamut starting with *A* as "the first.") *GS* I, p. 260: "Sane secundam nonam ♮ ideo adamavit, quia ad eius finem diapente est: maxime autem ideo, quia ad acutissimam eius, id est e. diatessaron reddit." By inference, *b-flat* would form an augmented fourth with the highest tone *e*; therefore, it is omitted.

The presence of both *b-natural* and *b-flat* in the authentic *tetrardus* diagram might appear to contradict my speculation, since the author makes this statement: "It should be noted, however, that if the first ninth [step] *b-flat*, is joined to it, nothing remains, except that from the sixth step [*F*] to it [*b-flat*] a diatessaron arises. And it will be the first [mode] throughout because it will have a tone, a semitone and then two tones, a semitone, and two tones [above], and it descends from the final by one tone as was said in the first [mode]. Thus, it will not be the seventh but the first [mode]." *Ibid*., p. 262: "Notandum est autem, quodsi ei prima nona b. concedatur, nihil restat, nisi ut a sexta ad eam diatessaron fiat, eritque per omnia primus, quia habebit tonum et semitonium, ac deinde duos et semitonium et duos tonos, et deponitur a fine tono uno, sicut in primo dictum est, et iam non erit septimus, sed primus."

Similarly, the author points out how *b-flat* changes mode eight into mode two. *Ibid*., p. 263. Although it is clear that he disapproves of both of these, he includes them for sake of illustration of what certain "of the stupidest cantors" do. Thus, the presence of both *b-natural* and *b-flat* in the *tetrardus* diagrams can be explained as the author's observation of a practice he has observed.

30. *Ibid*., pp. 263-64. This passage is translated by Strunk in *Source Readings*, pp. 115-16.

31. The *Dialogus* author does not make any general statement on the limits within which the modal likeness occurs. However, at least for the *D-a* and *E-♮* pairs, he spells out common movement within the range of a

sixth, paving the way for Guido's recognition of modally related six-note units (see later in this chapter).

32. Ibid., p. 264: ". . . si eam cum prima nona b. perpendas, habebit in depositione tonum, in elevatione vero semitonium, et tres tonos . . . si secunda nona ♮ privetur, habebit post se tonum, semitonium et duos tonos, ante se vero duos tonos et semitonium, . . ."

33. Ibid.: ". . . ideoque neque cantum neque distinctionem in ea principium vel finem habere probabis, nisi vitio id fiat."

34. Ibid., p. 262: "Iterumque si una tantum voce depravata finiatur in octava a. rursus fit per omnia primus: habebit enim a fine tonum et semitonium, et duos tonos, et reliqua, quae sunt primi."

35. Strunk, Source Readings, pp. 111-12.

36. Ibid. The three sources of "Domine" are LR 382, WA 395, and LA 475.

37. The continued importance of chant beginnings is also revealed in his solution. Having recommended the shift of melody to G, he adds, "For this reason, some begin 'Domine' as in 'Amen dico vobis.'" The latter is an antiphon of mode eight, and thus the author seems to be reporting that some musicians change "Domine"'s beginning to agree with mode eight beginnings. It is unclear whether or not he recommends this change. In her New Grove article "Introit," Ruth Steiner comments on and refers to examples in chant repertory of this procedure of giving a melody a new beginning after it has been modally analyzed and either transposed or emended. Cf. Steiner, "Introit (i)," The New Grove, vol. 9, p. 282.

38. An edition of the Prologus is found in GS II, pp. 62-79. Hans Oesch suggests that the work was written between 1021 and 1048, the date of Berno's death. Berno und Hermann von Reichenau als Musiktheoretiker, Publikationen der schweizerischen Musikforschenden Gesellschaft, ser. 2, vol. 9 (Bern: Paul Haupt, 1961), p. 46.

39. The first attempt to link octave species and modes occurred in the treatise Alia musica dating from the end of the ninth century. Referring to Greek theory as transmitted through Boethius, the compiler mistakenly (?) interpreted the Greek tonoi, today believed to be transposition scales, as analogous to modes. Since the tonoi were illustrated as octave segments moving successively within the fixed gamut, the Alia author made a one-to-one correspondence between the tonoi segments and the medieval modes. One result was the provision of modes with Greek names (Dorian, Phrygian, etc.).

The Alia compiler also discussed species of fourths and fifths, but he did not recognize their disposition within, and division of, the octave as Berno and other German writers were to do. See the edition of Alia musica prepared by Edmund B. Heard, "Alia musica: A Chapter in the History of Music Theory" (Ph.D. diss., University of Wisconsin, 1966).

Hans Oesch has pointed out that the passages in Berno's treatise dealing with species are interpolations drawn from the writings of the tenth-century Anonymous I and pseudo-Bernelius. Oesch, Berno und Hermann, pp. 86-87.

40. GS II, pp. 74-75: "Notandum vero est, quod quinto semper loco superioribus cum inferioribus finalibus quaedam talis concordia est, ut aliqua mela in eis quasi regulariter inveniantur finire: velut hoc responsorium: Factum est dum tolleret. quod quidem regulariter incipiens, sed extra regulam ultra nonum in decimum sonum ascendens, nequaquam terminat in lichanos hypaton finali, sed in mese eius sociali. Eodem modo clauduntur R. Terribilis est. communio: Cantabo Domino. Hoc ergo socialitatis foedus obtinet lichanos hypaton cum mese, hypate meson cum paramese, parypate meson cum trite diezeugmenon, lichanos meson cum paranete diezeugmenon. Cum inferioribus quoque quartis, et in quibusdam quintis parem habitudinem habent; quamvis hoc magis ad initia illorum, quam ad finem pertinere soleat. Fit etiam miro quodam modo, ut finales non solum in quintis, ut diximus, regionibus suos habeant sociales, verum etiam in quartis superioribus locis sibi inveniant compares: ut quemadmodum membra cantionum, quae sunt cola et commata, in finalibus et in quintis locis, ita per arsin et thesin consistant saepius in quartis."

Note that the opening sentence, the one beginning "Hoc ergo socialitatis . . .," and the next, "Cum inferioribus . . .," are almost word-for-word like Hucbald's (see ns. 7 and 9 above). The last sentence "Fit etiam . . ." reads as a paraphrase of the Scolica passage quoted in n. 18.

Hans Oesch verifies that parts of earlier chapters of the Prologus are taken word-for-word from, or are paraphrases of, Hucbald's De harmonica, but he does not mention the passage I have described here. Oesch, Berno und Hermann, pp. 85-86.

41. See previous footnote for context.

42. "Factum est" is found in LA 272 and WA 167, both of which preserve the melody with an ending on D. Neither version agrees with Berno's description of the melody ascending to a tenth above the final, since the range in both sources is C to c.

43. The references by other theorists are discussed on pp. 38 and 46 in Chapter Two. In Cambrai, Bibliothèque municipale C 38 (40), fols. 189-189v, "Terribilis est" is found in a version that moves in a higher region from the words "porta coeli" all the way to its ending on a. The versions in LR 235 and WA 317 also move around a at the words "porta coeli," but they return to D during the melisma on the syllable "ve-" of

"vere," and end on that note. Bamberg, Staatsbibliothek lit. 25, fol. 122^v preserves a version in which even the words "porta coeli" move around D, thus a fifth lower than in the other sources.

44. In addition to its appearance in GR 323 and GrS 143, "Cantabo Domino" is also found in LU 963, SYG 240, and GB 248. The version in GB is striking, since E-flat is actually notated in the first phrase. Fr. Dominique Delalande discusses "Cantabo Domino" in his study comparing Dominican, Cistercian, and Gregorian versions of selected chants. Cf. Vers la version authentique du Graduel Grégorien: Le Graduel des Prêcheurs (Paris: Les Editions du Cerf, 1949), pp. 55, 256-57. Delalande reduces the Gregorian versions he has examined to two forms that are essentially those of GR and GrS (see his Table XI). In his reconstruction of the melody, he includes an E-flat in the first distinction, a b-flat in the third, and a low B-natural in the fourth and final one moving around D (p. 257).

45. GS II, p. 75: ". . . pleraque mela ab ipsis finalibus seu dextera laevaque apta incepta minus conveniant propter semitonia, quae desunt per loca; a superioribus vero inchoata absque ullius soni diminutione decurrant modeste, finiantque in socialibus honeste."

46. "Beatus servus" is found in GR [45], LU 1203, GrS 223, SYG 28, and GB 29, in all of which it ends on a.

"De fructu" is found in GR 353, LU 1031, SYG 247, GB 254, and GrS 155. The version in GrS ends on c, but is classified as mode six, not eight, as Berno states. GR and GB end on F and are also designated as mode six. Urbanus Bomm offers an explanation for this variant classification in Der Wechsel der Modalitätsbestimmung in der Tradition der Messgesänge im IX. bis XIII. Jahrhundert (Einsiedeln: Benziger & Co., 1929), pp. 60-62, 96-103. By comparing sources, Bomm concludes that the communion was transmitted primarily in two forms, one containing only a semitone below the final (represented by Vat. 302) and one having both a tone and a semitone below the final (represented by Montpellier). He believes that Berno knew a version like the one in Montpellier, but while the latter designated it as mode six in spite of the appearance of a tone under the final in the last two distinctions, Berno referred to it as mode eight. Berno was concentrating on the chant ending. Keith Fleming offers additional variant readings to those available in Bomm's study, in "The Editing of Some Communion Melodies in Medieval Chant Manuscripts" (Ph.D. diss., Catholic University of America, 1979), pp. 41-42. For further discussion of "De fructu," see n. 106 in Chapter Three.

47. The sources of "Domine qui operati sunt" are given in n. 36. "Alias oves" appears in AR 472 and AM 486 classified as a mode eight chant ending on G. This solution recalls the modal reclassification carried out

by the Dialogus author with regard to "Domine." See p. 14.

48. The sources of each chant are: "Factus sum," OHS 613, LU 770, WA 126, LA 204. "O mors ero," AR 440, OHS 618, LU 773, AM 445, WA 127, LA 206; "Sion renovaberis" AR 229, LU 1083, AM 201, WA 13, LA 12; "Sion noli," AR 223, LU 1081, AM 194, WA 9,20, LA 22; "Vade iam," WA 90; "Ad te Domine levavi," AR 242, AM 217, WA 20, LA 27; "Ex Egypto," AR 222, LU 1083, AM 194, WA 16, LA 7. WA presents each of these chants in a version ending on a.

49. Gevaert, La mélopée antique dans le chant de l'église latine, reprint ed. (1895; Osnabrück: Otto Zeller, 1967), p. 322. In his introduction to the Antiphonale Sariburiense, Walter Frere remarks that this theme is the main one assigned to fourth-mode antiphons in this thirteenthcentury source. Walter Frere, Antiphonale Sariburiense. A Reproduction in Facsimile of a Manuscript of the Thirteenth Century, with a Dissertation and Analytical Index (London: Plainsong & Mediaeval Music Society, 1901-1924; reprint ed., London: Gregg Press Limited, 1966), p. 70.

50. Regino, calling these chants nothae - that is, "degenerate and illegitimate," named "Ante me more est," "Ex quo facta," "Ex Egypto," "Ad te Domine," "Sion renovaberis," "O mors ero," and "Vade iam." Cf. Sister Mary Protase LeRoux, R.S.M., "The 'De Harmonica Institutione' and 'Tonarius' of Regino of Prüm" [Latin Text with English Translation], Studies in Music 22 (Ph.D. diss., Catholic University of America, 1965), pp. 24-25. Pseudo-Hucbald, in De Modis Musicis, names two chants, "Benedicta tu [in mulieribus]" and "Rorate caeli," that belong to Gevaert's theme 29. He calls them examples of the third parapter, a word which at that time seems to have been a generic term for extra psalm tones designed to fit modally problematic chants. Cf. Terence Bailey, "De Modis Musicis: a New Edition and Explanation," Kirchenmusikalisches Jahrbuch 61-62 (1977/78), p. 54.

51. GS II, p. 75: "Quod quidam minus intuentes, magis has & huiusmodi putant septimo, quam quarto regi tono; quamquam non negent, easdem finem sortiri in quarto."

52. Michel Huglo devotes several pages to a summary of Regino's handling of dual mode chants in his Tonarius. Huglo, Les Tonaires (Paris: Société Française de Musicologie, 1971), pp. 83-85.

53. This dating is based on internal evidence of Guido's writings. In the dedication letter of the Micrologus to Bishop Theodaldus, Guido praises him for having "created by an exceedingly marvelous plan the church of St. Donatus." It is known the church was commissioned in 1026, so this year is the terminus post quem for the treatise. In Guido's Epistola, written after his trip to Rome at the request of Pope John XIX, he mentions the Micrologus. Since John died in 1033,

the trip must have taken place before then, and accordingly, the writing of the Micrologus as well. Cf. Joseph Smits van Waesberghe, De musico-paedagogico et theoretico Guidone Aretino eiusque vita et moribus (Florence: L.S. Olschki, 1953), pp. 13-23. Another interpretation of the evidence is offered by Hans Oesch in Guido von Arezzo, Publikationen der schweizerischen Musikforschenden Gesellschaft, ser. 2, vol. 4 (Bern: Paul Haupt, 1954), pp. 118-20. Oesch dates Micrologus c. 1025-26.

A critical edition of the Micrologus is found in Joseph Smits van Waesberghe, Guidonis Aretini Micrologus, Corpus Scriptorum de Musica 4 (Rome: American Institute of Musicology, 1955). Warren Babb presents an English translation of the Micrologus in Hucbald, Guido, and John on Music, pp. 57-83.

54. A published edition is found in GS II, pp. 43-50. The writing is translated in part by Strunk in Source Readings, pp. 121-25. The Epistola is dated c. 1032, again because of the timing of Guido's trip to Rome.

55. Although Guido uses the word vox (pitch) in the title and several times throughout the discussion, he explains the affinity concept using specific note designations. Thus, Babb's title translation "Concerning the Affinity of Notes . . ." does not inaccurately convey the sense of Guido's theory, contrary to Calvin Bower's claim in his review of the Babb translation, JAMS 35 (Spring 1982), pp. 163-64. Bower correctly notes that in some cases Guido carefully chooses between the terms vox and nota, the first referring to a distinct sound identifiable by its surrounding intervals, the second referring to the letter symbol that fixes the tone in the gamut. But even in one of the cases that Bower cites, Guido is not so consistent. Bower: "In Chapter 4 Guido discusses the six intervals by which pitches are joined to each other; in the following chapter he argues that there are only seven notes." If one reads further in Chapter 5, one recognizes that Guido argued for seven notes because there are only seven pitches (voces). Apparently Guido had begun to mesh the concept of a distinct pitch with that of the symbol representing it. A particularly blatant instance of this meshing occurs in Chapter 9, Micrologus, p. 131: "Utpote si quis vellet antiphonam cuius principium esset in .D., in .E. vel in .F., quae sunt alterius modi voces, incipere, mox auditu perciperet quanta diversitatis transformatio fieret."

56. Smits van Waesberghe, Micrologus, pp. 117-18: "Primus modus vocum est, cum vox tono deponitur et tono et semitonio duobusque tonis intenditur, ut .A. et .D. Secundus modus est, cum vox duobus tonis remissa semitonio et duobus tonis intenditur, ut .B. et .E. Tertius est qui semitonio et duobus tonis descendit, duobus vero tonis ascendit, ut .C. et .F. Quartus vero deponitur tono, surgit autem per duos tonos et semitonium, ut .G."

57. Jacques Handschin stresses the idea that Guido followed the viewpoint of the Enchiriadis author who linked the tones in his gamut with four modal qualities through consecutive designations of protus, deuterus, tritus, tetrardus, protus, etc. Der Toncharakter: Eine Einführung in die Tonpsychologie (Zurich: Atlantis Verlag, 1948), pp. 323-24.

58. The passages on "Tu patris" are found in GS II, p. 47 and Schmid, Musica, p. 36.

59. His calling attention to both upper and lower related notes reinforces the prominence given to octave relationships in his theory. In the Aliae regulae (GS II, p. 36), Guido includes a chart modeled after that of the Dialogus author:

VIII	I	III	V	I	III	V	VII	I	III	V	I	III	V	VII	I	III	V	VII
Γ	A	B	C	D	E	F	G	a	♮	c	d	e	f	g	aa	♮♮	cc	dd
VIII	II	IV	VI	II	IV	VI	VIII	II	IV	VI	II	IV	VI	VIII	II	IV	VIV	III

This clearly shows the duplicate function of notes at all octave locations within the gamut.

60. Smits van Waesberghe, Micrologus, pp. 124-26: "In eodem vero cantu maxime .b. molli utimur, in quo .F.f. amplius continuatur gravis vel acuta, ubi et quandam confusionem et transformationem videtur facere, ut .G. sonet protum, .a. deuterum, cum ipsa .b. sonet tritum. Unde eius a multis nec mentio facta est; altera vero .♮. in commune placuit. Quod si ipsam .b. mollem vis omnino non habere, neumas in quibus ipsa est, ita tempera, ut pro .F.G.a. et ipsa .b. habeas .G.a.♮.c.; aut si talis est neuma, quae post .D.E.F. in elevatione vult duos tonos et semitonium, quod ipsa .b. facit, aut post .D.E.F. in depositione vult duos tonos, pro .D.E.F. assume .a.♮.c. quae eiusdem sunt modi et praedictas depositiones et elevationes regulariter habent. Huiusmodi enim elevationes et depositiones inter D.E.F. et a.♮.c. clare discernens confusionem maxime contrariam tollit."

61. GS II, p. 49: ". . . utpote prima, si eam semitonium sequitur, de proto transit in deuterum; si autem duorum vel plurimorum modorum unam vocem esse liceat, videbitur haec ars nullo fine concludi, nullis certis terminis coarctari."

62. In Chapter 9, Guido states: "But on D and a, which are of the same mode, we can most often begin or end the same song. I say 'most often' and not 'always,' because likeness is not complete except at the octave." Smits van Waesberghe, Micrologus, pp. 131-32: "In .D. vero et .a. quae unius sunt modi, saepissime possumus eundem cantum incipere vel finire. Saepissime autem dixi et non semper, quia similitudo nisi in diapason perfecta non est."

63. Ibid., pp. 137-38: "Cantoris itaque peritiae esse debet quo loco vel modo quamlibet neumam incipiat, ut ei vel si motione opus est, affines voces inquirat."

64. *Ibid*., p. 156: "Plagae vero proti, deuteri, et triti aliquando in .a.♮.c. acutas necessario finiuntur."

CHAPTER 2: THE ELEVENTH- AND TWELFTH-CENTURY COMMENTATORS: TRANSPOSITION AND TRANSFORMATION

1. Both treatises are edited by Smits van Waesberghe in *Expositiones in Micrologum Guidonis Aretini* (Amsterdam: North-Holland Publishing Co., 1957): *Liber argumentorum*, pp. 19-30; *Liber specierum*, pp. 31-58. Smits provisionally concludes that the treatises were written in Italy in the second half of the eleventh century, probably by different authors, p.9.

2. *Ibid*., p. 22: "Item dicit Guido b. molle videtur confusionem et transformationem facere, ut G. sonet protum, .a. deuterum, cum ipsa b. sonet tritum, c. vero, ut ratio probat, tetrardum. Unde a multis, subaudis ignorantibus, eius nec mentio facta est. Sed ut videtur pro ignorantibus non est respuenda, sed magis scientibus assumenda."

3. *Ibid*., p. 50: "Propter autenticas elevationes et plagales depositiones finales voces modorum et plagalium statutae sunt in .D.E.F.G. Sed aliquando plagae proti vel triti, deuteri vel tetrardi propter necessitatem in acutas finiuntur."

4. Guido too used the term *acutae* in his analogous statement, but he spelled out the exact pitches as *a*, *♮*, and *c*. For an explanation of the designation *acutae*, see n. 4 of the Introduction.

5. A modern edition with English translation was prepared by Leonard Ellinwood in *Musica Hermanni Contracti* (Rochester: Eastman School of Music, 1936). Hermannus was born in Swabia in 1013 and died at Reichenau in 1054. Ellinwood has surmised that Hermannus probably did not write *Musica* until after 1048 since its contents do not always agree with the theories of Berno, his abbot at Reichenau, who died that year. Ellinwood, p. 16.

6. See *GS* II, p. 63 for Berno's passage naming the tetrachords. Hermannus' analogous passage is found in Ellinwood, *Musica*, p. 22.

7. Translation Ellinwood, *Musica*, p. 27: ". . . duorum quadrichordum id est IV troporum bis positorum voces pro sorte ordinis propriis denotemus literis, . . . Nam cum nulla praedictarum vocum cum alia concordet, quamvis quarto loco eadem positio, et ideo idem tropus redeat; . . ."

8. For example, for *protus* the four principal pitches are *A*, *D*, *a*, and *d*. *A* to *a* and *D* to *d*, as first *gravis* to first *superior* and first *finalis* to first *excellens*, respectively, are the two octave species belonging to *protus*. *D* to *a*, as first *finalis* to first *superior*, is the species of fifth, and *A* to *D*, as first *gravis* to first *finalis*, is the species of fourth, peculiar to *protus*. In functional terms, *A* and

d are outer notes of the combined plagal and authentic forms; D is the final note and a the beginning of the differentia for the authentic form. Hermannus also calls a the "middle pitch" of authentic protus, meaning the note where the juncture of its diapente and diatessaron occurs. In like fashion, D is the "middle pitch" of plagal protus, in addition to being the final.

9. Ellinwood, Musica, pp. 57-61.

10. Specifically, Hermannus describes each maneria according to its melodic movement by tone or semitone plus some species of fourth or fifth. Accordingly, the protus modus vocum, for example, consists of one tone in descent and a first species of fifth in ascent. Medieval writers generally expressed the species of fifths as the following ascending patterns: first, T-S-T-T; second, S-T-T-T; third, T-T-T-S; fourth, T-T-S-T. Similarly, the species of fourths were the ascending patterns: first, T-S-T; second, S-T-T; third, T-T-S.

11. Oesch, Berno und Hermann, p. 239.

12. Translation Ellinwood, Musica, p. 57: "Ut vero coepimus ad huc unam de agnitione troporum regulam a maioribus quidem ut rudem massam effossam, sed non pleniter a rubigine excoctam videamus . . ."

13. Translation Ellinwood, ibid., p. 60: ". . . quartum demum tropum per solum G tono remissum, duobis tonis semitonioque intendebant, . . ."

14. Richard Crocker discusses this issue in his article, "Hermann's Major Sixth," JAMS 25 (1972), pp. 21-24.

15. Handschin, Der Toncharakter, p. 334.

16. Translation Ellinwood, Musica, p. 57: "Accipe tetrachordum quodcumque volueris, verbi gratia gravium, addito utrinque tono, habes terminos modorum qui fiunt sedes troporum."

17. Translation Ellinwood, ibid., pp. 57, 59: "Primus modus vocum . . . hic habet agnitionem in hac antiphona, Prophetae praedicaverunt, et In tuo adventu, et similibus quae sex chordas non excedunt. Hic modus in principalibus proti chordis, A, D, a, d, agnoscitur."

18. For citation of the sources in which these chants appear, see ns. 28, 29, 30, and 32.

19. Translation Ellinwood, Musica, p. 49: "Has species facile etiam una voce cantabis; si eas per consuetam saeculorum amen melodiam inceperis, et propria diffinitione terminaveris. Quae quidem diffinitiones licet pleniter et perfecte in finalibus cantentur et superioribus; tamen ultimae neumae in unoquoque quadrichordo a suo non discordant tropo."

20. Translation Ellinwood, ibid., p. 28: ". . . erit prima D, G, sed ratione perversa; nam quamvis D propter communionem possit esse prima tamen G numero septima, tropice quarta, numquam potest esse prima. Secunda ab E quae est deuteri incipiens; in a quae est proti desinit. Tercia ibi si natura inspiciatur nulla est. Quarta a G quae est tetrardi inchoans; in c quae est triti terminatur."

By Hermannus' definition, formal species connect two tones that are not similarly placed in two different tetrachords. By contrast, the outer notes of "natural" species occur in the same position within two tetrachords. Hermannus reckons natural species from the *graves* tetrachord; e.g., *A* to *D* is the first natural species, stretching from the first *gravis* to first *finalis*. As opposed to the tones of formal species, those of natural species share the same mode.

21. *Ibid*., p. 50. By the eleventh century, *synemmenon* is used to refer specifically to the tone *b-flat*, and thus has been extended beyond its original meaning of the tetrachord in which *b-flat* appears.

22. A published edition is found in *GS* II, pp. 154-82. It has been superseded by that of Denis Harbinson, *Willehelmi Hirsaugensis Musica*, *Corpus Scriptorum de Musica* 23 (Rome: American Institute of Musicology, 1975). There is also a German translation by Hans Müller, *Die Musik Wilhelms von Hirschau. Wiederherstellung Übersetzung und Erklärung seines musiktheoretischen Werkes* (Frankfurt am Main: B.G. Teubner, 1883).

It is known that Wilhelm became abbot of the monastery at Hirsau in 1069 and died there in 1091. Müller surmises that Wilhelm wrote his treatise before 1069, probably at the monastery of St. Emmeran in Regensburg, because, according to Müller, Wilhelm was engaged in many time-consuming endeavors once he assumed the post of abbot. Müller, p. v. If Müller's speculation is correct, Wilhelm's treatise may have followed Hermannus' by as few as fifteen years.

23. Wilhelm takes the expression *biformes* from Hermannus and emphasizes it in his argument supporting *D* to *d* as the eighth octave species corresponding to the eighth mode. Harbinson, *Willehelmi*, pp. 40-49.

24. *Ibid*., p. 51: "Modi vocum sunt proprietates quaedam specierum cantilenae, id est troporum."

25. *Ibid*., p. 59: "Sedes vel metae troporum octo, legitimae autem non nisi in quatuor locis esse noscuntur, id est in C. in G. in a. in c. Videamus igitur quot metae vel intervalla metarum in monochordo fieri possint, et cur in praefatis locis magis legitimae esse dicantur quam in aliis. Sicut superius dictum est."

The naming of the four sites as *C*, *G*, *a*, and *c* presents an inconsistency, since the lowest note of the four *sedes* would be *Γ*, *C*, *G*, and *c*, as Wilhelm himself acknowledges later in the same passage. Wilhelm does, incidentally, provide some insight into the relative importance of the four principal positions. Those passages and commentary on them are found in Appendix A.

26. *Ibid*. p. 60: "Quinta in medio posita propter minus regulare synemmenon penitus non recipitur."

27. *Ibid*., p. 68: ". . . modus proto indifferenter aptatur, . . ."

28. "Prophetae praedicaverunt" appears in _AR_ 240, _AM_ 215, _LA_ 24, 377, and _WA_ 18. Except for _LA_, the others classify it as mode one. The other _protus_ antiphon mentioned by Hermannus, but not by Wilhelm, is "In tuo adventu," found in _WA_ 8 as mode one.

29. Harold Powers points out that "Gloria haec est" is found in the Petershausen Antiphoner on fol. 147r as mode four. Powers, "Mode," p. 389.

30. "Modicum et non videbitis" is found in _AR_ 473, _LU_ 820, _AM_ 487, _WA_ 143, and _LA_ 231, 236. _AR_, _LU_, _AM_, and _WA_ list this antiphon as mode six beginning and ending on _F_, while _LA_ uses the _c_ position.

31. Harbinson, _Willehelmi_, p. 68: "Qui modus hoc speciale inter caeteros obtinet, quod non solum hac autentica antiphona _Si vere fratres_, sed et hac plagali antiphona _Multi veniunt_, potest dinosci."

32. "Si vere fratres" is found in _AR_ 351, _LU_ 509, _AM_ 323, _WA_ 79, and _LA_ 119, in all of which it is listed as mode seven ending on _G_. Powers has located "Multi veniunt" in the Petershausen Antiphoner, fol. 34v, where it is designated mode eight ending on _G_. Cf. "Mode," p. 390.

33. Harold Powers offers another explanation: "Hermannus was able to follow up on Hucbald's hint to attend 'not to the end but to beginnings' in d' and in g, and use the same _modus vocum_ from d' as a module for the authentic _tetrardus_ mode 7, even though mode 7 ends on g." Powers, "Mode," p. 390.

34. The modern edition is by Joseph Smits van Waesberghe, _Aribonis De musica_, _Corpus Scriptorum de Musica_ 2 (Rome: American Institute of Musicology, 1951). See Andrew Hughes' article "Aribo" in _The New Grove_, vol. 1, pp. 579-80 for a résumé of the factors pointing to Freising as the most likely monastic site for Aribo's work.

35. Smits van Waesberghe, _Aribonis_, pp. 65-72.

36. _Ibid_., p. 16: "Principales quoque dicuntur chordae, quia principium sunt eiusdem habitudinis. Habitudinem autem appello ascensionis vel descensionis, aut utriusque similitudinem."

37. _Ibid_.: ". . . quia talis est concordia non solum quartis, sed quintis infra et supra, ut media alterius elevat, alteriusque sumat depositionem, et si ad quartam supra confertur cum elevatione, ad quintam superius respondet cum depositione; ac e contrario cum quarta inferiori per remissionem, cum quinta concordat per intensionem, excepto gravi deutero et superiori, . . ."

38. In order for Aribo's description to be understood, all comparisons have to be reckoned from the _graves_, as was true for Hermannus. Accordingly, his sentence "If it is compared . . ." would signify, for _protus_, a shift from _A_ to _D_. Since the melodic pattern for _protus_ consists mainly of ascent, that is, a fifth upward from either point, Aribo points out that a common descent would be obtained by relating _A_ to _E_, the note a fifth above.

That Aribo recognizes the modi vocum as spelled out by Hermannus and Wilhelm is evidenced in a later passage entitled "De proprietate protorum, deuterorum, tritorum, tetrardorum." Ibid., p. 32. Aribo uses the term proprietas or "property" instead of modus vocum. He spells out those for protus, deuterus, and tritus in Hermannus' terms. However, in prefacing his attempt to explain the dual nature of the D to d octave, he describes the tetrardus movement uniquely: "The property of tetrardus [notes], in order that they are contrasted to protus [notes], exists insofar as the ascent of the latter [protus] is the descent of the former [tetrardus]." "Proprietas est tetrardorum, ut protis opponantur, quatenus horum elevatio istorum sit remissio." That is, the protus modus vocum contains an ascent of a fifth, while the tetrardus modus vocum contains a descent of a fifth.

39. Ibid., pp. 17-20. In his accompanying discussion, Aribo imposes the metaphor of male and female chori sharing certain common materials as if in nuptial chambers. Accordingly, he names the final of each maneria thalamus or "marriage bed."

40. Smits van Waesberghe has edited the treatise under the title Commentarius Anonymus in Micrologum Guidonis Aretini in Expositiones in Micrologum Guidonis Aretini, pp. 99-172. His edition supersedes that of P. Cölestin Vivell (Vienna: Alfred Hölder, 1917).

Smits van Waesberghe notes that the anonymous commentator follows his discussion of Chapter Fifteen with Aribo's commentary ("Expositio") from the Musica. Aribo, in the Musica, first discusses the subject matter of Chapter Fifteen in an early section entitled "De opportunitate modulandi," while "Expositio," placed near the end of the treatise, is in a more subjective style and may have been a later addition in reaction to the anonymous commentator's interpretation.

41. Smits van Waesberghe, Expositiones, pp. 95-97. See also Smits van Waesberghe's article, "Some Music Treatises and their Interrelation: A School of Liège c. 1050-1200? (Part 2)" Musica Disciplina 3 (1949), pp. 95-98.

42. Smits van Waesberghe, Expositiones, p. 115: "Et sciendum quod hae depositionis vel elevationis proprietates, per quas hic discernit modos primum a secundo et ceteros a se, servari debent in cantibus maxime in fine distinctionum vel fine ipsorum cantuum, ut secundum proprietates sibi naturales descendatur vel ascendatur ad modos finales, . . ."

43. This reference stands in contradistinction to the discussion of modus vocum by Hermannus and Wilhelm. They both mention chants that move entirely within the range of the sixth of the modal pattern and which can thus be transferred in toto to related positions in the gamut. Since the entire chant shows the modus vocum, there is no need to single out phrase endings.

44. Smits van Waesberghe, _Expositiones_, p. 115: ". . . hae duae voces .A. et .D. sunt primus modus, .D. per naturam, .A. per affinitatem."

45. Since the word _socialis_ appears in some manuscript sources of Aribo's treatise that we know of, and may have appeared in others, it is possible that the anonymous commentator borrowed the word from Aribo's work.

46. Smits van Waesberghe, _Expositiones_, p. 120: "Sicut in illa facit Antiphona 'Urbs fortitudinis nostrae Sion,' primam distinctionem facit esse proti, cum tamen sit tetrardi; . . ." The sources of this chant are _AR_ 224, _LU_ 332, _AM_ 195, _WA_ 12, and _LA_ 11. In _AR_, _LU_, _AM_, and _WA_, the second phrase, not the first, contains _b-flat_, while the concluding phrases contain _b-natural_. All four sources classify it as mode seven. _LA_, however, notates the chant at the _D_ position and calls it mode one. See n. 82 for further discussion.

47. The sixth-mode example is the antiphon "O admirabile commercium." It is found in _AR_ 294, _LU_ 442, _AM_ 271, _WA_ 50, and _LA_ 64. In all except _LA_, it occurs as mode six with _F_ final and includes _b-flats_. (_WA_ has what appears to be a pre-placed _b-flat_ near the word "humani.") In _LA_, the antiphon is shifted up a fifth to end on _c_, and thus, the anonymous commentator's prescribed transposition is realized.

For a chant requiring _B-flat_ in descent below _D E F_, the author names the gradual "Haec dies." This gradual is designated mode two ending on _a_ in several chant sources, with both _b-flat_ and _b-natural_ _acutae_. See _GR_ 241, _LU_ 778, and _GrS_ 117. If this version were notated a fifth lower, it would require _B-flat_, as the author states, but also _E-flat_ (_b-flat_ = _E-flat_). The author does not mention the avoidance of _E-flat_ as a reason for transposition. _GB_ 125 contains a version that better fits his description; it is designated mode two ending on _a_, but without the _b-flat_ in the first phrase. See further Chapter Five, pp. 100-101.

48. Smits van Waesberghe, _Expositiones_, p. 122.

49. _Ibid_., pp. 122-23: "Sciendum vero est quod affinitas vocum, quam ponit, maxime utilis est in instrumentis musicis constantibus ex octo vocibus vel VII, ut in cymbalis reperimus aut organis. Cum enim non sint ibi tam multae variationes vocum depositione vel elevatione per ordinem, quod non possumus post illas octo voces deponere vel elevare in acutis, quod ibi non sunt sicut ordo exigebat, per affines suas idem prosequamur in gravibus; verbi gratia si in cymbalis a .G. finali per diapente ascendere debemus, eandem diapente speciem in .c. affinali sua habebimus, ideoque pro .G.c. assumamus et eundem cantum non inconcinne habebimus; cantum tamen .b. mollis, nisi ibidem .b. molle sit, ut a quibusdam novis ponitur, non inveniemus."

It is not certain which c is intended. Smits van Waesberghe indicates c acuta, but this does not agree with the direction to proceed in the graves, nor with the range of bells (see next footnote).

50. It is thought, according to research done by Smits van Waesberghe, that bells were used in churches of monasteries to accompany chant, in addition to their function in teaching intervals. Joseph Smits van Waesberghe, Cymbala. Bells in the Middle Ages. Edition of Texts and Introduction, Musicological Studies and Documents 1 (Rome: American Institute of Musicology, 1951), pp. 18-19. Thus, the quoted passage can be viewed as describing a practice to which the affinities could be applied.

The most common series of tones in bells was C, D, E, F, G, a, b-flat, b-natural. Sometimes b-flat was missing, as this anonymous writer indicates in the last sentence of the quotation.

51. See Appendix B for the Latin text.

52. See n. 63 in Chapter 1. The equivalent passage in the anonymous commentary occurs in Smits van Waesberghe, Expositiones, pp. 131-32.

53. Ibid., p. 131: "Et quia vel per vicium incautorum vel per inconcinnitatem vocum pravarum cantus transformatur, itaque adversus ista debet cantor esse peritus, . . ."

54. Ibid. p. 132: "Dixi quatuor modos esse in quibus potest fieri transformatio et dissonantia pravitate vocum, . . ."

55. Ibid., p. 127.

56. Karlheinz Schlager, Alleluia-Melodien 1 bis 1100, Monumenta Monodica Medii Aevi, vol. 7 (Kassel: Bärenreiter Verlag, 1968), p. 586. Schlager transcribes one version ending on a on pp. 256-57.

57. Confirmation of his disapproval is found in the earlier passage mentioning "Judicabunt": "Although certainly it ["Judicabunt"] is set down below D by a tone and is ended above D through the diapente on a, we find no song which is set down below its proper final, whether legitimate or affinity, more than through a diapente, if it was properly assigned that final. Thus, because it ["Judicabunt"] descends below a by one tone more than a diapente, it shows that it might not have the proper final, but rather [should have] D, below which it is set down by a tone." Smits van Waesberghe, Expositiones, p. 127: "Cum enim sub .D. tono deponatur, super .D. vero per diapente in .a. finiatur, nullum cantum invenimus qui sub proprio modo seu legali seu affini plus quam per diapente deponatur, si proprie illum modum sortitus fuerit. Quia ergo plus quam per diapente tono descendit sub .a., quod illum modum proprium non haberet ostendit, sed .D. potius sub qua deponitur tono."

In spite of his circumlocution, the author ultimately indicates a preference for a D final.

58. This treatise is edited by Heinrich Sowa under the title *Tractatus Anonymus de Musica et de Transformatione Specialiter* in *Quellen zur Transformation der Antiphonen: Tonar- und Rhythmusstudien* (Kassel: Bärenreiter Verlag, 1935), pp. 154-60. Sowa's discussion of dating and origin is found on pp. 5-10.

59. Compare, for example, pp. 116-17 of the anonymous commentary with p. 156 of the Leipzig treatise.

This view is a corollary to Smits van Waesberghe's discussion of a possible "school of Liège," flourishing between 1050 and 1125. He noted that the *Commentarius anonymus*, the *Quaestiones in musica*, and the *Anonymous Wolf* treatises, among others, appear to be interrelated in contents; this supports other evidence that they originated in the same area, that of Liège. Cf. Smits van Waesberghe, "Some Music Treatises and their Interrelation," pp. 95-115. As to the objection that might be voiced because of the apparent German origin of the Leipzig treatise, Smits van Waesberghe explains: ". . . many witnesses of the eleventh century can be adduced testifying not only to the high level of scholarly attainment at Liège but to the powerful attraction of the place on clerics and laymen in Bavaria." *Ibid*., p. 97. According to Sowa, a likely place of origin for the Leipzig treatise was a monastery at Lake Constance, bordering on Bavaria. Sowa, *Quellen*, p. 9. Following Smits van Waesberghe's reasoning, the Leipzig author could have sojourned in Liège where he saw the anonymous commentator's work, or perhaps the source from which it drew some material.

60. Sowa, *Quellen*, p. 156.

61. *Ibid*.: ". . . propter deficientiam ditoni ut vides in graduali Hec, vel propter deficientiam semitonii ut patet in introitu Exaudi domine, vel propter acutionem cantus. Quando tamen acuitur, ut ad finalem naturalem redire non possit, sibi scilicet in affini, vel gemina ut in responsorio Terribilis, vel simplici transpositione terminetur, . . ." *Gemina* could be a modifier of *transpositione*, but appears to be used here as a synonym for *affinis*.

62. "Exaudi Domine vocem meam" is found in *GR* 287, *LU* 854, *SYG* 181, *GB* 182, and *GrS* 136. This introit, which begins and ends on *a* in *GR* and *LU*, includes *b-flat* in the opening phrase, which suggests the reason for its transposition to the affinity: to accommodate the *E-flat* of the original position. *GrS* presents the chant at the normal *D* level, except for the beginning neumes, which appear one tone higher so that the *D*-*E-flat* movement is preserved as *E*-*F*. *GB* also uses the *D* position but simply replaces *E-flat* with *E-natural*.

‿ indicates the notes connected in neumes.

```
GR   241   a a b  G c c d e d e f e e
           D D Eb C F F G a G a b a a   (GR transposed
                                         down a fifth)
GrS  136     E F  D G G   a G a ♮ a a
GB   182     D E  C F F G a G c a a a
```

63. As mentioned earlier, Guido, and perhaps more so, the anonymous commentator from Liège, may have recognized transposition to preserve anomalous tones within the modus vocum. However, for both authors, a primary concern was establishing an understanding of the gamut and modal relationships in diatonic terms. Hence, neither one directly described "distorted tones" in conjunction with chant examples.

64. See Appendix B for the Latin text.

65. Sowa, Quellen, pp. 158-59: ". . . transformatio est quando G sonat prothum, a sonat deuterum cum ipsa b mollis que sonat tritum."

66. Sources of the antiphon "Angelus Domini nuntiavit" are AR 219, AM 191, LR 251, LA 7, 380, WA 8; of the antiphon "Dum complerentur," AR 503, LU 884, AM 520, WA 153, LA 261, 264; and of the antiphon "Vox clamantis," AR 228, LU 1082, AM 200, WA 13, LA 12.

67. Sowa, Quellen, p. 159: "Alia secunda autem transformatio nulla prorsus necessitate fit, quando cantus in naturali finali regulari cursu finiri, et in affini transponi potest, sicut in autenti prothi patet antiphona Angelus domini nuntiavit. In hac autem transformatione et in huic similibus dicam e converso b mollem maximam mihi meique similibus confusionem incutere, cum cantum istum autento protho naturaliter ascribendum in litteram septimi et octavi modi in G videlicet quasi regulariter transformat."

68. Ibid.: "Transformatio igitur ex necessitate fit, quando cantus nec in naturali finali regulari tramite finiri, nec in equivoca transponi potest ut verbi gratia patet in antiphona quarti toni Apud dominum. In huiusmodi autem transformationibus b mollem non solum dicam nullam confusionem facere immo maximam tollere . . ."

69. The sources that contain this version are AR 271, LU 412, AM 246, and WA 33. LA 39 presents "Apud" with a D final; at the point where the transposed version has b-natural to c, LA has F to G. Thus, LA emended the anomalous semitone F-sharp to G, rather than transpose the chant.

70. The author's only example is that for deuterus (E) transferred to a. Because of his several statements that G is final only for the seventh and eighth modes, it seems reasonable to assume that he would not accept G as a protus final. It is unlikely that he or any other writer of the eleventh century would have recognized b-flat as final in a tritus mode. On the other hand, c as related tone to G tetrardus was

acknowledged in limited terms by the anonymous commentator from Liège and outspokenly accepted by Berno. The Leipzig author falls between them in his attitudes towards modal identity. All in all, he would be likely to accept this "transformation" of c for the same reason he acknowledged it for a, to notate a chant that could otherwise not be accommodated at the final or affinity position.

71. It is somewhat ironic that he insists on distinguishing transposition and transformation about which, he states, many have said there is no difference. Sowa, Quellen, p. 158: "Quia sunt plerique simplices musice artis nimirum ignari, qui inter transformationem et transpositionem nichil distare prorsus existimant, caritati eorum satisfacere cupiens in quo distent ab inviem dicere caritate magistra compellor."

72. Ibid., p. 3. The tonary is found on pp. 90-154.

73. The use of the term sociales does not necessarily separate the tonary from the apparent Liègois influence of the treatise (see n. 59). As mentioned earlier, the anonymous commentator from Liège uses sociales at least once in his treatise, as does Aribo, for whom we also cannot dismiss the possibility of Liège associations, according to Smits van Waesberghe.

Finally, Michel Huglo considers this tonary to be a copy of one composed at Reichenau c. 1075. Huglo, Les Tonaires, p. 254. The significance of this connection will not be examined in the present study.

74. Edited by Rudolf Steglich, Die Quaestiones in musica: ein Choraltraktat des zentralen Mittelalters und ihr mutmasslicher Verfasser Rudolf von St. Trond (1070-1138) (Leipzig, 1911; reprint ed., Wiesbaden: Breitkopf & Härtel, 1970). For discussion of the attribution, see pp. 5-11.

75. Smits van Waesberghe discusses Vivell's argument and lends support to it in "Some Music Treatises and their Interrelation," pp. 98-101.

76. Ibid., p. 98.

77. Steglich, Quaestiones, p. 50: "Qui sint transformati modi, qui sint transpositi, vel quare qualiterve dicantur transformari ac de propriis sedibus transponi."

78. Ibid., pp. 52-53. The two antiphons are "Si cognovissetis me" and "Salvator mundi." The sources of these are, respectively: AR 695, PM 152, LU 1465, AM 893, WA 307, LA 394; and OHS 584, LU 747, LA 463, SYG 141. According to the author, "Si cognovissetis me" requires F-sharp at the words "et patrem meum" and "Salvator mundi" does likewise at "per crucem." In the named sources, all of which end on G, those positions use F-natural or another note.

79. Steglich, Quaestiones, p. 53: ". . . quia absurdum sit et inconcinnum, septimum tonum in sextum transformare et adulterari."

80. Ibid.: "Tu quid eligas e duobus, tuo arbitrio relinquimus."

81. *Ibid.*, pp. 51-52. Steglich shows the similarity of wording to the analogous passage in the *Dialogus*.

82. "Urbs fortitudinis" presents a thorny problem for modal classification. The earliest mention of it by theorists reveals the difficulty: Regino assigns it to mode one; the author of *Alia Musica* states that it begins in mode one and ends in mode eight; the tonary of Odo of Arezzo assigns it to mode seven. Beginning with the Liège anonymous commentary, the chant is described as occurring on *G*, where, through the use of *b-flat*, *G* is transformed into *protus*.

A number of writers have attempted to trace the possible modal development of this chant. The most extensive investigation was undertaken by Jacobsthal in *Die chromatische Alteration im liturgischen Gesang der abendländischen Kirche*, pp. 198-205. Steglich added further comments in his edition of the *Quaestiones in musica*, pp. 148-50, and Walther Lipphardt has done additional analysis in his edition, *Der karolingische Tonar von Metz* (Muenster: Aschendorff, 1965), pp. 264-66. Lipphardt disagrees with Jacobsthal's (and it seems, Steglich's) belief that the chant had a *tetrardus* cadence and that concern for the modal primacy of this ending prompted the change to the *G* or *tetrardus* level. He believes, rather, that the chant had a *protus* beginning and ending on *D*, and only in the middle was there a modal incongruity, namely, the melodic figure *F-sharp E F-sharp G* at "portas." To make this notationally acceptable, the chant was moved to *G*, where both the *F-sharp* and *F-natural* could be realized as *b-natural* and *b-flat*; however, the *protus* cadence then had to be changed to a *tetrardus* one in deference to the *G* final.

Neither theory can be proven, but both seem to assert that modal identity according to the movement around the final was the ultimate concern of musicians in the Middle Ages. From the point of view of this discussion, the importance of "Urbs fortitudinis" lies in its need for *b-flat* above *G* early in the chant. From the *Dialogus* treatise onward, *b-flat* was excluded from *G tetrardus* lest it assume a *protus* character. Rather, each modal final was to keep its basic diatonic identity. This may explain why even the broader-minded theorists such as Berno do not suggest *G* with *b-flat* as an alternative position to *D protus*, even though they accept *a* and *c* for *deuterus* and *tetrardus* respectively.

83. The sources of the antiphon "Magnus sanctus Paulus" are *PM* 163, *WA* 330, and *LA* 423. In both *WA* and *LA*, "Magnus" ends on *G*, and in *WA*, *b-flat* is notated at two points. For further discussion, see Chapter Three, pp. 67-68.

84. Steglich, *Quaestiones*, p. 53: ". . . triplex ipsius causae perpenditur divisio, quia fit aut voluntate aut necessitate aut voluntate simul et necessitate."

85. Ibid.: ". . . partem comitatur voluntas simul et necessitas. . . . ex parte vero ita fit, cum cantus quidem secundum regimen propriae finalis incipit et aliquandiu circa eandem finalem versatus postea voluntate musici in acutis lasciviendo exaltatus et diutius, quam debuerat, immoratus, cum iam eum ad propriam sedem reduci sit inconcinnum, necessitate, quasi lassus et anhelus in proximum sotialis suae divertit hospitium."

See Appendix B where the similarity between the anonymous commentator's and Leipzig author's statements on partial transposition and this passage are apparent.

86. Both this opinion and the use of the word socialis suggest that the author knew Berno's work; indeed, although there is no direct quotation from Berno in the discussion of transposition, Steglich shows that passages in other parts of the treatise were derived from Berno's Prologus.

87. See Appendix B for the Latin text.

88. "Domine fac mecum" is found in GR 133, OTT 37, SYG 96, GB 85v, and GrS 58. In all these sources, it ends on ♮ and would require B-flat if notated at the original E position.

"Honor virtus" is found in WA 160 as mode six beginning and ending on c. There are numerous b-flats (= E-flats) up until the final cadence, which shows a tritus subsemitonium movement.

89. Steglich, Quaestiones, p. 53: "Totum sequitur aliquando voluntas, nonnunquam necessitas; partem comitatur voluntas simul et necessitas."

90. Ibid., p. 54: "Sunt alii ut tertius, quintus, septimus, octavus, quibus adhoc naturalis ptongorum positio plenariam usquequaque non dedit concordiam. Itaque modi isti voluntate transponuntur . . ."

91. There is a third point regarding a question of practice: is the psalm-tone formula transposed in instances where an antiphon is transposed? The Quaestiones author states: "The 'saeculorum amen' and psalms, which must be adapted to the antiphons, prohibit the transposition of the antiphons [in their entirety], because if the antiphons are transposed, the affixed parts themselves suffer a defect in the higher [notes]. However, an antiphon is transposed in part, as in 'Scindite corda.'" Steglich, Quaestiones, p. 55: "Nam antiphonas prohibent [ex toto] transferri 'seculorum amen' et psalmi, qui eis sunt aptandi, quia, si antiphonae transferantur, ipsae subiunctiones defectum in superioribus patiuntur. Ex parte autem transponitur ut antiphona: 'Scindite corda.'" (Bryden and Hughes' Index does not have an entry for an antiphon of this name.)

The author thus states that antiphons, unlike the graduals, responsories, and offertories cited earlier, should not be transposed completely, because the concomitant change in the psalm tone would be unacceptable. This statement is problematic in view of other theorists' citing of antiphons transposed in their entirety, and the manuscript evidence showing _differentiae_ in two positions a fifth apart. Such dual positioning occurs in the twelfth-century Lucca antiphoner.

92. See n. 71 above.

93. Johannes Wolf, "Ein anonymer Musiktraktat des elften bis zwölften Jahrhunderts, "_Vierteljahrschrift für Musikwissenschaft_ 9 (1893), pp. 186-234.

94. _Ibid_., p. 201-202: "Prius autem huius modi cantus diligenter debet considerari, si vel in transpositis vel transformatis possit cantari. Unusquisque enim tonus transformatos habet modulos vel transpositos, ut si quis cantus in membris finalium propter deficientia ibidem semitonia non possit decurrere, in transpositis vel transformatis decenter possit procedere, quod studiosus cantor diligenter debet attendere."

95. The sources of "Domine qui operati sunt" are given in n. 36 of Chapter One. "Turba multa" is found in _AR_ 423, _LU_ 585, _AM_ 401, _PM_ 58, _OHS_ 73, 98, _WA_ 113, and _LA_ 182, in all of which it ends on _E_. _AM_ notates a low _B-flat_ at the word "Domini," while _AR_, _LA_, and _OHS_ alter the neume to avoid _B-flat_. _WA_ is unclear at that point.

96. A published edition is found in _GS_ II, pp. 287-369. _Ibid_., p. 365: "Cum vero propter mutatam aliquam consonantiam per occursum semitonii transpositi compellimur cantum alicuius toni non in loco sibi proprio et naturali incipere aut finire, sed in consimili, tunc dicitur cantus sive tonus transformatus sive transpositus, ut superius proxime dicebatur. Dicitur autem ideo transpositus, quia sua inceptio et terminatio transponitur a sua sede naturali ad consimilem: et dicitur transformatus, quia ex tunc, cum est transpositus, non decantatur in natauralibus speciebus diatessaron et diapente, et diapason illius toni, sed in consimilibus secundum formam, . . ." _Consimilis_ could be translated as "[note] similar in all respects." I have left it untranslated to show Engelbert's distinctive wording.

97. Wolf, "Ein anonymer Musiktraktat," pp. 191-93; Smits van Waesberghe, "Some Music Treatises and their Interrelation," p. 95.

98. Chapter Thirty of Engelbert's _De musica_ is, in part, a commentary on Berno's passage regarding the transposition of certain fourth-mode antiphons to the fourth above. See _GS_ II, pp. 359-60. The Anonymous Wolf treatise glosses several passages from the _Prologus_. See Wolf, "Ein anonymer Musiktraktat," pp. 199-204.

99. For an edition, see Johannes Affligemensis, _De Musica cum tonario_, ed., Joseph Smits van Waesberghe, _Corpus Scriptorum de Musica_ 1 (Rome: American Institute of Musicology, 1950). For an English translation by Warren Babb, see John, _On Music (De Musica)_ in _Hucbald, Guido, and John on Music_, pp. 101-87.

The dispute over John's identity, and hence, the work's origin, has been longstanding. Even today, there remain three different hypotheses concerning its provenance: England, the Liège area, and a south German area between St. Gall and Bamberg. The dispute over English versus Liègois origin has been carried on by Smits van Waesberghe and Leonard Ellinwood in the following articles: Smits van Waesberghe, "Some Music Treatises and their Interrelation," pp. 101-7; Ellinwood, "John Cotton or John of Affligem? The Evidence of a Manuscript in the Library of Congress," Notes vol. 8, no. 4 (Sept. 1951), pp. 650-59; Smits van Waesberghe, "John of Affligem or John Cotton?" Musica Disciplina 6 (1952), pp. 146-53. In support of its English origin, Edwin Frederick Flindell has contributed two articles: "Joh[ann]is Cottonis," Musica Disciplina 20 (1966), pp. 11-30; and "Joh[ann]is Cottonis, corrigenda et addenda," Musica Disciplina 23 (1969), pp. 7-11. It was Michel Huglo (Les Tonaires, pp. 299-301) who first suggested a south German origin.

100. Smits van Waesberghe, De Musica, p. 102: ". . . quotiens opus fuerit, vice finalium affines haud incongrue subrogantur."

101. Ibid., p. 101: "Affines autem illas voces dicimus, quae in depositione et elevatione concordant, verbi gratia .D. finalis proti cum .a. acuta concordat. Ambae enim tono deponuntur et tono et semitonio elevantur. Item .E. finalis deuteri cum .♮. quadrato affinitatem habet, cum similiter deponantur et eleventur. Sed et .F. finalis triti cum .c. acuta in depositione et elevatione convenit."

102. Ibid.: "Itemque fit ex cantorum vitio, plerumque ex irrefutabili antiquitate."

103. Ibid., pp. 102-3: "Hoc autem quidam evitare volentes ponunt inter .A. et .B. graecum .S., quod etiam synemmenon id est adiunctum appellant, ut ita sub .C. tonum habeant. Vertumtamen nulla id auctoritate confirmare queunt." This writer has found no mention of the addition of low B-flat to the gamut in the other eleventh- and twelfth-century treatises examined.

104. The protus chants with B-flat are "Gaudendum est nobis" and "Magnum hereditatis mysterium." There are no sources for the former listed in Bryden and Hughes' Index. The latter appears in AM 275, 716, AR 297, AS 79, LA 66, LU 444, and WA 51, in all instances transposed to a. The protus chants requiring E-flat are the communion "Aufer a me" and the antiphon "Germinavit." "Aufer a me" appears in GB 258, GR 370, GrS 170, and SYG 252. In GrS and GR it ends on D with no E-flats notated. GB follows this reading except for the final neume which appears to be shifted up one tone. "Germinavit" appears in AM 272, AR 295, AS 79, LA 65, LU 443, and WA 50. All end on D with no E-flats included. However, AM has a final phrase without the E's that are found in other versions, which suggests that it might have been here that E-flat was once found.

The *deuterus* chant mentioned is the antiphon "Tu Domine universorum." It is found in *LA* 300 where it appears as mode one ending on *D*, not *a*.

The *tritus* chant is the communion "De fructu operum tuorum." Its sources are given in n. 46 of Chapter One. John's designation of the communion as *tritus* ending on *c* agrees with the reading in *GrS*.

105. Smits van Waesberghe, *De Musica*, pp. 147-48: ". . . et communio *Dicit Andreas* in affinibus canenda est secundum illos qui eam hypolydio asscribunt. Secundum illos vero qui eam plagali tetrardo attribuunt, in proprio cursu bene cantatur." "Exaudi domine vocem . . . Alleluia" is found in *GB* 182, *GR* 288, *GrS* 136, *LU* 854, and *SYG* 181. "Dicit Andreas" is found in *GB* 245v, *GR* 392, *GrS* pl. g, *SYG* 231.

106. Bomm, *Der Wechsel der Modalitätsbestimmung*, pp. 81-82; Fleming, "The Editing of Some Communion Melodies," pp. 41-42.

107. Smits van Waesberghe, *De Musica*, p. 111.

108. *Ibid*., p. 106: ". . . plerique delinquunt in eo loco ubi est *et porta coeli*: elevant enim hoc subito ad acutas transilientes, cum potius circa finalem .D. sit canendum."

109. In support of this speculation, there is a statement in his tonary regarding the respond "Factum est dum tolleret": "Berno considers that this [the respond "Factum est dum tolleret"] should end on mese [*a*] and that "patet mi" should begin on trite hyperbolaeon [*f*]. But since it should be emended, it seems to me more fitting that it be emended to the natural final. Now this can be done if "Heliseus" is begun on hypate meson [*E*] . . ." *Ibid*., p. 166: "Hoc Berno in mese emittendum esse censet, et patet mi in trite hyperboleon incipiendum. Sed cum emendandum sit, convenientius mihi videtur, ut ad propriam finalem emendetur. Hoc autem ita fieri potest, si *Heliseus* in hypatemeson incipiatur . . ." While John's exact solution does not emerge clearly through a comparison of his description with extant versions, the passage elucidates the fact that he did not favor ending this chant in the *acutae*, just as he did not favor such a solution for "Terribilis est." The version of "Terribilis est" found in Bamberg, Staatsbibliothek lit. 25, fol. 122^{v}, moving entirely around *D*, confirms that John's opinion about how this responsory was to be sung was held by someone else.

110. Smits van Waesberghe, *De Musica*, p. 137.

111. *Ibid*., pp. 137-38. "Ex Egypto" and "Sion renovaberis" were discussed in Chapter One as needing *F-sharp* in their lower position. See pp. 17-18. "Custodiebant" is found in *LR* 140, *WA* 412, and *LA* 508. Like the other two chants, it belongs to Gevaert's theme 29.

112. A published edition of the *Regule de arte musica* is found in *CS* II, pp. 150-91. The *Prefatio seu tractatus de cantu* is edited and translated by Fran-

cisco J. Guentner, S.J. in _Epistola S. Bernardi et Tractatus Scriptus ab auctore incerto Cisterciense_, _Corpus Scriptorum de Musica_ 24 (Rome: American Institute of Musicology, 1974). An edition of the _Tonale Sancti Bernardi_ is found in _GS_ II, 265-77. The _Prefatio_ and _Tonale_ are also edited in Migne, _Patrologiae cursus completus: Series latina_, vol. 182, cols. 1121ff and 1153ff, respectively.

113. See Norman E. Smith's article "Guy de Cherlieu" in _The New Grove_, vol. 7, p. 858.

114. For the relevant passages in the _Tonale_, see _GS_ II, pp. 266-68; in the _Regule_, _CS_ II, pp. 157 _et passim_.

115. Translation Guentner, _Epistola_, p. 51; p. 32: "B quadratum tamen licet tam autentorum quam plagalium naturaliter susceptivum sit, nullum tamen autentum in antiphonario reperies, quam in ipso terminare valeas."

116. _Ibid_., p. 52.

117. _CS_ II, p. 173.

118. Translation Guentner, _Epistola_, p. 48; p. 29: "Nullus enim cantus qui sine ipso notari potest, per ipsum notari debet." S. R. Marosszeki, in his study, "Les origines du chant cistercien," _Analecta sacri ordinis cisterciensis_ 8 (1952), pp. 70-71, notes that the Cistercians transposed all _protus_ pieces of the type "Gaudeamus" and "O Doctor" (that is, with _b-flats_) to the fifth above. Similarly, they transposed plagal _deuterus_ chants with _b-flat_ to ♮.

119. In spite of this theoretical claim, the Cistercian chant books show instances where they transposed such chants to the fifth above anyway, emending the _b-natural_ which could not be realized at the transposed level. There are also instances where such chants are transposed up a step to avoid _b-flat_, but at the point where a _b-natural_ would occur, the phrase is kept at its original level. A shift to the higher level occurs when _b-flats_ return. Marosszeki, "Les origines," p. 70.

120. Translation Guentner, _Epistola_, p. 50; p. 30: "Horum ergo cantuum in A terminantium in quibus naturam suffocat similitudo, necessaria correctio est, quia dissoluti per oppositionem quae partes compositionis contaminat, alterum in principio, alterum in fine tonum redolent."

121. He thus follows Regino who characterized these chants as "degenerate and illegitimate" because of their lack of unity. He acknowledges his predecessor, in fact, by beginning his discussion, "I once read a most elegant treatise on the art of music which begins thus: _Quoniam pauci sunt_." Guentner, _Epistola_, p. 50; p. 30: ". . . elegantissimum quoddam artis musicae breviarium repperi quod sic incipit, _Quonaim pauci sunt_." He then proceeds to quote Regino's description of the _nothae_ chants.

122. The Cistercian emendation of the cadence of the fourth-mode antiphon "Benedicta tu" is shown in Delalande, _Le Graduel des Prêcheurs_, p. 30.

123. For the statement in the Prefatio, see Guentner, Epistola, pp. 53-54; in the Regule, CS II, p. 164.
124. Marosszeki, "Les origines," p. 89.
125. Delalande provided evidence of these practices in his study, Le Graduel des Prêcheurs, p. 32 et passim. A more recent examination of Cistercian sources has been carried out by Cecily Pauline Sweeney in her edition of a later Cistercian treatise found in London, British Library, Lansdowne 763 and Oxford, Bodleian Library, Bodley 77. Cf. Sweeney, "The Musical Treatise Formerly Attributed to John Wylde and The Cistercian Chant Reform" (Ph.D. diss., University of California at Los Angeles, 1972). Appendix I of her study lists the chants subject to transposition in the twelfth-century Cistercian Antiphonale.

CHAPTER 3: HEXACHORDS: SEATS OF THE MODES

1. The word "hexachord" was not used until the sixteenth century. Medieval theorists referred to the unit as cantio, deductio, and voces musicales. Such expressions will be rendered as "hexachord" in this study.
2. Figure 4 is reproduced with the permission of the University Library in Ghent. This representation, entitled "Figura scalae musicalis," or "Drawing of a Music Scale," shows the twenty degrees of the gamut (on the right column "graduum numerus") divided into the traditional categories graves, acutae, and superacutae (see half circles on the left column). The inflection on b acuta and bb superacuta is counted as only one scale degree. The central portion of the figure presents the seven overlapping hexachords. Below the gamut, under the rubric "Sequuntur proprietates," the author labels each of the hexachords as hard, natural, or soft, and of the graves, acutae, or superacutae. More frequently, theorists referred to the position of a hexachord within the gamut by number. For example, the hexachord beginning on Γ was "first hard," while that beginning on G was "second hard."
3. Andrew Hughes, in his New Grove article on "Solmisation," states: "Until the sixteenth century, there seems to be no evidence linking the hexachord and modal systems, although the latter, in common with many other descriptions, uses the syllabary of solmisation for convenience." The New Grove, vol. 7, p. 462. Contrary to Hughes' statement, one thirteenth-century discussion relates each mode to two hexachords -- Jerome of Moravia's Tractatus de musica, ed. Simon M. Cserba, Freiburger Studien zur Musikwissenschaft 2 (Regensburg: Friedrich Pustet, 1935), pp. 168-70. See p. 58 of this study for further discussion.
4. Richard Crocker believes that the resemblance of Guido's affinities and Hermannus' sedes troporum with

the later hexachord is too strong to be ignored. He discusses Handschin's reluctance to recognize in the earlier theories the concept of a transposable unit. Crocker, "Hermann's Major Sixth," p. 35.

5. The edition appears in CS I, pp. 157-75. The opening words are, "Incipit introductio musice plane et eciam mensurabilis secundum magistrum Joannem de Garlandia musice sapientissimum." The wording "according to" suggests that Garlandia may not have been the author, but rather the source for the contents of this treatise.

6. There are two other treatises about which there is little question of Garlandia's authorship, De plana musica and De mensurabili musica. See Rebecca Baltzer's article "Johannes de Garlandia" in The New Grove, vol. 9, pp. 662-64.

7. CS I, p. 173: "Non enim ut stultissimi cantores putant, gravitate vel acumine unus modus ab alio discrepat; nihil enim impedit quodcunque volueris modum, si acute vel gravitater decantaveris, id est, primus in A; tertius in ♮; quintus in c; quomodo pauciores habent voces, sed tonorum ac semitoniorum quibus et alie consonantie fiunt. Diversa positio diversos ab invicem ac differentes modos constituit." The first letter A should read a to be consistent with the lower case designation of the following two letters. See the following footnote for the significance of the underscoring.

8. GS I, p. 262: "Non enim, ut stultissimi cantores putant, gravitate vel acumine unum modum ab alio discrepare scimus; nihil enim impedit, quemcunque volueris modum, si acute vel graviter decantaveris; sed tonorum ac semitoniorum, quibus et aliae consonantiae fiant, diversa positio diversos ab invicem ac differentes modos constituunt."

I have underscored the differences in wording between the two versions. Further, I have changed the punctuation in the translation of Garlandia's passage to agree with that of the Dialogus, which clearly provides superior Latin.

9. I recognize the possibility that the underscored lines in Garlandia's passage may appear in some version of the Dialogus. However, in the absence of a critical edition of that work, I have relied on Gerbert's reading, which does not include the additional phrases and clauses.

10. The Latin for this passage appears in n. 34 of Chapter One.

11. The present comparison lends support, I believe, to a speculation that the Dialogus author did not view the affinities as a means to notate anomalous tones that occurred within the normal interval set surrounding a final (Cf. pp. 13-14 above).

12. Gilbert Reaney discusses Petrus' identity in "Petrus de Cruce," MGG, vol. 10, cols. 1142-43.

13. See the edition by Denis Harbinson: Petrus de Cruce Ambianensi, Tractatus de tonis, Corpus Scriptorum de Musica 29 (Rome: American Institute of Musicology, 1976).

14. Ibid., p. vi: "Tres sunt litterae affinales, scilicet a.b.c., et dicuntur affinales quia suppleant vices aliarum quatuor; et hoc est quando aliqui tonorum, qui non possunt in finalibus litteris finiri propter suum ascensum vel propter sua principia, tunc finiuntur in istis."

15. Ibid., p. xv.

16. F. Alberto Gallo, "Amerus," The New Grove, vol. 1, p. 325. Practica is edited by Cesarino Ruini under the title Ameri Practica artis musice, Corpus Scriptorum de Musica 25 (Rome: American Institute of Musicology, 1975).

17. Ibid., p. 77: ". . . tonus quidem regula que de omni cantu in principio, medio, in fine diiudicat."

18. Ibid., p. 94: "Et nota quod d,e,f,g sunt finales, a,b,c,d confinales et affinales vel consociales sunt."

19. See Appendix B for the Latin text.

20. The sources for "Haec dies" were given in n. 47 of Chapter Two. An entry for the offertory "Dominus dixit" does not appear in Bryden and Hughes' Index. "Ostende" is found in GR 11, SYG 2, GB 8, and GrS 7. GR presents it as mode two ending on a. The chant moves within a range of C to f, which could be viewed as a protus plagal range shifted up a fifth. There are several prominently placed F's, which, as B-flats in the lower position, could account for the transposition. Further, if the entire chant was transposed, as Amerus claims, then the several C's in the first half might also explain the need for transposition: at the original level, they would be extra-manum F's. GrS and SYG follow the reading in GR; however, both end unexplainably before the completion of the melisma on "nobis." Also, SYG alters two neumes, apparently to avoid the F's (= B-flats).

21. Ruini, Ameri, p. 95: "Quatuor voces vocantur finales ex quibus similis nova vel vetus cantio nisi finiatur irregularis esse non legitima sine dubio iudicatur. Sed nota quod, apud veteres quinto semper loco superioribus cum inferioribus finalibus, talis condicio fuit ut aliqua viella in eis quasi regulariter finiri invenirentur. Sed cum omnis musica quatuor tantum finales esse testentur quorum lege omnes octo modorum cantus regantur, sollercie modernorum placuit huius cantus quasi per negligenciam depravatos corrigi suisque finalibus legitime cantari velut istos: Terribilis est locus et Cantabo domino qui tribuit et cetera huiusmodi."

22. See n. 40 in Chapter One for Berno's wording.

23. In ns. 43 and 44 of Chapter One, it was noted that "Terribilis est" and "Cantabo Domino" do exist in versions that end on their normal final.

24. Coussemaker edited this Tractatus de musica, CS I, pp. 251-81, referring to it as "cujusdam Aristotelis," an attribution based on Jacques de Liège's reference when he cited the authority of Tractatus de musica. For further explanation of the pseudo-Aristotle attribution, see Gilbert Reaney's article on Lambertus in MGG, vol. 8, col. 130.

25. CS I, p. 261: "Voces finales illorum sunt re, mi, fa, sol; sedes finales horum D,E,F,G."

26. Ibid. Coussemaker incorrectly prints B for D in this sentence.

27. Ibid.: "Quarti vero modi finis quandoque reperta est in a la,mi,re, cui donat regula nomen, quod per b mollem finire videtur ibidem. Sic sexti finis c sol fa ut est aliquando."

28. He confirms this in his later discussion of mode four where he cites "Benedicta tu" as ending on a with b-flat. Ibid., p. 265.

29. Frederick Hammond, "Jerome of Moravia," The New Grove, vol. 9, p. 607. Coussemaker edited the treatise in CS I, pp. 1-94. Simon M. Cserba re-edited it in 1935 (see citation in n. 3); his edition will be cited here.

30. Cserba, Tractatus, pp. 157-60.

31. Ibid., p. 157. Earlier, on p. 56, he spelled out the members of each tetrachord.

32. Ibid., p. 59: "Omnis igitur cantus ecclesiasticus in mediis clavibus terminatur, hoc est in D E F G gravibus et in a ♮ et c acutis."

33. Ibid., p. 157: "Secunda sedes est tetracordum scilicet acutarum, in quo sicut et in primo dicti toni terminantur. Nam primus et secundus tonus terminantur in a cum re, tertius autem et quartus ibidem, sed in mi, item tertius et quartus in ♮ quadro et acuto, quintus et sextus in c acuto, septimus et octavus in d acuto similiter."

34. Ibid., pp. 168-73.

35. Ibid., p. 170: "Primi toni in a acuto terminati melodiam efficit ♮ duralis secundus, naturalis secundus et secundus b mollis licentialem, . . ."

36. The Greeks presented this interval pattern in descending order of tone-tone-semitone: hence, d c b-flat a.

37. Cserba, Tractatus, p. 173: "Licet autem in discantibus synemmena sint utilia, tamen cantus ecclesiasticus ipsa non recipit ullo modo."

38. See Heinrich Besseler, "Studien zur Musik des Mittelalters," Archiv für Musikwissenschaft 7 (1925), pp. 180-81.

The modern edition of the complete work is Jacobus of Liège, Speculum musicae, ed. Roger Bragard, Corpus Scriptorum de Musica 3 (Rome: American Institute of Musicology, 1955-73). An earlier edition of Books Six and Seven appears in CS II, pp. 193-433.

39. Besseler, "Studien," pp. 180-81.

40. For a discussion of all three scholars' contribution to the question of provenance, see Roger Bragard's article, "Le _Speculum musicae_ du Compilateur Jacques de Liège (Part 1)," _Musica Disciplina_ 7 (1953), pp. 59-104.

41. Smits van Waesberghe, _Muziekgeschiedenis der Middeleeuwen_, 1- (Tilburg: W. Bergmans, 1938-), p. 64.

42. Steglich, in his edition of the _Quaestiones in musica_, discussed the organization of book six of the _Speculum_ (94). He noted that Chapters One through Fourteen are based on Boethian principles, Chapters Fifteen through Fifty-Nine on Guido's and his followers', and Chapters Sixty through One Hundred and Eleven on more contemporary solmization theory.

43. Bragard, _Speculum_, pp. 100-104.

44. _Ibid_., p. 100: "Praeter quattuor voces tetrachordi finalium saepe tactas, quae principalius finales dicuntur, sunt et aliae in quibus cantus aliqui finiuntur, scilicet .A.B.C. Hae, etsi non dicantur finales, nomen aliarum usurpando dicuntur tamen affinales vel sociales."

45. _Ibid_., p. 104: ". . . cum non sint nisi septem vocum discrimina, et illarum quattuor sunt proprie et naturaliter finales, cum non restent nisi tres, non potuerunt esse nisi tres affinales, nisi coinciderent cum finalibus."

46. _Ibid_., p. 100: "Affinitas est aliquarum vocum ad voces vere, proprie et naturaliter finales similitudo, quaedam societas vel vicinitas. Haec autem societas, vicinitas vel similitudo provenit vel ratione concordiae inter voces dissimiles, vel ratione cuiusdam conformitatis inter voces similes.

Prima affinitas dici potest triplex: perfecta, perfectior, et perfectissima. Illa dicitur perfecta, quae est per diatessaron et, quantum ad hoc, G. affinis est ad .D., .a. ad .E., .b. ad .F. Continetur enim, inter tactas voces vel claves, diatessaron consonantia. Perfectior affinitas est illa quae est per diapente et, hoc modo, .a. et .D. sunt affines, similiter .♮. et .E., .c. et .F. Distant autem tactae voces ab invicem per diapente. Perfectissima affinitas dicatur illa quae est per diapason. Quo modo, .d. affinis est ad .D., .e. ad .E., .f. ad .F., .g. ad .G."

47. _Ibid_., pp. 100-101: "Affinitas . . . inter illas reperitur claves quae in aliquibus vocibus sunt similes. Et, quantum ad hoc, ad _re_, de _D solre_, omnis clavis affinis est in qua reperitur _re_. Et hoc modo clavis quaelibet, continens _mi_, affinis est ad _E lami_, et quae continet _fa_ ad ._F faut_., et quae continet _sol_ ad _G solreut_."

48. _Ibid_., p. 103: "Iam autem in antiphonariis et cantuum libris ecclesiasticis hoc male servatur in quibus quasi passim cantus multi notantur in affinalibus clavibus vel vocibus qui in propriis finalibus convenienter possent notari, et tunc maior confusio et maius inconveniens nascitur, . . . ut fieret de cantu

qui convenienter notari potest et terminari in .E., si notaretur et finem faceret in .a., vel si notaretur in .G. cum notari posset in .D."

49. *Ibid*., pp. 103-4.

50. Jacques' discussion occurs on pp. 101-2, *ibid*. The comparable portion of the *Quaestiones* is found in Steglich, pp. 53-55.

Whereas the *Quaestiones* author used the words *transpositus* or *transpositio* in his discussion, Jacques uses *translatio* as the primary noun throughout his passages. This was also the primary noun used in the Leipzig tonary (see p. 39 above). Jacques begins his discussion, however, by using *translatio* and *transpositio* as synonyms: "Et tunc dicitur fieri cantus translatio vel transpositio a propria finali ad affinalem."

51. *Ibid*., p. 101: ". . . vel quando quis proprio motu notat cantus aliquos in affinalibus quae, sine aliquo impedimento, notari possent in propriis finalibus. Hoc autem, etsi possit fieri, non tamen oportuit; unde vitiosum est et irregulare."

52. See Appendix B for the Latin text.

53. Jacques' passage is as follows, *ibid*., pp. 101-2: "Voluntate autem et necessitate transfertur cantus aliquis ad affinalem, quando videlicet cantus aliquis circa propriam finalem se tenuit, postea voluntate musici actoris illius cantus in acutis lasciviendo exaltatus et diutius quam debuerat immoratus, cum iam eum ad propriam finalem terminari sit incontinuum, in proximum socialis suae, quasi fessus, divertit hospitium, ut patet, quantum ad saeculares leodienses ecclesias, in *Alleluia, iudicabunt sancti*."

For the comparable passage in the *Quaestiones*, see n. 85 of Chapter Two.

54. Smits van Waesberghe, "Some Music Treatises and their Interrelation," pp. 30-31.

55. Bragard, *Speculum*, p. 102: "Primo, qui idem cantus et modus non [debent] habere duos fines."

56. *Ibid*.: "Secundo, quia nulli tono competit sub fine suo ultra diapente descendere, quod non est verum de cantu illo, cum in .a. finaliter terminatur, quia descendit in .C."

57. See n. 57 of Chapter Two.

58. *Ibid*.: "Tertio, quia de cantu regulari irregularis fit cantus . . . Ideo in aliis multis ecclesiis ille cantus correctus [est]; finitur enim in .D., non in .a." Amerus, writing in Italy, had also noted that some musicians were emending these chants. The manuscript sources of both "Terribilis est" and "Alleluia. Judicabunt" preserve versions ending on *D* and on *a*.

59. *Ibid*.: "Secus autem est de quibusdam aliis cantibus qui, alte ascendendo, sic diu ibi morantur et usque ad finem suum, vel prope, ut non convenient, sic subito et praecipitanter de loco sic alto ad proprium redeant finem. Ideo magis excusari tales cantus sunt si in proximam affinalem terminentur."

60. Ibid., p. 139: "Rarissime igitur utendum est .b. rotundo, nisi in quinto, vel in sexto tono, . . . Utinam advertissent hoc qui multos cantus per .b. molle destruxerunt et cantus illos in suo sustinent errore."

61. Ibid., pp. 140-42. The comparable passage in the Dialogus is found in GS I, pp. 263-64. Jacques obviously considered the Dialogus to be a work by Guido since he begins, "Dicit igitur Guido sic."

62. Ibid., p. 140: "Habemus ex tacta Guidonis sententia quod vox, quae est ut, non repugnat voci finali septimi toni, quae est sol."

63. Ibid., pp. 142-43. For the comparable passage in Guido's Epistola, see GS II, p. 47. In the Epistola, Guido does not actually use the term modus vocum, although the explanation is almost identical to that in the Micrologus, where modus vocum does appear.

64. Ibid., p. 143: ". . . patet quod nec primus tonus, nec secundus quantum ad formulas suas regulares prius tactas terminari possunt in primam .A., vel octavam .a., et ideo multi cantus primi quantum ad aliquid corrumpuntur qui non in propria notantur finali, sed in affinali. Patet in aliquibus libris de illo responsorio Christi virgo, vel illo Circumdederunt me viri mendaces et de multis aliis."

65. The responsory "Circumdederunt me viri mendaces" is found in WA 113 ending on a. It ends on D in LA 183, PM 52, and OHS 63, 303. There is no responsory entitled "Christi virgo" listed in Bryden and Hughes' Index. However, there is an antiphon "Christi virgo" found as "Christi mater" in WA 303 ending on a. In WA, both chants have a range E to f, with the f occurring in the melodic figure:

If one attempts to locate a place where the normal protus pattern is lost, this figure seems to be the only possibility: f forms a minor sixth instead of the normal major sixth with the final. Following Jacques' statement, one has to conclude that the chants would have been written with a major sixth above their proper final - with b-natural above D. Such is their notation in other sources. However, the question remains, why did Worcester notate both chants up a fifth? It is noteworthy that the figure given above uses f as an embellishing tone at the top of the chant's range. The basic range E to e, if transferred to the normal mode two position, would become A to a, for which an upper embellishing tone of b-flat did occur in some chant repertory. Might the compiler of Worcester have known these chants, or preferred them, in a version containing the upper b-flat, but in accordance with a desire to avoid that tone in notation, he transposed them to the affinalis? The possibility also exists that Worcester transposed "Circumdederunt" to avoid the need for low B-flat at "domine" (F = B-flat).

66. Bragard, Speculum, pp. 143-44: ". . . in distinctis locis decantari possunt et notari . . ." Guido's comparable passage is found in GS II, p. 49. The chant example is missing from Gerbert's edition, but it is found within manuscript copies of the Epistola, e.g., London, B.M. Add. 17808 and Vienna, Nat. Bibl. (Cpv) 51.

"Spera in Domino" is found in WA 63 and LA 87 as mode six ending on F.

67. Bragard, Speculum, p. 146.

68. Ibid.: "Si enim .b. molle, etiam in acutis vocibus, magnam in multis cantibus faciat confusionem, ut supra visum est, quanto faceret ampliorem si etiam in gravibus vocibus poneretur. Unde, sicut minus quam possimus, in cantibus uti debemus .b. molle, . . ."

69. Ibid., pp. 219-24.

70. Ibid., p. 219: "Dicendum igitur quod cantus qui finiuntur in ut sunt quinti vel sexti toni, septimi vel octavi, non primi vel secundi, tertii vel quarti. Dico specialius quod, si finem habeant in ut de .C. vel .F. gravibus et in .c. acuta, quinti sunt vel sexti toni. Si vero cantus aliqui terminentur in .Γ. graeca, quod visum non est, vel in .G. gravi, vel .g. acuta, septimi sunt toni vel octavi."

71. Ibid.: "Sed secus est de .c. acuta, quia in illa iungitur ut non solum cum fa, sed etiam cum sol."

72. Ibid.: ". . . videtur tamen quod tales cantus potius dici debeant quinti vel sexti toni quam septimi vel octavi, primo quia .c. acuta, secundum Guidonem, dicitur clavis affinalis, sicut ceteris tonis; secundo quia sol de .c. acuta cum cantetur per .b. molle, non sic naturaliter inest illi clavi sicut fa. Ideo ibidem ut maiorem affinitatem habet ad fa quam ad sol."

73. Ibid., p. 220: ". . . sunt primi toni vel secundi, tertii vel quarti, non quinti vel sexti, septimi vel octavi; primi vel secundi, tertii vel quarti, si terminentur in .a. acuta vel .aa. superacuta, quia iungitur in illis clavibus la cum re quae est finalis primi toni et secundi, et cum mi quae finalis est tertii et quarti."

74. Ibid., p. 222: "Quodsi qui cantus obtineant duos fines, ut terminentur primo in propria finali et postmodum in affinali, vitium et irregularitas quaedam est; sic sunt quaedam Alleluia et quaedam Responsoria in aliquibus ecclesiis et illi secundum Antiquos cantus sunt transpositi. De quibus supratactum est."

75. Ibid., p. 223.

76. Ibid.: "Generalius igitur fieri videtur tonorum denominatio a tactis vocibus quam a quattuor finalibus clavibus, quia voces illae non solum respiciunt tetrachordum finalium, sed et alia. Septies enim continentur in gammate et propterea alibi terminari possunt cantus quam in illis quattuor clavibus proprie finalibus."

77. Ibid.: "Dixi autem 'si convenienter' propter quosdam cantus qui finem habent in re de .G. gravi per .b. molle, sed non convenienter. . . . Et consimiliter est de quibusdam aliis antiphonis et responsoriis quae in finali voce per .b. molle depravantur."

78. See n. 83 of Chapter Two for the source citations. Steglich notes that "Magnus" has always been classified as tetrardus, Quaestiones in musica, pp. 148-50.

79. An edition of the Lucidarium is found in GS III, pp. 64-121. That edition, based on only two sources, has been superseded by Jan Herlinger's, which collates fifteen complete and twelve fragmentary sources. Herlinger's edition with English translation is found in his dissertation, "The Lucidarium of Marchetto of Padua: A Critical Edition, Translation, and Commentary" (University of Chicago, 1977).

80. Ibid., p. 572: "Sunt nonnulli qui absque specierum lege cantus dijudicant cujus toni sint solum propter ascensum et descensum inspecto fine, quorum judicium pluribus rationibus nullum est."

81. Ibid., p. 594: ". . . nam quilibet tonus debet in finali sua proprie terminari, et tunc talis tonus dicitur regularis, eo quod juxta sibi datam regulam modulatur. Si autem, ut dictum est, in finali finiri non potest, debet in confinali, et tunc talis tonus irregularis dicitur, eo quod propter accidens quod in eo est, vel esse potest, secundum sibi datam regulam propriam non incedit, ut est Graduale Nimis honorati sunt et cetera et similes, . . ."

As distinct from Jacques', Marchetto's usage of "irregular" agrees with that of the majority of medieval theorists' before and after him. It reflects a recognition that the total modal unfolding a fifth above the final is not the "regular" one associated with that mode. Jacques, on the other hand, who was ultimately concerned with the modal nucleus as defined within the hexachord, considered a mode intact as long as it ended on a syllable associated with that mode. He did recognize chant irregular with regard to its ending, but here he referred to a structural situation -- the chant operated on two tonal levels, ending on a higher one than where it began.

82. Ibid. The chant is found in five sources, GR 391, LU 1326, SYG 54, GB 235, and GrS plate W. In all except SYG, it ends on a. SYG does not include the last two distinctions of the response. Only GR contains b-flat, which would be equivalent to E-flat at the untransposed level, as shown in Example 5.

83. See Herlinger, Lucidarium, pp. 600-608.

84. Ibid., p. 606: ". . . dicimus quod quilibet tonus potest terminare in quolibet loco manus ubi ejus species possunt proprie reperiri."

85. Ibid., p. 608: ". . . et talis tonus dicitur acquisitus, eo quod acquiruntur ejus species per variationem signorum b rotundi et ♮ quadri, et in alio loco quae improprie terminantur."

86. See n. 84 above.

87. Coussemaker's edition of the treatise appears in CS IV, pp. 201-298. For a discussion of its possible author, see Gilbert Reaney, "The Question of Authorship in the Medieval Treatises," Musica Disciplina 18 (1964), pp. 10-11.

88. CS IV, p. 233: "Notandum quod plagales prothi, deuteri, et triti, quia ad quintas voces elevantur, aliquando contra auctoritatem in a, ♮, c, acutis finem ponunt, ut patebit inferius; sed quia raro accidit, non regula, sed abusio est. Istae tres litterae collaterales vocantur."

89. The general sense of abusio is "abuse," "misuse," or "irregular use." Further, in rhetoric, it is a term for a false or harsh use of tropes or figures of speech. Thesaurus linguae latinae, editus auctoritate et consilio academicarum quinque Germanicarum, Gottigensis, Lipsiensis, Monacensis, Vindobonensis, 1- (Lipsiae: Teubner, 1900-), vol. 1, p. 238.

90. See, for example, Jacques de Liège: Bragard, Speculum, p. 242.

91. CS IV, p. 237: "Et aliquando facit finem suum in A. acutam causa toni vel semitonii."

92. Heinrich Hüschen, "Heinrich Eger," MGG, vol. 3, cols. 1154-67. The modern edition is also by Hüschen, Das Cantuagium des Heinrich Eger von Kalkar (1328-1408), Beiträge zur rheinischen Musikgeschichte 2 (Cologne: Staufen-Verlag, 1952).

93. Ibid., p. 49: "Quicumque enim cantus secundum principium suum vel medium dubius videat [sic] et vagus, in sua tamen finali, si regularis est, capitur et certus dijudicatur, . . ." Videat should read videatur.

94. Ibid., p. 50: "Quapropter, si cantus aliquando in aliis locis finalem habuerit, scilicet in quarta vel in quinta, octava vel alia supra loca praedicta, quod permittitur, quia superius saepe cantatur aptius vel dulcius propter vel semitonium vel b-molle ibidem existens, hoc tamen fit pro eo, quod praedictae syllabae terminales seu finales in illis proportionaliter reperiuntur clavibus. Sicque ex hoc primus et secundus a-lamire pro finali propter re ipsius habere possunt, similiter et tertius et quartus propter mi ipsius et sic de aliis. Et si aliquando cantus terminatur in ut, sicut saepe fit in octavo tono et quandoque in quinto, hoc tantum fit propter sol vel fa ibi latentes, ex quibus talis cognoscitur cantus."

95. There is an intermediary passage on chant beginnings that contains one citation relevant to a discussion of affinities. Eger wants to emphasize that when a chant is elevated to the fourth or fifth above the final, the beginning is raised proportionately to the end: ". . . the antiphon "Dominus regit me" and similar ones, which are of the fourth [mode] and are ended on a lamire because of the mi within it, are

begun from b fami." Ibid., p. 51: ". . . antiphona 'Dominus regit me' et similes, quae quarti sunt et terminantur in a-lamire propter mi ipsius, inchoantur a b-fami."

The version of the chant in the Worcester antiphoner (WA 60) begins on b-natural and ends on a. If this version were begun a fourth lower, the opening figure would read F-sharp D E G, and thus the reason for beginning on b-natural becomes evident. The other source of "Dominus regit me" is LA 80. Here it ends on E, its proper final. Whereas the beginning in WA would demand F-sharp at the untransposed level, LA has altered the chant so that it begins E D E, thereby eliminating the necessity for transposition. LA similarly alters the music at "loco," which would require an F-sharp in WA's version.

96. Hüschen, Das Cantuagium, p. 56: "Cantus quidam dicuntur praeceptivi, . . . qui regulariter incipiunt, mediant et finiunt servantes ea, quae servari ars praecipit aut regula."

97. Ibid.: "Permissivi dicuntur qui, licet ab arte quodam modo deficiant; excessus tamen ipsorum seu defectus excusabiles sunt. Quorum quidam dicuntur transpositi, scilicet illi, qui olim in gravibus facti ibidem duriter cantabantur et dissone. Postea a modernioribus in acutorum regionem propter dulcedinem vel b-mollis vel toni vel alterius (modi) ibidem convenientiorum translati, et hoc per diapente sicut antiphona 'Germinavit radix' vel per diatessaron sicut antiphona 'Oculi mei' et similes."

The sources of "Germinavit radix Jesse" are AR 295, LU 443, AM 272, WA 50, and LA 65. Its range is that of a sixth, C to a, and the ending is on D in all sources. There is no apparent reason for transposing this chant.

The antiphon "Oculi mei semper ad Dominum" occurs in WA 60 and LA 80. As with "Dominus regit me," it is transposed to a in WA, but remains on E in LA. LA alters the beginning to avoid F-sharp, just as happened in "Dominus regit me."

98. In this context, Eger says a tone is involved, whereas he said semitone in the earlier quotation. Either would make sense.

99. Hüschen, Das Cantuagium, p. 56: "Defecti quidam (nominantur), illi scilicet, . . . finalem non habentes proprium, sed vocem terminalem suo tono consonum, ut si cantus primi toni terminaretur in G-solreut propter re ibidem latens."

100. The treatise is found in CS II, pp. 434-83. For the latest thought on attribution, see Lawrence Gushee, "Anonymous Theoretical Writings," The New Grove, vol. 1, p. 445.

101. Heinrich Hüschen, "Anonymi," MGG, vol. 1, col. 495.

102. CS II, p. 438. This interest in ambitus is distinct from the interest in species expressed by

other writers, including Jacques de Liège and Marchetto of Padua. Beginning with the _Dialogus_ author and Guido, many writers gave general rules for the ascents and descents of plagal versus authentic modes. Berno was one of the first who attempted to establish criteria and nomenclature by which to judge ambiguous cases -- those with limited or excessive ranges. The Cistercians followed suit in the reforms they undertook leading to a revised system of codification and classification. No attempt has been made here to determine to what degree Anonymous I bases his rules and designations on those of his predecessors.

103. _Ibid_., p. 439: "Et si aliquis cantus inveniatur qui nec incipiat, nec finiat in suis gradibus regularibus, sed in suis affinibus de quibus infra dicetur. Dicendum est quod talis cantus non sit simpliciter regularis; sed magis irregularis, sicut de illo responsorio: _Job scio Domine_, qui cantus deputatur sexto tono, ut patet ex melodia versus; nec tamen ipsum responsorium regulariter incipit nec finit regulariter."

Bryden and Hughes' _Index_ does not list any sources of "Job scio Domine."

104. _Ibid_., pp. 440-42. When Anonymous I refers to the four principal final degrees (specifically _gradus seu claves finales_), he uses the same designations as Heinrich Eger, _D solre_, _E lami_, _F faut_, and _G solreut_, one of the few features common to their discussions of the affinities.

Anonymous I provides a somewhat traditional statement on alternative finals. He names three, _a lamire_, _b fa♮ mi_, and _c solfaut_, which agree, according to their ascents and descents, with _D_, _E_ and _F_ respectively. Interestingly, he spells out the corresponding movement only within the interval of a fourth, as did the monk John and the Cistercians. Finally, he states that _G_ has no related degree, the reasons for which he gives later.

105. _Ibid_., p. 441: "Commoditatis dico, ut cantores in compositione cantuum ad omnes gradus superiores liberius discurrere possint, coacte restringantur." The relative pronoun _qui_ seems to have dropped out after _cantores_.

106. All three of the chants were cited by John in his discussion of the affinities. See n. 104 of Chapter Two. Anonymous I assigns different modes from John to two of them. John designated "Tu Domine universorum" as _deuterus_, while Anonymous I calls it mode two. Although still not in agreement, this latter designation approaches more closely than John's the assignment of the chant to mode one in _LA_. There it ends on _D_, not on _a_, as Anonymous I suggests it should. At the words "Qui nullam," Lucca has neither a _B-flat_ nor _B-natural_, so it appears that the copyist may have altered the chant to avoid the need for transposition.

Anonymous I also assigns "De fructu operum tuorum" to mode two, while John calls it tritus. Keith Fleming identifies a version of "De fructu" ending on D and classified as mode one in Lat. 903. Cf. "The Editing of Some Communion Melodies," pp. 101-2. Bomm discusses a similar version found in both a Cistercian and a Dominican source. He concludes that a process of emendation was carried out, whereby the appearance of a strong protus cadence in the middle of the communion prompted changes in other phrases, especially the last, to reflect a protus character. Cf. Der Wechsel der Modalitätsbestimmung, pp. 101-3. Delalande corroborates Bomm's interpretation and cites "De fructu" as a "magnificent instance" of the Cistercians' concern for unity of mode. Faced with modally varied cadences throughout the communion, they carried out emendations so that all the cadences occurred on D. Delalande comments that the Cistercian efforts towards unity of mode most often resulted in modification of a chant's ending to agree with its beginning, although they also changed intonations and internal cadences at times. Cf. Le Graduel des Prêcheurs, p. 45.

107. CS II, p. 441: "Et quia tetrardus, id est, quartus tonus [sic], in suis cantibus supratactum impedimentum non patitur, transponi non indiget; . . . autentus tetrardus, id est, septimus tonus, quamvis in ultimo graduum principalium finiatur, semper tamen in acutis versatur. Etiam plaga tetrardi, id est, octavus tonus, quamvis ad graves infra finalem descendat, in usitatis gradibus tamen semper se revolvit; ergoque transferri non indiget." In the first sentence, tonus appears to have been substituted incorrectly for maneria.

108. Ibid.: "Unde si ex errore ignorantis tetrardus transpositus inveniatur, per prudentem cantorem ad proprium finalem reducatur." Later, Anonymous I returns to the issue of tetrardus chants and the affinities. He remarks that another reason why d solre is not affinalis to G solreut is to "prevent doubt in boys," because if a chant ended on d solre, they would be unsure whether it were in mode one or two, or in seven or eight. Ibid., pp. 441-42. This argument is weak, since by the syllable rule he himself espouses shortly after, the final syllable associated with D would identify it as either protus or tetrardus. Nowhere does Anonymous I offer the most obvious argument, that D as tetrardus provides only limited ascent.

109. No doubt in the calligraphy of the original source, the formation "coniuncta" might look very much like "conventa." In several treatises to be discussed below, a concept expressed by the term "coniuncta" appears in a context similar to the one under discussion here. The term "conventa," however, enjoys no such currency. It is quite likely that "conventa" represents a misreading on the part of Coussemaker or of the treatise's copyist.

110. CS II, p. 441: ". . . omnia que supradicta sunt de causa necessitatis affinium salvari possunt hujusmodi cantus, in gravibus per conventas, ita quod cantaretur perfectam musicam; sed ad hoc potest responderi, quod tales convente, vel talis ficta musica, in communibus cantibus faciliter et de levi non sunt admittende, cum ipsa ficta musica ex solo componentis arbitrio dependeat et curiositate nullo fulta misterio."

The connotations of communis cantus cannot be definitively established by means of a dictionary. Although some theorists use it as a term for chants of a limited range, equally attributable to authentic and plagal, Anonymous I calls those chants "of mixed mode" (442). I have translated communis as "common," referring to the known chant repertory versus the organa to which he later refers.

111. Ibid.: "Quare potius hujusmodi cantus de quibus supra juxta beatum Gregorium et Guidonem monachum justius transferendi sunt de gravibus gradibus ad acutos, . . ."

112. See discussion in Chapter Four, p. 80ff, for more on this point.

113. Ibid., p. 442: ". . . quando cantus est b mollaris, ut patet illis antiphonis: Rorate celi et Emitte agnum." The sources of "Rorate celi" are AR 238, AM 213, WA 17, and LA 23. The sources of "Emitte agnum" are AR 239, AM 214, WA 17, and LA 23. Aside from minor variants owing to text setting, the two chants are identical.

114. Anonymous I refers to a semitone that could not be supplied at the lower level, Ibid.: ". . . hoc est propter quoddam semitonium in illis cantibus inclusum, quo ibi finiuntur, quod tamen alibi quam ibi nulltenus commode fieri posset."

115. Ibid.: "Etiam contingit septimum tonum finiri in F fa ut, in linea; et hoc quando cantus est b mollaris et utrumque fit magis ex gratia quam ex jure." The author seems to be playing with two meanings of gratia, the notion of arbitrariness and that of loveliness.

116. Ibid., p. 444: ". . . cantus regularis est ille qui metas sibi prescriptas de principio, medio et fine non excedit." The entire discussion of regular and irregular songs occurs on pp. 444-45.

117. These references to materia and form are borrowed from the discipline of grammar, which, in turn, had adapted them from the current philosophical language. Beginning in the thirteenth century, the scholastic philosophers had proposed a metaphysical theory of reality that contrasted matter and form. This theory, or at least its terminology, was then applied to the analysis of partes orationis, in particular by a group of grammarians known as the "modistae." See discussion by G. L. Bursill-Hall in Speculative Grammars

of the Middle Ages. The Doctrine of Partes Orationis of the Modistae (The Hague: Mouton and Co., 1971), p. 39 et passim.

Although one can say with some certainty that Anonymous I was familiar with a grammar of this sort, it is not within the scope of this study to determine which it might have been.

118. CS II, p. 445: ". . . commode aliter fieri posset . . ."

119. For the analogous citation in John's work, see p. 46 above.

120. CS II, p. 445: ". . . quia non est facile contra usum longevum, quamquam perversum, aliquid attemptaret."

CHAPTER 4: CONUINCTAE OR TRANSPOSITION

1. Oliver Bryant Ellsworth, The Berkeley Manuscript. A New Critical Text and Translation (Lincoln, Nebraska: University of Nebraska Press, 1984). Ellsworth's dissertation will also be referred to during my discussion: "The Berkeley Manuscript (olim Phillipps 4450): A Compendium of Fourteenth-Century Music Theory," 2 vols. (Ph.D. diss., University of California, Berkeley, 1969).

2. An edition of the treatise was prepared by Albert Seay, Anonymous Ex Codice Vaticano Lat. 5129, Corpus Scriptorum de Musica 9 (Rome: American Institute of Musicology, 1964).

3. Coussemaker edited Anonymous XI under the title Tractatus de musica plana et mensurabili in CS III, pp. 416-75. A new edition has been completed by Richard J. Wingell, "Anonymous XI (CS III): An Edition, Translation, and Commentary" (Ph.D. diss., University of Southern California, 1973). I refer to Wingell's edition throughout my discussion.

4. The Szalkai treatise was edited by Dénes Bartha in Das Musiklehrbuch einer ungarischen Klosterschule in der Handschrift von Fürstprimas Szalkai (1490), Musicologia Hungarica 1 (Budapest, 1934).

5. Petrus Tallanderius, Lectura, ed. Albert Seay, Critical Texts, no. 4 (Colorado Springs: Colorado College Music Press, 1977).

6. Ellsworth, "The Berkeley Manuscript," vol. 2, pp. 32-33.

7. Ibid., vol. 2, pp. 213-14.

8. Ibid., vol. 2, pp. 211-12.

9. Ibid., vol. 2, p. 215.

10. Translation Ellsworth, The Berkeley Manuscript, pp. 50-53: ". . . potest unusquisque voces cuiuscumque cantus discernere easque secundum racionem debite iudicare, nisi forsitan intervenerit aliquis inusitatus cantus, quem aliqui sed male falsam musicam appellant, alii fictam musicam, alii vero coniunctas eum nominant

et bene. Est enim quasi coniunctus proprietatibus regularibus supradictis. Et propterea invente fuerunt ipse coniuncte ut cantus antedictus irregularis per eas ad regularitatem quodammodo duci posset. Est enim coniuncta quedam acquisita canendi actualis attribucio in qua licet facere de tono semitonum, et e converso. Vel aliter: coniuncta est alicuius proprietatis seu deduccionis de loco proprio ad alienum locum secundum sub vel supra intellectualis transposicio. Pro cuius evidencia notandum est, quod omnis coniuncta aut signatur per b aut # in locis inusitatis positum. Item ubicumque ponitur signum b debet deprimi sonus verus illius articuli per unum maius semitonum, et dici fa. Et ubi signum # ponitur, sonus illius articuli debet per maius semitonum elevari, et dici ibidem mi."

11. CS I, p. 166: "Falsa musica est, quando de tono facimus semitonium, et e converso."

12. His assignment of this function to accidentals is noteworthy in view of Margaret Bent's comment, "Nowhere in the period up to 1450 is there any direct theoretical admission that b lowers or that ♮ raises a note: ♮ simply denotes mi and b fa (that is, they indicate where the semitone lies in relation to the accidental)." "Musica ficta," The New Grove, vol. 12, p. 804.

13. See pp. 58-59 in Chapter Three for a discussion of Jerome's use of the word synemmenon. Ellsworth also comments on Jerome's treatment of the subject in "The Berkeley Manuscript," vol. 2, pp. 28-30.

14. Translation Ellsworth, The Berkeley Manuscript, pp. 56-57: ". . . et incipit eius deduccio in A gravi, finiens in F gravi, et cantatur ista deduccio per #. Nam ista coniuncta nichil alius est quam illius proprietatis seu deduccionis, que in Γ incipit, . . ."

15. Seay discovered two later treatises (both found in fifteenth-century MSS) which do contain the definition -- one by Florentius de Foxolis entitled Liber musices, Milan, Biblioteca Trivulziana, MS 2146, fol. 43v, the other in Rome, Biblioteca Apost. Vaticana, MS Capponi 206, fol. 21r. Albert Seay, "The 15th-Century Coniuncta: A Preliminary Study," Aspects of Medieval and Renaissance Music, ed. Jan LaRue (N.Y.: W.W. Norton and Co., Inc., 1966), pp. 730-32.

16. The question of when and to what degree altered tones were integrated into the hexachord system is a difficult one. In 1430, Ugolino outlined a series of hexachords on pitches other than C, F, and G, and labeled them ficta hexachords. In the last quarter of the fifteenth century, Tinctoris, on the other hand, defined a coniuncta as the alteration of a tone, with no reference to hexachord placement. As discussed above, coniuncta is used as a mitigating term to that of ficta in the Berkeley MS of 1375 and in other treatises, with or without the reliance on a hexachord framework. A thorough study of the sources discussing

coniuncta from the point of view of their chronology and their interrelationships would seem to be a fruitful starting point for answering the question posed here.

To date, the relevant articles on this issue are: Albert Seay, "The Beginnings of the Coniuncta and Lorenzo Masini's 'L'Antefana,'" L'ars nova italiana del Trecento (Certaldo: Edizioni Centro di Studi Sull 'Ars Nova Italiana Del Trecento, 1969), pp. 51-65; Seay, "The 15th-Century Coniuncta: A Preliminary Study," op. cit.; Oliver Ellsworth, "The Origin of the Coniuncta: A Reappraisal," Journal of Music Theory 17 (1973), pp. 86-109.

17. Ellsworth, The Berkeley Manuscript, pp. 52-53.

18. We are reminded that Anonymous I knew about coniuncta theory around this time (see p. 77 above), and although he might have known it through the Berkeley author, it is also possible that he was reporting on an idea of general currency.

19. WA 85 transposes the chant up a fifth to account for B-flat, while LA 128 alters the melodic line at the level of the final to erase it.

20. The second-mode responsory "Sancta et immaculata virginitas" is transposed in its entirety to a in AM 1184 and from "non poterant" to the end in WA 29. The transposed versions would account for a B-flat at "non poterant" at the final location.

The sixth-mode responsory "Gaude Maria Virgo" ends on c in AM 1195, LA 354, and WA 271. AM and WA show a b-flat at "interemisti" that would be an E-flat at the lower level. LA, although at the c position, alters the melodic line to avoid the b-flat.

"Beatus servus" has been discussed in Chapter One as a third-mode communion transposed to a to account for F-sharp at the lower level. See p. 16 above.

The sixth-mode responsory "Conclusit vias meas" ends on c in WA 115. It was apparently transposed to account for a chromatic tone, but not a-flat as stated by the Berkeley author. Near the middle of the chant, WA has a b-flat that would become E-flat at the lower level.

21. They are the antiphons "Liberavit" and "Caro mea," the communion "Si consurrexistis," "Ave," and the alleluias "Multifarie olim Deus loquens" and "Vidimus stellam."

22. The reading in Berkeley mentions only "Liberavit" in the text, but includes the incipit for both chants in the examples. Ellsworth, The Berkeley Manuscript, pp. 64-65.

23. Ibid. The remaining example mentioned by the author, "Alleluia. Multifarie olim Deus loquens," presents a complicated picture of multiple partial transpositions, each at a different interval, joined with shortened versions of the chant. GrS, SYG, and GB are particularly subject to such changes. Examination of

them has not revealed, however, that an e-flat might have existed at the place named by the Berkeley author, that is, at "nobis."

24. Translation Ellsworth, *ibid.*, pp. 75-77: "Unde omnis cantus ecclesiasticus primi vel secundi toni regulariter finiri debet in D gravi; potest tamen licencialiter in A acuta finiri. Omnis eciam cantus ecclesiasticus tercii vel quarti toni finiri debet in E gravi; tercius licencialiter in B acuta finiri potest, et quartus in A acuta, dum tamen ibi cantetur mi per b. Omnis autem cantus ecclesiasticus quinti vel sexti toni finiri debet regulariter in F gravi; licencialiter tamen in C acuta potest finiri. Similiter omnis cantus ecclesiasticus septimi vel octavi toni debet regulariter in G gravi finiri; tamen potest licencialiter in D acuta finiri."

25. *Ibid.*, pp. 84-85.

26. Richard Crocker, "A New Source for Medieval Music Theory," *Acta Musicologica* 39 (July-Dec. 1967), p. 165.

27. Ellsworth, *The Berkeley Manuscript*, pp. 84-85. In accordance with the Berkeley author's discussion, this figure gives for each possible final its syllable and a designation for the hexachord in which it occurs. Accordingly, *re ♮* refers to *re* in the natural hexachord, *re b* to *re* in the soft hexachord, and *re #* to *re* in the hard hexachord.

28. *Ibid.*, pp. 85-87. The only other puzzling final is *c* for *protus*. As part of the soft hexachord, it would require *e-flat* above to produce the identifying interval movement of *protus*. The author does not elucidate this point.

29. Seay arrives at this date because of the treatise's use of black notation for its mensural examples; the change to white notation took place in the mid-fifteenth century. Also, the treatise offers no discussion of mensuration signs, an important topic in the fifteenth century. Seay concludes that, even if the author were not himself of the fourteenth century, he is describing fourteenth-century practices still in use at the time and place in which he was writing. Seay, *Anonymous*, pp. 11, 15.

30. *Ibid.*, p. 27: "Prima signatur per B molle in gravi, sicut patet in Rx, "Sancta et immaculata," in loco qui dicitur, 'non poterant,' et in Rx, "Emendemus in melius," in loco qui dicitur, 'miserere,' et in Antiphona, "A timore," in loco qui dicitur, 'eripe Domine animam meam.'"

31. The sources of "A timore" are *AR* 192, *AM* 52, 53, *WA* 67, and *LA* 95. All end on *D* and contain no apparent transposition. The words "eripe Domine animam meam" are set in various ways in each of the sources, but in none of them does a *B-flat* appear. If an emendation is present, it is not revealed by a comparison of these four versions.

32. A point that perhaps bolsters the prototype argument is the fact that the example for "Adorate Deum" does not agree closely with what appears in the Berkeley MS.

Vat. Anonymous Berkeley MS (pp. 62-63)

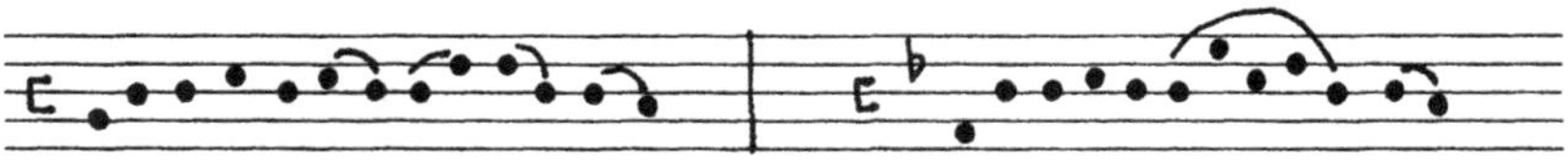

33. Seay, Anonymous, p. 32: "Quid est coniuncta? Est facere de tono semitonum, aut de semitono tonum, aut de duobus tonis tonum et semitonum, aut de tono et semitono duos tonos."

34. Ibid., p. 17.

35. Ibid., p. 47: "Modo quaeritur quid est coniuncta in musica? Coniuncta in musica est signum seu figura per quem in deductione secundum vocem hominis facere de tono semitonum et de semitono tonum.

Quare fuit inventa coniuncta? Fuit inventa duabus de causis; prima causa fuit causa necessitatis, secunda ad faciendum et e converso, vel secunda causa fuit ad habendum vocem pulchriorem seu semitonum dulciorem."

36. Anonymous II wrote: "Musica falsa, however, has been invented for two reasons, namely, a reason of necessity and a reason of the beauty of song alone." Anonymous II, Tractatus de discantu, ed. Albert Seay, Colorado College Music Press Texts/Translations, no. 1 (Colorado Springs: Colorado College Music Press, 1978), p. 32: "Fuit autem inventa falsa musica propter duas causas, scilicet, causa necessitatis et causa pulchritudinis cantus per se."

37. Wingell, "Anonymous XI," p. 357.

38. Wingell, ibid., p. 9: ". . . D,E,F,G, dicuntur finales, quia omnis cantus regulariter compositus et non transpositus in eius terminatur. Post haec sequuntur quattuor, scilicet a,b,c,d, quae dici possunt afinales, quasi ad fines, ex eo quod sicut cantus principaliter potest terminari in quattuor clavibus praecedentibus, sicut in his quattuor terminari potest minus principaliter."

It is noteworthy that Anonymous XI refers to the tetrachord traditionally called superiores as affinales, thus underscoring the significant functional importance held by those tones.

39. For example, for the eighth coniuncta (Berkeley's ninth), Anonymous XI reads: "Octava coniuncta accipitur inter g acutum et aa superacutum, hoc est inter g sol re ut et aa la mi re, et signatur in a superacuto per b molle, sic quod ibi erit fa." Ibid., p. 37. Berkeley reads: "Nona coniuncta accipitur inter G acutam et A superacutam, et signatur in A signo b, ubi dicetur fa, . . ." Ellsworth, The Berkeley Manuscript, p. 64. Note that Anonymous XI identifies the tones parenthetically by means of solmization syllables.

40. Wingell, "Anonymous XI," p. 29: "Sed tamen si aliquis evitare vellet praedictas coniunctas, tunc hoc responsorium, scilicet "Sancta et immaculata," incipi debet in a acuto, id est in a la mi re; sed sequencia duo responsoria, scilicet "Fuerunt sine querela" et "Emendemus" incipi debent in E finali, id est in E la mi."

41. The responsory "Sancta et immaculata" and the responsory "Emendemus" were discussed in connection with the Berkeley MS, see p. 82 above. The second-mode responsory "Fuerunt" begins on *E* in *WA* 413, and therefore ends on *a*. *LA* 509 presents it at the lower level, but appears to have altered the melodic line to erase *B-flat*.

42. *B-flat* has been treated above, n. 41.

As for *E-flat*, the responsory "Gaude Maria" was discussed in n. 20. The antiphon "O crux gloriosa" is found in *WA* 370, partially illegible. However, at the beginning of each staff, a *b-flat* appears, which would be equivalent to *E-flat* at the lower level. Although the ending of the chant, and thus the final, cannot be made out, it seems safe to assume that the chant is transposed; it moves in the range *G* to *g*, which, in order to accord with its sixth-mode designation, would have to be a transposition from the normal range, *C* to *c*.

The third *E-flat* example, "Gloriosa sanctissimi," is a hymn found in the twelfth-century Reichenauer MS 60 and in the Brev. Constant. v. 1495, f. 254.

The communion "Beatus servus" has been discussed earlier. The second example for *f-sharp* has not been identified.

43. The transposition that yields *c-sharp* is to the fifth above, ending on *b*. Other theorists, including Marchetto, rejected this as a solution for the notational problems of "Beatus servus." For the other *c-sharp* example, the "Alleluia. Assumpta est Maria," *GR* and *LU* contain a version that begins and ends on *C*. The range *C* to *c* would appear to be a transposition down a fourth of the normal fifth-mode range *F* to *f*. This use of the lower affinity position would eliminate the need to use numerous *b-flats* at the *F* level. Anonymous XI's reference to *c-sharp* when the chant begins on *a* seems to be a hypothetical positioning. He recommends instead beginning and ending on the *F* final with its *b-flats*.

The seventh-mode communion "Fidelis servus" begins and ends on *G* in all sources named in Bryden and Hughes' *Index*. Such is the solution Anonymous XI offers to avoid *a-flat* at "in tempore." However, his musical example shows *F-sharp*, not *a-flat*:

Fidelis servus et prudens   in tempore

Indeed, *F-sharp* would result if the chant were begun on *E lami* as he shows it.

Further, he mentions *a-flats* occurring in the responsory "Jesum tradidit impius" if it begins on *G solreut*. *LU* 711 begins on *e*, ends on *c*, and classifies it as mode eight; transposed a fourth lower to *G*, it would require *F-sharp*. The situation is complicated by the way in which this chant is transmitted in *LA* 199, where it begins on *a*, ends on *F*, and is assigned to the sixth mode. It would seem that the presence of a semitone and tone under the final (*F-sharp* and *F-natural*) resulted in the different modal designations. But, in any event, there is no indication that the chant ever contained *a-flat*.

The third example cited for *a-flat*, the responsory "Conclusit vias meas," also shows no evidence of having contained that tone, but rather *E-flat* (see n. 20). Thus, Anonymous XI gives no clear example containing *a-flat*, although he does select two chants that are likely to have contained some altered tone.

The first *e-flat* example, the introit "Adorate Deum" was discussed in n. 32. The second example, the *protus* antiphon "Immutemur," is a puzzling one. In *GR* 65 the chant begins on *G* and ends on *D*; from "ieiunemus" onward there are *b-flats*. The version in *GrS* 30 begins on *G* and ends on *G*; from "ieiunemus" on it is transposed up a fourth in comparison to *GR*, but contains no *e-flats* corresponding to the *b-flats* at the lower level. Anonymous XI shows "ieiunemus" exactly as it appears in *GrS*, but describes it as having an *e-flat*:

ieiunemus

He offers no alternative here. Delalande discusses the role of *b-flat* in the variant readings of this introit. Cf. *Le Graduel des Prêcheurs*, pp. 206-7.

The eighth-mode antiphon "Hodie Maria virgo" is found in *WA* 272 beginning on *F*, ending on *G*, with a limited range of *F* to *d*. This version corresponds to the solution given by Anonymous XI to avoid *f-sharp*. In order to have *f-sharp*, it would have been found a fifth above the extant version, with an ending on *d*. This seems unlikely and suggests that Anonymous XI was inventing a transposition of the chant to illustrate *f-sharp*.

44. Wingell, "Anonymous XI," pp. 28-29: ". . . cognicio talium coniunctarum necessaria sit in cantu plano, et eciam organico, . . ."

45. *Ibid*., p. 38.

46. *Ibid*., p. 369.

47. *Ibid*., pp. 42-43: ". . . sed eciam in aliis, scilicet in a, b, c, d, acutis, id est in a la mi re, b fa b mi, c sol fa ut, d la sol re, quae alio nomine dicuntur affinales. Et ideo quia sicut principaliter terminari in quattuor clavibus prius enumeratis, sic in his quattuor terminari potest minus principaliter. Et illo modo in hac arte simplices huiusmodi cantus solent in dubiam provocari ex eo quod in clavibus finalibus regulariter non terminantur. Ex hoc eos nonnuli irregulares affirmantur esse, quum tamen quamplures cantus diversorum tonorum in propria sua sede aliquando causa b mollis nec causa effectus toni vel semitonii stare non possunt. Ideo ad loca tranferunt antiphona propterea irregulares iudicare non debemus, sed cantus transpositos nominare."

48. *Ibid*., p. 43. The sources of "Benedicta tu" are *AR* 221, *AM* 193, *LR* 246, 375, *WA* 268, and *LA* 7, 444; of "Stetit Angelus," *AR* 724, *LU* 1659, *AM* 1058, *WA* 379, and *LA* 465; of "Exaltata es," *LR* 374 and *LA* 442. "Benedicta tu" and "Stetit Angelus" end on *a* in all the sources except *LA*. *LA* presents the identical third distinction of each chant without the *F-sharp* that the other versions would contain if transposed down to the *E* level:

LA	E	a	F	G	E	D	E	D
others	a	d	♮	c	a	G	a	G
transposed down	E	a	F#	G	E	D	E	D

LA also presents "Exaltata es" ending on *E*.

49. *Ibid*., p. 84: "Haec autem differencia unam habet litteram inicialem, scilicet G finale, id est G sol re ut, sed quia antiphona huius differenciae inchoata in G sol re ut vadit per coniunctas minus perfecte; et illo modo propter veritatem sol fa mi, et propter evitare coniunctas, sumit inicium in c acuto, id est in c sol fa ut; et tunc EVOVAEN huius differenciae debet ponere suum tenorem in d la sol re . . ." For this *differentia* Anonymous XI cites "Sion renovaberis" and "O mors ero." The sources of these two chants are given in n. 48 of Chapter One.

50. Bartha, *Das Musiklehrbuch*, p. 33.

51. Bartha devotes a two-part article to the question of interrelationships among five fifteenth-century MSS. Among these are the Trier MS and the Szalkai MS. He concludes that Trier could not be the direct source of Szalkai, but also considers it unlikely that Szalkai copied from any of the other related sources. Dénes Bartha, "Studien zum musikalischen Schriftum des 15. Jahrhunderts (2 parts)," *Archiv für Musikforschung* vol. 1, nos. 1 and 2 (1936), pp. 59-82, 176-99.

52. Wingell," Anonymous XI," p. 28: "Sequitur de naturis coniunctarum. Pro quo advertendum: possit aliquis quaerere, quid est coniuncta; . . ."

53. Bartha, *Das Musiklehrbuch*, pp. 84-85: "Sequitur nunc de naturis coniunctarum (causa autem inventionis coniunctarum est transpositio vel non transpositio cantuum, unde si aliquando aliquis cantus transponeretur, non indigeret huiusmodi coniuncta et econverso, si non transponeretur, indigeret), propter quod sciendum, possit quis quaerere, quid sit coniuncta, . . ."

54. With regard to "Quae est ista," *WA* 355 appears to offer the solution suggested by Szalkai for avoiding *F-sharp*, transposition of this fourth-mode responsory to *a*.

55. The sixth-mode responsory "Ite in orbem" appears in *LA* 258 beginning and ending on *c*. The reason for its positioning is not apparent. However, this version fits the description given by Szalkai. The word "universum" reads:

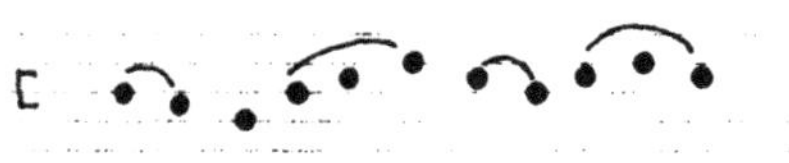

and Szalkai says that *e-flat* occurs on that word when the chant begins on *c*. It would appear that Szalkai is adding *e-flat* here, as did Anonymous XI in "Immutemur" (see n. 43).

56. "Ingressus Pilatus" is found in *Les manuscrits musicaux de Jumièges*, ed. René Jean Hesbert, *Monumenta musicae sacrae* 2 (Macon: Protat frères, 1954), plates XXIX and LX, photographs of Rouen, U. 135, fol. 95 and Rouen, A. 205, fol. 135v, respectively.

57. Bartha, *Das Musiklehrbuch*, p. 77: ". . . affinales, quasi adfinales id est confinales . . ." Compare with Wingell, "Anonymous XI," p. 9: ". . . afinales, quasi ad fines . . ."

58. Bartha, *Das Musiklehrbuch*, p. 91.

59. Specifically, in giving the characteristics of *cantus irregularis* or *vulgaris*, he says: ". . . firstly, because it does not stop in regular seats as it should, namely in *finales* or *affinales*, in which all song of authentic and plagal modes regularly formed ends." Cf. *ibid*., p. 90: ". . . primum est, quia non consistit in sedibus regularibus, sicut deberet, scilicet in finalibus vel affinalibus, in quibus omnis cantus tonorum autentorum et plagalium regulariter formatus terminatur."

60. *Ibid*., pp. 102-3.

61. Tallanderius, *Lectura*, p. i. Seay refers to Higini Anglès' research in this regard. Angles concludes that Petrus may be the grandson of one Antoni Taillandier (c. 1360-1446), a musician of the Aragonese court. *Scripta Musicologica*, 3 vols. (Rome: Edizioni di Storia e Litteratura, 1976), vol. 3, p. 1328. If one accounts for three generations, grandfather, father, and son, Petrus would have flourished in the mid-fifteenth century.

62. Ibid. p. 1: "Incipit lectura per Petrum Tallanderii ordinata tam super cantu mensurabili quam immensurabili."
63. Ibid., p. i.
64. Ibid., pp. 10-11.
65. Ibid., pp. 12-13: "Praeterea toni ubilibet finire possunt, duntamen suorum cantum armoniam non admittant. Quamvis plures asserant cantus irregulares esse qui finiunt alibi praeterquam in litteris quatuor supradictis. Animadvertum est quod siquis cantus finiat in A la mi re, potest esse ibi primi, secundi, tertii vel quarti; ex hoc exemplum: de primo, "Cunctipotens," etc.; de secundo, "Requiem aeternam," etc.; de tertio, "Beatus servus"; de quarto, " . . ." See n. 69 for discussion of the word armonia.

A hiatus occurs in the MS where Tallanderius intended to place a fourth-mode example. The reference to "Cunctipotens" may be to the Kyrie trope "Cunctipotens genitor." The untroped Kyrie is found in LU 25 ending on a and designated mode one; the troped version is transcribed in Archibald T. Davison and Willi Apel, Historical Anthology of Music, 2 vols., rev. ed. (Cambridge, Mass.: Harvard University Press, 1970), vol. 1, no. 27b. The second-mode gradual "Requiem aeternam" is found in GR 95, LU 1808, SYG 235, GB 265v, and GrS 232. GR, LU, and GrS end on a and have a b-flat which would translate as E-flat at the lower level. GB is set a fifth lower, but alters the melodic line where E-flat would be required in the other versions. The communion "Beatus servus" has been discussed earlier.

66. Ibid., p. 13: "Sed illud simpliciter mutare speciem debet dici."
67. Shortly after, he also gives dual maneriae status to C faut, in partly mistaken fashion. Loc cit.: "Finit etiam aliquotiens cantus in C fa ut et tunc est primi, secundi, septimi vel octavi." He should have associated C faut with modes seven and eight and five and six, not modes one and two. This apparent mistake is difficult to reconcile with the otherwise generally precise information provided by Tallanderius in the Lectura.
68. Ibid.: "Fit ut coniunctas alicubi non deceat assignare, verumtamen opinor quod notantes planum cantum melius opus peragerent, si loco debito tonos quoslibet situarent, nec staret propter mutationes specierum, hoc etiam propter evitationem coniunctae, nam coniunctarum ignorantia destruit cantus armonicos et facit regulares enormes."
69. Both here and in the earlier quotation, Tallanderius speaks of preserving the armoni(c)a of a song. I am assuming that he is loosely using two forms of the word, with and without c, as Walter Odington also did, CS I, p. 212. At the beginning of the treatise, Tallanderius defines armonia as "the sweet

harmony of songs, arising from a given likeness in different voices, breaths, strikings, and tones." Tallanderius, Lectura, p. 2: ". . . armonia est dulcis cantuum consonantia, proveniens ex proportione debita in diversis vocibus, flatibus, pulsibus et sonis." This definition seems to agree with that given by other writers who viewed armonia as synonymous with melodia or euphonia. See discussion by Hans Peter Gysin, "Studien zum Vokabular der Musiktheorie im Mittelalter: Eine linguistische Analyse" (Ph.D. diss., University of Basel, 1958), p. 149.

While it may be in this general sense that he uses armonia in the affinales passage, it should be pointed out that immediately after it there is a heading, "Hic de armoniis," followed by a listing of psalm-tone formulas, EVOVAE, and the like, for each mode. It is possible that he is using armoni(c)ae to refer to these specific melodies associated with each mode, rather than in a general sense. A third possibility is that the word refers to melodic intervals.

70. Tallanderius, Lectura, p. 19. Seay notes that the MS erroneously shows E instead of C in line three. This is noteworthy, because Anonymous XI did exactly the same thing in his verse, the wording of which is similar. See Wingell's edition, Anonymous XI, p. 43.

Also similar in wording is the verse found in Coussemaker's Anonymous II, CS II, p. 497. More significantly, that writer introduces his verse in a way that corresponds to Tallanderius' verse heading: "Qualiter toni finiunt indebite." Anonymous II reads: "Et in istis quatuor sedibus habet omnis cantus terminari, nisi aliquando cantus sit diversus vel indebite coactus, tunc poterit similiter cantus primi toni vel secundi terminari in A lamire, sed raro."

CHAPTER 5: THE RISE OF OCTAVE SPECIES THEORY

1. Albert Seay, "Ugolino of Orvieto," The New Grove, vol. 19, p. 320. Other relevant articles by Seay are "Ugolino of Orvieto, Theorist and Composer," Musica Disciplina 9 (1955), pp. 111-66; and "The Declaratio Musice Discipline of Ugolino of Orvieto: Addenda," Musica Disciplina 11 (1957), pp. 126-33. Seay edited the treatise, Ugolino of Orvieto, Declaratio Musicae Disciplinae, 3 vols., Corpus Scriptorum de Musica 7 (Rome: American Institute of Musicology, 1959-62).

2. Ugolino, Declaratio, vol. 1, pp. 89-90. In referring to modes, Ugolino employs the archaic term "tropi,"showing his reliance on Boethius and Greek-derived thought. At times he adds "seu toni," but rarely, if ever, "modi."

3. Ibid.: "Hae quidem voces et litterae graves sunt, et in eis troporum termini statuuntur, ut autenticorum perfectionibus atque plagalium eorumque formationibus satisfiat. . . . Si in superioribus locarentur

specierum ordo ex quibus consistit troporum formatio penitus perderetur, ut intelligenti patet. Necessario igitur his in sedibus trop sunt collocati. Sed propter quaedam quae interdum accidunt inferius declaranda tres acutae voces et tres litterae primis tribus gravibus vocibus et litteris respondentes, ubi sit etiam troporum finis et terminatio, sunt adiunctae, scilicet, re, mi, fa, A, ♮, et C sociatae, . . ."

4. In Gregorian Chant, Willi Apel devotes several pages to these graduals (357-63). He refers to the appropriateness of the designation "gradual type," since all the melodies concerned (19 in number) use the same standard phrases. Among the melodies are the "Haec dies" graduals, which differ from the model in their opening phrase. See n. 47 in Chapter Two of the present study for a citation of the sources of the Easter "Haec dies" gradual.

5. Ugolino, Declaratio, pp. 208-10.

6. Ibid., p. 209: "In primis namque terminationibus et secundis autentici tropi atque plagales possunt suum terminum figere, sed in primis hi tropi suam locant sedem qui formae suae convenientiam servant. Qui autem in his primis positi inconvenientiam patiuntur, in secundis terminationibus collocantur, quia eam neumarum seriem et tonorum, diphtonorum, aliarumque coniunctionum formam et ordinem quam in secundis habent terminationibus in primis habere non possent."

7. The use of inconvenientia in this context is reminiscent of a similar usage of accidentia by Marchetto in the Lucidarium (see pp. 69-70). Marchetto had also distinguished the two seats as to whether or not the proper species of fourth and fifth can be attained there. Finally, Marchetto discusses a "Justus ut palma" gradual, "Nimis honorati sunt," as well as "Beatus servus." Based on these similarities, it is likely that Ugolino based his discussion on the related passages in the Lucidarium.

8. In the Easter Sunday gradual "Haec dies" (LU 778), he specifies the need for a ditone under the final (D) in the beginning phrase. Also, for the word "Exsultemus" in the respond and for the word "Saeculum" in the verse, a perfect fifth (diatessaron plus a tone) is needed under c (c - F = F - B-flat). In the "Haec dies" gradual for the fifth day after Easter (LU 797), the last syllable of the word "mirabile" ends on c, from which the melody descends a perfect fifth to F. Again, c - F = F - B-flat.

9. The sources of the gradual are GR 42, LU 1201, SYG 195, GB 23, and GrS 202.

10. Ugolino, Declaratio, p. 210: ". . . quod non est secundum neumarum ordinem gradualis, . . ."

11. In support of this interpretation, one notes that at least one source, GrS 202, has the chant transposed to a, but with the tritone left uncorrected.

12. The three chants are "Exsultabant sancti in gloria," "Nimis honorati sunt," and "Exiit sermo."

"Nimis" was discussed above in connection with Marchetto, pp. 69-70. As was the case with "Justus ut palma," the tritone is not corrected in all the sources examined.

"Exsultabant" is found in GR 455, SYG 205, GB 210, and Grs 214. GR, GB, and GrS have the chant ending on a, apparently to accommodate the B-flats that would be needed at "laetabuntur in." SYG changed the melodic line at those words to avoid B-flat.

"Exiit sermo" is found in GR 637, LU 423, SYG 25, GrS 17, and GB 26. This chant is of a limited range, F to e, and ends on a in all sources but GB. GB retains the lower position B to G, with an ending on D, and uses B at the word "donec," whereas the transposed sources would require B-flat.

13. Ugolino, Declaratio, pp. 210-13.

14. For example, Ugolino shows that when the neumes indicate la, fa sol, la, sol fa, the actual solmization would be sol, mi fa, sol, fa mi. Thus, the neumes would show a, F G, a, G F, while the singers would solmize a, F-sharp G, a, G F-sharp.

15. Ibid., p. 211: ". . . quoniam in D secundo diceretur ut ubi non est ut, in E re ubi non est re, in F mi ubi non est mi, . . ." This quotation is evidence, incidentally, that Ugolino did not consider the possibility of transposing hexachords to accommodate the accidentals of chant. He confirms this shortly after by saying: ". . . on d a new proprietas would be placed in which the proper [one] would be changed, which cannot happen in plainchant." Ibid., p. 212: ". . . in D secundo nova poneretur proprietas in quam propria mutaretur, quae in plano cantu haberi non potest."

16. Ibid., p. 212: "Quidam aut volentes iam dicta inconvenientia evitare graduale praedictum alio in loco posuerunt, in quo figurarum seu notarum et prolationum conformitas haberetur, et ipsius tropi forma perfecta. Principium enim gradualis huius locant in A secundo, . . ."

17. Ibid. Ugolino includes b-natural and not b-flat in his outline of the perfect form for each mode. However, he explains that a mode may have a mixture of hexachords and hence can possess b-flat per se. A chant could also require b-flat to correct a tritone and accordingly have it per accidens. Ibid., p. 220.

18. Gustave Reese, Music in the Renaissance, 2nd ed. (New York: W. W. Norton and Co., Inc., 1959), p. 139.

19. An edition of the Diffinitorium is Dictionary of Musical Terms. An English Translation of Terminorum Musicae Diffinitorium Together with the Latin Text, trans. and annot. Carl Parrish (London: The Free Press of Glencoe, 1963).

The Expositio manus is edited by Albert Seay in Jean Tinctoris, Opera theoretica, Corpus Scriptorum de Musica 22 (Rome: American Institute of Musicology, 1975), pp. 27-57.

A modern edition of the <u>Liber de natura et proprietate tonorum</u> is found in the same volume, pp. 59-104. Albert Seay has translated it in Jean Tinctoris, <u>Concerning the Nature and Propriety of Tones</u>, <u>Colorado College Press Translations</u>, no. 2 (Colorado Springs: Colorado College Music Press, 1967).

20. Tinctoris still views mode as a linear attribute, assigned primarily to the tenor voice in a polyphonic complex. However, he does adjust his definitions to include harmonic aspects as well. For instance, the mixture of authentic and plagal forms of a mode (<u>mixtio tonorum</u>) may be successive in one voice, or simultaneous between voices. Cf. <u>Concerning</u>, pp. 16-20.

21. Translation Seay, <u>Concerning</u>, p. 37. <u>Liber de natura</u>, p. 98: "Et quamvis quatuor praedicta loca nostris octo tonis regulariter sint attributa, unde quando in eis finiunt regulares vocantur, ipsi tamen toni in omnibus locis aliis regularibus aut per veram aut per fictam musicam correspondentibus sive intra manum sive extra finire possunt, et tunc irregulares appellati sunt."

22. In the <u>Diffinitorium</u>, Tinctoris defines <u>coniuncta</u> as ". . . when a note that is normally a whole step is made an exceptional half step, or a note that is normally a half step is made an exceptional whole step, or else: a <u>coniuncta</u> is the placing of a flat or natural sign on an unaccustomed place." I have used Carl Parrish's translation in his edition of the <u>Diffinitorium</u>, (15) except that I have omitted his expression "chromatic alteration" for the word <u>coniuncta</u>. It imposes too narrow a restriction on the word, which Tinctoris also uses for the signs associated with <u>musica ficta</u>.

Lucy Balmer has noted that when one of the alternative positions requires a tone that is not in the gamut, Tinctoris refers to the latter as a <u>coniuncta</u>, without specifying an accompanying hexachord. For instance, when low <u>B-flat</u> is needed, Tinctoris simply calls it a <u>coniuncta</u> on ♮ mi. See her <u>Tonsystem und Kirchentöne bei Johannes Tinctoris</u> (Bern: Haupt, 1935), p. 247. This manner of designation suggests that Tinctoris did not consider <u>coniunctae</u> in terms of hexachord transpositions.

23. Tinctoris does not explain why he chooses <u>C faut</u> rather than <u>c solfaut</u>. The most plausible explanation rests on the fact that he was concerned with mode in polyphony, attributable to the tenor voice. It would seem that he has in mind the tenor range when he designates the lower <u>C</u> as final.

24. One may assume that practice preceded theory in this instance. In manuscript (and later printed) sources of polyphonic compositions, <u>b-flats</u> and <u>E-flats</u> were notated. Albert Seay points out that <u>E-flats</u> are present in certain compositions even in the thirteenth-century Notre Dame repertory. Cf. Seay, "The Begin-

nings of the Coniuncta," p. 52. Apparently, flats were added to correct certain melodic tritones and ones that occurred between the lowest voice and one of the upper voices. Flats might also be needed in an imitative voice seeking exact interval correspondence with its model. Frequently, altered tones were indicated by means of flat signatures. See Edward E. Lowinsky's Foreword to Musica nova, ed. H. Colin Slim, Monuments of Renaissance Music 1 (Chicago: The University of Chicago Press, 1964), pp. v-xxi. It seems plausible that Tinctoris provided the theoretical constructs of first- and second-level flat transpositions to account for the use of flats, both texted and in signatures, in the music of his time.

25. This treatise was edited by Albert Seay, Guilielmi Monachi: De preceptis artis musicae, Corpus Scriptorum Musicae 11 (Rome: American Institute of Musicology, 1965).

26. Ibid., p. 57.

27. Ibid., p. 58. Compare this verse with the similar one found in Petrus Tallanderius' Lectura, p. 96 above.

28. Ibid.: ". . . et tenere debet tunc temporis dictus quartus tonus mediationem propriam suam, scilicet, in D la sol re, dicendo re ut re mi re."

29. Ibid., p. 54: "Tonus . . . in omni cantu diiudicat et bene dico in omni cantu sive firmo sive figurato."

30. There is a facsimile of the 1497 Bologna edition, Nicolo Burzio, Musices opusculum, Bibliotheca Musica Bononiensis, ser. 2, no. 4 (Bologna: Forni, 1969).

31. Ramos held that solmization according to hexachords was outdated and useless because of the increasing use of chromatic tones in polyphony. In his treatise Musica practica (Bologna, 1482), he proposed a system that relied on eight syllables, and hence, on an octave division of the gamut. See Albert Seay, "Ramos de Pareia, Bartolomeo," The New Grove, vol. 15, pp. 576-77.

32. Musices opusculum, [d v]^{v}: "Nam cum iste antiphonae . . . sint plagales: tum respectu diatessaron: quam habent desuper reputantur de quarto potius: quam de alio tono . . ."

33. The available sources of these chants are as follows: "Dominus regit me," WA 60, LA 80; "Sicut myrrha," LR 246, WA 268, LA 347, 383; "Factus sum," OHS 613, LU 770, WA 126, LA 204; and "Benedicta tu," AR 221, AM 193, LR 246, 375, WA 9, LA 7, 444. WA presents a version of all four chants with an ending on a.

34. Ibid., [d vi]: ". . . tamen nonnulli ausi eos appellare commixtos. id est tam ex suis propriis diatessaron: et diapente spetiebus: quam ex alienis compactos . . ."

35. Practica musicae is available in a facsimile of the 1496 edition, Franchino Gafori, Practica musicae (England: Gregg Press Ltd., 1967). In addition, there

are two English translations: Franchinus Gaffurius, *Practica musicae*, translated and transcribed by Clement A. Miller, *Musicological Studies and Documents* 20 (Rome: American Institute of Musicology, 1968); and *The Practica musicae of Franchinus Gafurius*, translated and edited by Irwin Young (Madison: University of Wisconsin Press, 1969). I have adopted Miller's translation here.

36. Miller holds that the treatise was not completed in 1483, as formerly believed, but rather only after Gaffurius assumed the position of *maestro di cappella* in Milan in 1484. Clement A. Miller, "Gaffurius's *Practica Musicae*: Origin and Contents," *Musica Disciplina* 22 (1968), pp. 105-9.

37. Translation Miller, *Practica*, p. 51. *Practica*, [b v]^{v}: "Sunt enim quattuor confinales chordae: secundum scilicet octo tonorum combinationem . . . Septimus et octavus regulariter in Gsolreut gravem terminantur. Irregulariter in Dlasolre acutam: quanquam Antiphonis et gradualibus: caeterisque Gregorianis modulationibus raro concesserint confinalem: dicunt enim eos semper regulariter terminari. Ambrosiani autem saepius septimum hunc tonum in sua confinali conterminant: octavum raro."

38. Roy Jesson describes the Ambrosian practice of choosing a psalm tone according to the final note of an antiphon. There are four "series" or families of tones, one each for antiphons ending on *D*, *E*, *F*, and *G* or their transposed equivalents *a*, *♮*, *c*, and *d*. Cf. Jesson, "Ambrosian Chant," in Willi Apel, *Gregorian Chant*, pp. 471 and 480.

39. Translation Miller, *Practica*, p. 51. *Practica*, [b v]^{v}: "Potest insuper unusquisque tonus in introductorio concipi ubicunque eius latera seu species noscuntur extendi: quem extra naturalem ac primariam eius dispositionem ductum: possumus fictum vel acquisitum appellare."

40. His definition of *musica ficta* in Book Three reads as follows: "In Guido's diatonic *Introductorium*, *musica ficta* is shown by one interval, that is, where the soft b hexachord makes the fourth string *fa* by dividing the whole tone between *A la mi re* and *♮ mi* . . ." Translation Miller, *Practica*, p. 145. *Practica*, [ee ii]^{v}: "In Diatonico autem Guidonis introductorio musica ficta unico toni monstratur intervallo: ubi videlicet b mollis exachordum quartam disponit chordam fa quae toniaeam scindit distantiam inter Alamire et ♮ mi . . ."

41. According to early theorists' discussions of "Nos qui vivimus" and other related antiphons, the need for a special psalm tone arose because of the difficulty of joining a regular *tetrardus* recitation tone (authentic on *d* or plagal on *c*) with the low-lying tessitura of the antiphon, which has a characteristic *tetrardus* beginning. Not only would the recitation tone be comparatively high, but there also would not be

a smooth connection between a _tetrardus_ _differentia_ and the antiphon beginning. The _tonus peregrinus_, on the other hand, provides a smooth transition to the antiphon beginning. However, it confuses the modal picture since it borrows the first of its two recitation tones and possibly its _differentia_ from the plagal _deuterus_ psalm tone.

Charles M. Atkinson summarizes some comments made about these antiphons by theorists from Aurelian onward, "The _Parapteres_: _Nothi_ or Not?" _The Musical Quarterly_ 68 (Jan. 1982), pp. 41-44.

42. Two of these antiphons, "Martyres Domini" and "Angeli Domini," are classified as mode eight in the ninth-century Metz tonary and as mode four in the twelfth-centruy Lucca antiphoner. _Ibid_., p. 43.

43. Miller, _Practica_, p. 60.

44. Translation Miller, _ibid_., p. 61. _Practica_, [c iv]: "Hanc tamen primitus antiphonam a divo Ambrosio propriis septimi toni clavibus ductam. ubi et septimam diapason figuram et ipsum mixolydium demonstrat. videlicet in Gsolreut gravem. et in Dlasolre propria confinali (quod plurimum in auctenticis instituit) terminat . . ."

45. The question arises: Might the version of "Nos qui vivimus" ending on _d_ be an early, if not the earliest, form of the chant? Michel Gastoué supports such an interpretation in his article, "La Psalmodie traditionelle des huit Tons de l'Office (Pt. 4)," _La Tribune de Saint-Gervais_ 12 (1908), p. 272.

46. There are three other writers who share the vocabulary and approach of Wollick and Ornithoparchus -- Johannes Cochlaeus, Venceslaus Philomathes, and Georg Rhau. Since their writings present only minor variants to the ideas of Wollick and Ornithoparchus, they are treated in Appendix D rather than within the main text.

47. Leo Schrade has outlined the factors that suggest there was a distinctive school of thought among music theorists working in Cologne at the time of the Reformation; he concentrates on the influence exerted by Johannes Cochlaeus who was at the University of Cologne at least part of the time that Wollick was there. Schrade believes that the contribution of these writers was to view the study of music in the light of a higher philosophical study, in accordance with the goals of humanism. Leo Schrade, "Johannes Cochlaeus, Musiktheoretiker in Köln," _Beiträge zur rheinischen Musikgeschichte_ 20 (Cologne: Arno Volk Verlag, 1956), pp. 124-32.

48. For an edition of the _Opus aureum_ see Klaus Wolfgang Niemöller, _Die Musica Gregoriana des Nicolaus Wollick: Opus aureum, Köln 1501, pars I/II_, _Beiträge zur rheinischen Musikgeschichte_ 11 (Cologne: Staufen Verlag, 1955). _Enchiridion musices_ is available in a facsimile of the 1512 edition (Geneva: Minkoff Reprint, 1972).

49. Klaus Wolfgang Niemöller comments on Wollick's borrowing from Spechtshart in these passages and others. Nicolaus Wollick (1480-1541) und Sein Musiktraktat, Beiträge zur rheinischen Musikgeschichte 13 (Cologne: Arno Volk Verlag, 1956), pp. 230ff. Spechtshart's treatise is available in a modern edition with a German translation: Flores musicae omnis cantus gregoriani, 1332, ed. Carl Beck, Bibliothek des Litterarischen Vereins in Stuttgart 89 (Stuttgart, 1868).

50. Niemöller, Die Musica, p. 54. The parallel verse appears in Flores, p. 111.

51. Niemöller, Die Musica, p. 55.

52. Wollick, Enchiridion, d iiii.

53. Ibid.: ". . . et cum cantus in his apte neumari non posset: ad confinales transformaretur . . ."

54. It appears that he applies to confinales or affinales the traditional meaning of finals a fifth above the normal ones. Ibid., d iii: ". . . distat enim affinalis cuiusque toni a sua finali pleno diapenthes intervallo."

55. Ibid. Wollick names the sequence, "Congaudent angelorum" as an example of Ambrosian usage of d as confinalis to G. "Congaudent" is found in Le Prosaire d'Aix-la-Chapelle: manuscrit 13 du chapitre d'Aix-la-Chapelle, in Monumenta musicae sacrae 3 (Rouen: Imprimerie rouennaise, 1961), p. 53. Here only the incipit is given, so it is impossible to determine on what note the sequence ends.

56. Ibid., d iii and iii^{v}. In this discussion, Wollick refers his reader to Book Two, Chapter Six on musica ficta (c ii^{v} and c iii). That chapter amounts to an exposition on coniunctae that is most closely related to the one in the Szalkai treatise, as far as the chant examples are concerned: "Sancta et immaculata" is also named there for the coniuncta B-flat. Whereas Szalkai explained how each coniuncta could be avoided by transposition, Wollick describes how each one can be part of a hexachord. It seems that, once again, such a discussion using chant examples and suggesting that coniunctae are acceptable is merely a theoretical exposition. Otherwise, Wollick' comments on the need for transposition to avoid coniunctae would be meaningless, as would his reference to avoiding the error in "Sancta et immaculata" by means of emendation.

57. Ibid., d iii^{v}.

58. The sources of "Paradisi porta" are LR 374, VP 201, and LA 442. Sources of "Dominus veniet" have not been located.

59. Ibid., d iii^{v}: "Ceterum non nisi ob irregularem cantuum solmisationem que forsitan per coniunctas sive fictas in finalibus fieret: huiuscemodi transformatio inventa est. Tum propter diversas (quod michi magis placet) Contrapuncti partes in craticula manus constituendas. Tenor itaque qui bassum sub se collocet altius tollitur . . ."

60. A facsimile edition appears in Andreas Ornithoparchus, Musicae active micrologus, Together with John

Dowland's Translation, *Andreas Ornithoparchus His Micrologus, or Introduction: Containing the Art of Singing*, ed. Gustave Reese and Steven Ledbetter (New York: Dover Publications, Inc., 1973).

61. In several places, Ornithoparchus adds to "Joannes Pontifex" the number XXII, and thus it would seem that he attributes John's *De musica* to the French pope who reigned from 1316 to 1334. Although this attribution in no way helps solve the question of John's identity, it does provide a glimpse of the significant reputation held by Pope John XXII with regard to music. Throughout his papacy, he zealously worked for the preservation of chant against the inroads of polyphonic practice. See Mary Berry, "Pope John XXII," *The New Grove*, vol. 9, pp. 671-72.

62. Ornithoparcus, *Musicae*, [c vi]: "De transpositione Cantus. Est coniunctarum evitatio. Dum enim coniunctas (quoniam viciosum reddunt cantum) vitare intendimus, cantum ex loco proprio sui finis sursum ad quintam elevamus ut in responsorio, Ite in orbem, lucide claret."

63. The *coniuncta* given here may in fact represent the true cause of the chant's transposition, rather than the questionable *e-flat* discussed earlier (see n. 55 of Chapter Four). However, this cannot be confirmed by a comparison of Ornithoparchus' example with available sources.

64. Ornithoparchus, *Musicae*, [c vi]^{v}: "Fit autem ista cantuum illegalitas, ut scribit Pontifex .14. ca. musice sue, interdum venialiter, cantorum ignavia interdum, ex irrefutabili antiquitate nonnunquam, plerumque etiam contrapuctandi causa, ut Baritonus sub chorali Tenore locum descendendi habeat." The comparable passage in John's treatise is found in Babb, *Hucbald*, p. 127.

65. The Szalkai treatise also cited "Quae est ista" as containing *F-sharp*, and recommended a transposition to *a*, a fourth above (see n. 54 of Chapter Four).

66. Ornithoparchus, *Musicae*, d i: "Eaedem voces post transpositionem cantande sunt, que canebantur ante."

67. *Ibid*.: "Cantus in G solreut terminatus: signato fa in bfa♮ mi est primi vel secundi toni ad quartam transpositi. Et qui in alamire tertii vel quarti, ut Que est ista, et sic de aliis."

68. *Trattato* is available in a facsimile of the 1529 edition, Pietro Aaron, *Trattato della natura et cognitione di tutti gli tuoni di canto figurato*, *Bibliotheca Musica Bononiensis*, ser. 2, no. 9 (Bologna: Forni, 1972). Strunk has translated the first seven chapters, those most integral to this study, in *Source Readings*, pp. 205-10.

69. There is a facsimile of the 1516 edition, Pietro Aaron, *Libri tres de institutione harmonica*, *Bibliotheca Musica Bononiensis*, ser. 2, no. 8 (Bologna: Forni, 1970).

70. Toscanello is available in a facsimile of the 1529 edition, Pietro Aaron, Toscanello in musica, Bibliotheca Musica Bononiensis, ser. 2, no. 10 (Bologna: Forni, 1971). Peter Bergquist has translated the entire treatise, Pietro Aaron, Toscanello in Music, 3 vols., Colorado College Music Press Translations, no. 4 (Colorado Springs: Colorado College Music Press, 1970).

71. Aaron, Libri tres, 16^{v}-17.

72. Ibid., 16^{v}: ". . . ut scilicet primus ac secundus tonus in A la mi re terminetur acuto in quo speciem unam primi habemus & unam tertii: In b fa♮ mi tertium et quartum et species quinti habemus ac sexti: In C sol fa ut quintum ac sextum et septimi speciem et octavi. In D la sol re septimum et octavum et species primi habemus et octavi."

73. Aaron says that on b fa♮ mi the species of mode five and six are formed. That is the case when they are reckoned from b fa or b-flat, however, not when they are calculated from the usual affinalis b-natural. In his later treatise Lucidario (see citation in n. 90), in a passage analogous to this one, he describes the species formed from b-natural and acknowledges that they are not regular species associated with any mode.

74. Aaron, Libri tres, 16^{v}: "Ex quo quidem (ut mihi videtur) confusio magna suboritur ut et toni rectam formationem non habeant et potius de suis speciebus quam de fine iudicentur."

75. Ibid., 17: "Verum huiusmodi constitutionem irregularem magis puto cantilenis mensurabilibus: quam immensurabilibus necessariam."

76. Aaron, Toscanello, O i^{v}-[O $v]^{v}$.

77. Harold Powers discusses the question of whether mode was an a priori compositional choice or an a posteriori category with regard to late fifteenth- and early sixteenth-century polyphony. He concludes that, as far as Aaron's selection of polyphonic examples is concerned, the application of modal designations is ex post facto. Powers, "Tonal Types and Modal Categories," JAMS 34 (Fall 1981), pp. 433-35.

78. Translation Strunk, Source Readings, p. 207. Trattato, a $[i]^{v}$: ". . . di qua adunque nascera che el fine alcuna volta signoreggera, e alcuna volta la spetie, . . ."

79. Strunk, pp. 210-12, 215-16.

80. Translation Strunk, Source Readings, p. 208. Trattato, a [ii]: ". . . se nella positione chiamata A lamire termineranno alcuni canti, e che in essi canti non sia el segno del B molle tal fine sara commune al primo e secondo tuono rispetto alla confinalita, e anchora al terzo quanto alla differenza intendendo . . . pur che in essi sia el processo conveniente e atto alla confinalita, oucramente differenza come seguitando intenderai."

81. In his discussion of modes three and four, Aaron designates three compositions whose tenors end on

a with no flats in the signature as mode three, because, ". . . when these observe the appropriate procedure they will be assigned to the third tone." Translation Strunk, p. 215. *Trattato*, c [i]: ". . . negli quali essendo in essi el processo conforme saranno giudicati di esso terzo tuono . . ." In one of the works, Eustachio's "Benedic anima mea Dominum," Aaron confirms that the first part ends on the cofinal, the second on the final, and the third on the *differentia*, all three of which cadences would fall among those specified. This work by Eustachius de Monte Regali Gallus is found in Ottaviano Petrucci, *Motetti de la corona, Libro secondo* (Fossombrone, 1519), No. 11. Peter Bergquist has transcribed *pars* III of the composition in "The Theoretical Writings of Pietro Aaron" (Ph.D. diss., Columbia University, 1964), pp. 287-91.

82. The work is found in *Werken van Josquin des Prés*, ed. A. Smijers (Amsterdam: G. Alsbach and Co., 1925-), Bundel 8, vol. 21, pp. 58-76.

83. Aaron does not actually name the third example as such. He refers to "O Maria Rogamus te" in Petrucci's *Motetti C* (where the title is "Rogamus te piissima Virgo"). Martin Just has identified this motet as Isaac's "La mi la sol." Cf. Just, "Heinrich Isaacs Motetten," *Analecta Musicologica* 1 (1963), pp. 10-15. The composition (as "La mi la sol") is found in *Heinrich Isaac: Weltliche Werke*, ed. Johannes Wolf, *Denkmäler der Tonkunst in Österreich*, Jahrg. XIV/1, Band 28 (Vienna, 1907), pp. 87-89. See n. 81 for discussion of "Benedic anima mea Dominum."

84. Peter Bergquist comments on the association of cadences on *E* and *A* with the prominent fifth *A* to *e* in *deuterus* polyphonic works. Bergquist, "Mode and Polyphony Around 1500: Theory and Practice," *Music Forum* 1, ed. William J. Mitchell and Felix Salzer (New York: Columbia University Press, 1967), vol. 1, p. 107. See also Carl Dahlhaus, *Untersuchungen über die Entstehung der harmonischen Tonalität* (Kassel: Bärenreiter Verlag, 1967), pp. 201-2.

85. The two works are found in Ottaviano Petrucci, *Harmonice Musices Odhecaton A*, *Monuments of Music and Music Literature in Facsimile* 10 (New York: Broude Brothers Ltd., 1973), pp. 56^v-57 and 69^v-70, respectively. They are also found in the modern edition by Helen Hewitt, *The Mediaeval Academy of America Publication*, No. 42 (Cambridge, Mass.: The Mediaeval Academy of America, 1942), Nos. 51 and 64, respectively.

86. In his 1982 *JAMS* article, Harold Powers seems to be observing something akin to this when he describes features of compositions of the tonal type he designates $\flat$-g_2-A versus those he designates $\flat$-c_1-A. Both these types end on *A*, but the former usually is assigned to *protus* and the latter to *deuterus*. He notes the high occurrence of the modal fifth *re*-*la* in the *protus* examples and of the modal

fourth mi-la in the deuterus examples. Powers, "Tonal Types," p. 453.

87. Aaron designates Josquin's "Comment peut," which fits this description, tetrardus; for a modern edition, see Ottaviano Petrucci, Canti B Numero Cinquanta, Venice 1502, ed. Helen Hewitt (Chicago: University of Chicago Press, 1967), pp. 145-47. He also cites Josquin's (?) "Madame helas" which has a range of G to a, ends on c, and emphasizes c to g. "Madame helas" is found in Petrucci, Odhecaton A, fols. 71v-72, and in Hewitt's edition as No. 66. In two of the extant original sources, there is a b-flat notated in the tenor line, which strengthens the argument for tetrardus. Cf. Hewitt's edition, pp. 158 and 202.

88. Translation Strunk, Source Readings, p. 216. Trattato, c ii: "Alcuni altri in C solfaut saranno detti del quinto tuono o sia el B molle o no come Si sumpsero di Obretti, questo e solo per la differenza laquale alcuna volta el canto fermo dimostra, Per tanto el sesto tuono in tal luogo manchera dato che sia confinalita del quinto et sesto regularmente finiti, perche non si puo torre alcuna forma ne differenza conveniente a lui."

89. Translatin Strunk, ibid. See previous footnote for the Latin text.

90. There is a facsimile of the 1545 edition, Pietro Aaron, Lucidario in musica, Bibliotheca Musica Bononiensis, ser. 2, no. 12 (Bologna: Forni, 1971).

91. "Oppenionie" appears to be a variant spelling of "opinione," meaning opinion or view.

92. Ibid., [b iv] and [b iv]v.

93. Peter Bergquist, "The Theoretical Writings of Pietro Aaron," p. 254.

94. Powers mentions Aaron's disciple Illuminato Aiguino, in "Tonal Types," p. 458.

95. The Latin text of Musica choralis deudsch is available only in the original (Wittenberg: Georg Rhau, 1533). There is an English translation in Derq Howlett," A Translation of Three Treatises by Martin Agricola--'Musica Choralis Deudsch,' 'Musica Figuralis Deudsch,' and 'Von den Proporcionibus'--With Introduction, Transcriptions of the Music and Commentary" (Ph.D. diss., Ohio State University, 1979).

Rudimenta musices is also available only in the original (Wittenberg: Georg Rhau, 1539), as is Quaestiones vulgatiores in musicam (Magdeburg: Michael Lotter, 1543).

96. Translation Howlett, A Translation, pp. 131-34. Musica choralis deudsch, [D viii]v: "Welcher gesang sich inn einem andern schlüssel / ausserhalb der iiii. genanten / endet / der selbige wird ein vorsatzter gesang genennet. Darumb ein gesang / der fa hat im bfa♮mi / und endet sich im G / der selbige ist .1. odder .2. toni. Im a / 3. oder 4. Im bfa♮mi / so ist er 5. odder 6. toni. Im c .7. odder 8. Toni." E: "Ein gesang der mi im bfa♮mi hat / und endet sich im

a / der ist .1. odder .2. toni. Im c / 5. odder 6." E^{v}: "Wenn aber ein gesang ausgehet im a / und hat fa im befa♮mi / der gehört auch dem 3. odder 4. tono zu /wie im exempel folget."

97. Agricola, Rudimenta, [c vii]^{v}: "Est autem transpositio hoc loco, cantus alicuius e sede propria ad peregrinam translatio, quae in plano cantu (ubi singulorum tonorum harmoniae in peculiaribus suis regionibus commodissime accinuntur) raro, In figurato vero, quo concentus frequenter, necessitatis causa, ad diatessaron, diapenten, diapason a sedibus suis tolluntur, deprimunturque, maxime consideratur."

98. Ibid., [c viii].

99. Agricola, Quaestiones, F i^{v}: "Cur inventa est cantus transpositio. Figurati cantus causa, in quo potissimum primus et 2, tonus a sede D, saepenumero ad diatessaron G, in Scala b molli elevantur, ut scilicet mutuum Tenoris et Baritonantis, in Compositione, impedimentum tollatur."

100. Ibid., F ii: "Primo 2, 3, 4, 7, 8, tonis, Systema b durum in b molle variatum, dexterior est quartaria, quam quintaria cantuum translatio. Quando quidem tonorum ac semitoniorum digestio in solis octavis et 4tis omnimode aequalis existit. Verum quintus et 6, tonus, sub Scala b dura, quintariam requirunt transpositionem."

101. He adds, incidentally, that in measured music, mode five is more suitably located at C gravis that at c acuta.

102. There is a facsimile of the 1533 edition, G. M. Lanfranco da Terenzo, Scintille di musica, Biblioteca Musica Bononiensis, ser. 2, no. 15 (Bologna: Forni, 1970). Barbara Lee translated the work in "Giovanni Lanfranco's 'Scintille di Musica' and its Relation to 16th-Century Music Theory" (Ph.D. diss., Cornell University, 1961).

103. Scintille, pp. 102-3.

104. Ibid., p. 106: "Perche ciascun Tuono si puo transportare per quinta: Et con maggior convenientia alla quarta con la auttorita del, b, molle."

105. Ibid., p. 108: "La Trasportatione nel Canto si fa per quinta: quando il canto e formato di poche note: cio e che sopra la quarta del Tuono in acuto di poco passa. Ma per quinta si puo trasportare ciascun canto col soccorso del, b, molle, e dove si vuole simelmente, pur che dopo la trasportatione il Semituono minor non sia rimosso dal luogo, dove primi era, . . ."

106. Ibid.: ". . . nel canto Fermo non si fa per altro: se non per schiva re le voci fitte: Et nel Figurato, per havere piu spatio di consonanze: o pur per arbitrio del Componente."

107. There is a facsimile of the 1533 edition, Stefano Vanneo, Recanetum de musica aurea, ed. Suzanne Clercx, Documenta Musicologica, ser. 1, no. 28 (Kassel: Bärenreiter, 1969).

108. Ibid., 31-31^{v}.

109. Ibid., 31: "Nec audiendi sunt dicentes suam confinalem litteram D non esse acutum videlicet, in D la sol re, semperque terminari in littera finali videlicet, in G acuto, isti nempe perperam sentiunt, quorum adulterinae, vaneque sententie, Viri utique in hac disciplina insignes, apprimeque figurati cantus eruditi, refragantur."

110. See p. 115 above.

111. In his article, "The Dodecachordon: Its Origins and Influence on Renaissance Musical Thought," Musica Disciplina 15 (1961), pp. 161-62, Clement Miller challenges Hans Albrecht's hypothesis that Dodecachordon was compiled between 1510 and 1539. Miller believes it more likely that Glareanus gave serious attention to it only after he had had access to manuscripts at the St. George monastery in 1530. Dodecachordon is available in a facsimile of the 1547 edition, Monuments of Music and Music Literature in Facsimile 65 (New York: Broude Brothers, 1969). Clement Miller's English translation appears in Musicological Studies and Documents 6 (Rome: American Institute of Musicology, 1965).

112. The Latin text is available only in the original, Henricus Glareanus, Isagoge in musicen (Basel: Froben 1516). There is an English translation by Frances Berry Turrell, "The Isagoge in Musicen of Henry Glarean," Journal of Music Theory 3 (1959), pp. 97-139.

113. Turrell, "The Isagoge," pp. 129-31.

114. Translation Turrell, "The Isagoge," p. 129. Isagoge, [C 4]^{v}: "Verum cum naec scriberem videremque nec nobis plane constare, quo modo antiqui his usi sint, deinde quae nostro tempore celebrantur. non modo plurima aliena esse, sed nonnunquam diversa. non facile dictu est, quam invitus calamo indulserim."

115. Translation Turrell, "The Isagoge," p. 135. Isagoge, [D 4]^{v}: "Non enim omnis cantus toni primi et secundi in D finitur. sed nonnunquam etiam in a et d. frequentissime vero a Symphonistis in G. non tamen absque fa, in b clave per Tetrachordum synemmenon . . ."

116. Translation Turrell, "The Isagoge," p. 135. Isagoge, [D 4]^{v}: ". . . repugnant enim systematibus illorum et supernae, et infernae claves, . . ."

117. Translation Turrell, "The Isagoge," p. 135. Isagoge, [D 4]^{v}: "Quanquam hoc consilium sanum magis est, quam necessarium. Quippe quae possent extra scalam quoque locum habere."

118. Translation Turrell, "The Isagoge," p. 135. Isagoge, [D 4]^{v}: "In ecclesiasticis vero cantibus non est opus transponere cantus propter unam vel alteram voculam fictam, quae consuetudine nonnunquam potius quam ratione introducitur."

119. Translation Miller, Dodecachordon, p. 70. Dodecachordon, C 4: "Aliquando etiam alamire, sed dumtaxat in cantibus quae diapente non egrediuntur, alioqui neque primus modus superne, neque secundus

inferne suam diatessaron servarint, denique lami, pro solre eveniet, contra horum modorum naturam."

120. Thus, *la mi* (upper note first) refers to *aa*-*e* or *a*-*E* belonging to the *a* position, whereby *la* and *mi* are within the natural hexachord. *Sol re* refers to *d*-*a* or *D*-*A* belonging to the *D* position, whereby *sol* and *re* are in the hard hexachord. *La mi* (descending T-T-S) is the usual species of fourth for modes three and four, not modes one and two, and hence his comment "*la mi* . . . which is contrary to the nature of these modes."

121. Translation Miller, *Dodecachordon*, p. 70. *Dodecachordon*, C 4: "Unde quidam καθολικῶς canonem prodiderunt. Omnem modum posse in quinta supra finalem clavem, aliam habere confinalem, quam finalem appellant. Verum illud prorsus in nullo modo verum est, ubique enim diatessaron repugnat."

122. Glareanus adopts the names *Aeolian* and *Ionian* (*Iastian*) principally from the writings of Aristoxenus, who, in the fourth century B.C., added five modes, or more correctly "tonoi," to the original Greek model. Glareanus acknowledges his borrowing, Miller, *Dodecachordon*, p. 110. Also, Glareanus uses the Greek names *Dorian*, *Phrygian*, *Lydian*, and *Mixolydian* for the traditional authentic modes, with the prefix *Hypo*- added for their four plagals. These designations were first applied to the eight medieval modes by the *Alia musica* compiler in the late ninth century.

123. Turrell, "The *Isagoge*," p. 134.

124. The four undesirable interval progressions are as follows: 1) four successive whole tones; 2) five successive whole tones; 3) only one whole tone between two minor semitones; and 4) two successive minor semitones. Cf. Miller, *Dodecachordon*, pp. 106-8.

125. Translation Miller, *Dodecachordon*, p. 114. *Dodecachordon*, G 2: "Quare si octavus vulgo alius est Modus ab septem illis veris atque in dubitatis, ideoque ob unicum systematis inversionem, necesse est quatuor reliquos Modos, nonum, decimum, undecimum, ac duodecimum, quos nos ita nominamus, etiam in Modorum numerum admittere, quod erat ostendendum."

126. Translation Miller, *Dodecachordon*, p. 113. *Dodecachordon*, G 2: "Qui propter unum alterumve semitonii mutationem neutique totum systema mutari contendunt. Nam Synemmenon hunc esse cantum aiunt, ac velut adventicium, de substantia Modi nihil mutantem. . . . Itaque undecimum ac duodecimum nostros a quinto ac sexto veteribus nullo pacto, propter unius semitonii in diapente eorum immutationem separandos esse. Et quos nos nonum decimumque fecimus, illi non dubitant primo ac secundo Modis annumerare."

127. One such theorist was Heinrich Faber in his *Ad musicam practicam introductio* (Nürnberg, 1550).

128. Powers, "Tonal Types," p. 467. He refers in particular to Palestrina and Lasso. Powers analyzes Palestrina's approach to *a* endings in his "Vergine"

madrigals in "The Modality of 'Vestiva i colli,'" *Studies in Renaissance and Baroque Music in Honor of Arthur Mendel*, ed. Robert L. Marshall (Kassel/Hackensack, 1974), pp. 31-46.

129. Miller, "The *Dodecachordon*: Its Origins," pp. 163-65. Elaine Friedman Farrant discusses Herpol's work in "The *Novum et insigne opum musicum* . . . (Nuremberg, 1565) of Herman Herpol" (Ph.D. diss., Case Western Reserve University, 1973). Another collection influenced by Glareanus' theories is Tschudi's Songbook; see Donald G. Loach, "Aegidius Tschudi's Songbook (St. Gall MS 463): A Humanistic Document from the Circle of Heinrich Glarean" (Ph.D. diss., University of California at Berkeley, 1969).

130. Walter Atcherson discusses the German theorists so influenced in his dissertation, "Modal Theory of Sixteenth-Century German Theorists" (Ph.D. diss., Indiana University, 1960). Zarlino and Thomas Morley are, respectively, the most well-known Italian and English followers of Glareanus' theories. See further Miller," The *Dodecachordon*: Its Origins," pp. 164-65.

APPENDIX C

1. Herlinger, *Lucidarium*, p. 612: "In ♭ gravi, et iterum mixte, incipitur primus tonus, ut Graduale Salvum fac servum, cujus Versus est Auribus percipe. Sed sunt nonnulli qui hoc Graduale incipiunt in F gravi, et tunc terminatur in confinali primi, . . ." The sources are *GR* 105, *GrS* 41, *SYG* 80, and *GB* 72. In none of these sources does the chant begin on *B-flat* and end on *D*, as in Marchetto's description. Only *GB* transposes the chant to *F* with an ending on *a*. The other versions end on *D*, *SYG* beginning on *F*, whereas *GrS* and *GR* begin on *C*. These three sources seem to use partial transposition, i.e., transposition of only the beginning, rather than transposition of the chant in its entirety.

2. *Ibid*., p. 616: ". . . talis additio naturaliter non est ibi, sed melioris sonoritatis causa."

3. *Ibid*., p. 614.

4. *Ibid*., p. 618: ". . . et talis tonus dicitur artificialis, eo quod artificialiter locatur unus tonus ubi naturaliter non exsistit."

5. The sources are *GR* 445, *LU* 1182, *SYG* 37, *GB* 41, and *GrS* 200.

6. Herlinger, *Lucidarium*, p. 622: "Respondemus quod talis tonus a parte compositionis dicetur proprius, eo quod ex speciebus suis propriis sit formatus, sed dicetur improprius a parte locationis, quia in loco alio quam in proprio collocatur."

7. *Ibid*., p. 646.

8. The version in *LA* 22 ending on *D*, contains *F-natural* at two of the three places where *WA* 9 would require *F-sharp* if it were transposed down a fifth. At

the third place, LA alters the melodic line to eliminate F. Marchetto may have known a version such as the one in LA.

9. Herlinger, Lucidarium, p. 670. The known sources of "Tradiderunt" are LU 710, OHS 505, LA 197, and WA 123. The source of "Aspiciebam" is LA 3.

10. In the transposed version of "Tradiderunt," there is one F that would sound as low B-flat at the lower level. However, it occurs in a melodic figure for which B could easily be a preferred tone:

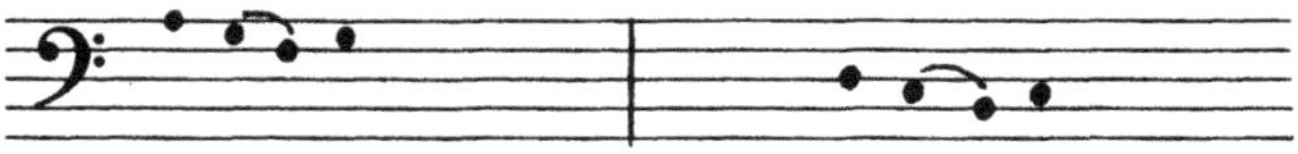

et inter = et inter

Still, there are a number of f's (=b-flats) that could not so easily be taken as b-naturals.

APPENDIX D

1. The treatise is available in a facsimile of the 1512 edition, Johannes Cochlaeus, Tetrachordum musices (Hildesheim: Georg Olms, 1971); there is also an English translation by Clement A Miller, Musicological Studies and Documents 23 (Dallas: American Institute of Musicology, 1970).

2. Miller, pp. 3-5. There are apparently three editions of the Musica, only the second of which is available in a modern edition by Hugo Riemann, "Anonymi Introductorium Musicae," Monatshefte für Musikgeschichte 29 (1897), pp. 157-64; 30 (1898), pp. 1-8. Joseph Mantuani did the pioneer work in dating the three editions. Cf. "Ein unbekanntes Druckwerk," Mitteilungen des österreichischen Verein für Bibliothekswesen 6 (Vienna, 1902), unpaginated (15 pp. total).

3. Johannes Cochlaeus, Musica, 3rd. ed. (Cologne, 1507), [A ii]^{v}.

4. Ibid.: "Nonnumquam tamen ad effugiendam musicam fictam vel nimis in sollemnitatem cantus declivitatem in clavibus transponitur cantus a finali ad confinalem per quintam (ut communiter licet non semper) distantem."

5. Riemann, "Anonymi," p. 161: ". . . quas sibi cantus in proprio cursu deficientes usurpant."

6. Ibid.: "Verum qui mensurabiles cantilenas describunt ad nutum sili [sic] confinales vendicent. dum modo eadem consonantia cantus persistere poterit." Sili: sibi? illis?

7. Ibid.: ". . . ecclesiasticis pernotationibus raro consesserint has quatuor confinales. dicunt enim

quamlibet confinalem diapentes intervallo debere distari a voce finali."

8. Translation Miller, *Tetrachordum*, p. 48. *Tetrachordum*, c ii: "At cum septimus et octavus in G. finiantur, non habent confinalem sursum propter nimium clavium ascensum."

9. There is no modern edition of the treatise. Present references are to the third edition, Venceslaus Philomathes, *Musicorum libri quatuor* (Vienna, 1523).

10. *Ibid*., b i: "Initio, medio, tonus est et fine notandus. Fine per extremas voces nam definit in re Cum deutro primus, cum quarto tertius in mi. Quintus cum sexto in fa, octavo septimus in sol. Exitus ist idem, variatur origo tonorum."

11. *Ibid*., a iv. The *protus* antiphon "Jesum autem transiens" is found in *AR* 391, *LU* 1089, *AM* 366, *WA* 99, and *LA* 154, in all of which it ends on *D*.

12. *Ibid*., c iv. In Philomathes' drawing, the symbols in the left column represent clef signs. ʒ and γ stand for *F* and *FF*, respectively. Each time the syllable *re* appears, it signals a hexachord beginning (one line or space below is *ut*). The two editorial arrows point to *e-flats* that occur within hexachords beginning on *b-flats*.

13. There is a facsimile of the 1538 edition, Georg Rhau, *Enchiridion utriusque musicae practicae*, ed. Hans Albrecht (Kassel: Bärenreiter Verlag, 1951).

14. *Ibid*., F i: "Per quartam tamen aut quintam transponimus illos sedibus aut [sic] propriis si non possunt modulari." Philomathes' treatise correctly reads *in* instead of *aut*. See Philomathes, *Musicorum*, b i.

15. *Ibid*., F ii: "Transpositio cantus, est coniunctarum evitatio. Dum enim coniunctas vitare intendimus, cantum ex loco proprio sui finis sursum ad quintam elevamus, interdum ad quartam. Non enim omnis cantilena primi et secundi tonorum in D exit, sed nonnunquam etiam in a et d, Frequentissime in cantu mensurali in G, non tamen absque fa in b clave, Quod potissimum ea ratione symphonistae faciunt, ne voces extra Guidonis scalam expatiari videantur."

16. *Ibid*., F ii^{v}: ". . . aiunt enim eruditi musici, corruptas esse cantilenas cantorum inscicia, quae vel in d, vel C, terminantur."

Bibliography

Primary Sources

The Treatises: Editions, Translations, and Facsimiles

Aaron, Pietro. Libri tres de institutione harmonica. [Reproduction of the 1516 edition] Bibliotheca Musica Bononiensis, ser. 2, no. 8. Bologna: Forni, 1970.

________. Lucidario in musica. [Reproduction of the 1545 edition] Bibliotheca Musica Bononiensis, ser. 2, no. 12. Bologna: Forni, 1971.

________. Toscanello in musica. [Reproduction of the 1529 edition] Bibliotheca Musica Bononiensis, ser. 2, no. 10. Bologna: Forni, 1971.

________. Toscanello in Music. 3 vols. Translated by Peter Bergquist. Colorado College Music Press Translations, no. 4. Colorado Springs: Colorado College Music Press, 1970.

________. Trattato della natura et cognitione di tutti gli tuoni di canto figurato. [Reproduction of the 1529 edition] Bibliotheca Musica Bononiensis, ser. 2, no. 9. Bologna: Forni, 1972.

Agricola, Martin. Musica choralis deudsch. Wittenberg: Georg Rhau, 1533.

________. Quaestiones vulgatiores in musicam. Magdeburg: Michael Lotter, 1543.

________. Rudimenta musices. Wittenberg: Georg Rhau, 1539.

Anonymous II. Tractatus de discantu. Edited by Albert Seay. Colorado College Music Press Texts/Translations, no. 1. Colorado Springs: Colorado College Music Press, 1978.

Bailey, Terence. "De modis musicis: A New Edition and Explanation." Kirchenmusikalisches Jahrbuch 61-62 (1977/78), pp. 47-60.

Bartha, Dénes. Das Musiklehrbuch einer ungarischen Klosterschule in der Handschrift von Fürstprimas Szalkai (1490). Musicologia Hungarica 1. Budapest, 1934.

Burzio, Nicolo. Musices opusculum. [Reproduction of the 1497 edition] Bibliotheca Musica Bononiensis, ser. 2, no. 4. Bologna: Forni, 1969.

Chartier, Yves. "La Musica d'Hucbald de Saint-Amand (traité de musique du IXe siècle). Introduction, établissement du texte, traduction et commentaire." Ph.D. diss., Sorbonne, 1973.

Cochlaeus, Johannes. Musica. 3rd ed. Cologne, 1507.

________. Tetrachordum musices. [Reproduction of the 1512 edition] Hildesheim: Georg Olms, 1971.

________. Tetrachordum musices. Introduction, Translation and Transcription by Clement A. Miller. Musicological Studies and Documents 23. Dallas: American Institute of Musicology, 1970.

Coussemaker, Edmond de. Scriptorum de musica medii aevi. 4 vols. Paris, 1864; reprint ed., Hildesheim: Georg Olms, 1963.

Ellinwood, Leonard. Musica Hermanni Contracti. Rochester: Eastman School of Music, 1936.

Ellsworth, Oliver Bryant. "The Berkeley Manuscript (olim Phillipps 4450): A Compendium of Fourteenth-Century Music Theory." 2 vols. Ph.D. diss., University of California at Berkeley, 1969.

________. The Berkeley Manuscript. A New Critical Text and Translation. Linclon, Nebraska: University of Nebraska Press, 1984.

Expositiones in Micrologum Guidonis Aretini. Edited by Joseph Smits van Waesberghe. Amsterdam: North-Holland Publishing Co., 1957.

Faber, Heinrich. Ad musicam practicam introductio. Nürnberg, 1550.

Gafori, Franchino. Practica musicae. [Reproduction of the 1496 edition] Farnsborough, Hants.,England: Gregg Press Ltd., 1967.

________. Practica musicae. Translated and transcribed by Clement A. Miller. Musicological Studies and Documents 20. Rome: American Institute of Musicology, 1968.

Gerbert, Martin. Scriptores ecclesiastici de musica sacra potissimum. 3 vols. St. Blasien, 1784; reprint ed., Hildesheim: Georg Olms, 1963.

Glareanus, Henricus. Dodecachordon. [Reproduction of the 1547 edition] Monuments of Music and Music Literature in Facsimile 65. New York: Broude Brothers, 1969.

________. Dodecachordon. Translation, Transcription, and Commentary by Clement A. Miller. Musicological Studies and Documents 6. Rome: American Institute of Musicology, 1965.

________. Isagoge in musicen. Basel: Froben, 1516.

Gushee, Lawrence A., ed. Aureliani Reomensis Musica Disciplina. Corpus Scriptorum de Musica 21. Rome: American Institute of Musicology, 1975.

________. "The Musica disciplina of Aurelian of Réôme: A Critical Text and Commentary." 2 vols. Ph.D. diss., Yale University, 1963.

Harbinson, Denis. Willehelmi Hirsaugensis Musica. Corpus Scriptorum de Musica 23. Rome: American Institute of Musicology, 1975.

Heard, Edmund B. "Alia musica: A Chapter in the History of Music Theory." Ph.D. diss., University of Wisconsin, 1966.

Herlinger, Jan. "The Lucidarium of Marchetto of Padua: A Critical Edition, Translation, and Commentary." Ph.D. diss., University of Chicago, 1977.

Heironymus de Moravia. Tractatus de musica. Edited by Simon M. Cserba. Freiburger Studien zur Musikwissenschaft 2. Regensburg: Friedrich Pustet, 1935.

Holladay, Richard Lee. "The 'Musica Enchiriadis' and 'Scholia Enchiriadis': A Translation and Commentary." Ph.D. diss., Ohio State University, 1977.

Howlett, Derq. "A Translation of Three Treatises by Martin Agricola--'Musica Choralis Deudsch,' 'Musica Figuralis Deudsch,' and 'Von den Proporcionibus' --With Introduction, Transcriptions of the Music and Commentary." Ph.D. Diss., Ohio State University, 1979.

Hucbald, Guido, and John on Music: Three Medieval Treatises. Translated by Warren Babb. Edited, with Introductions, by Claude V. Palisca. Index of Chants by Alejandro Enrique Planchart. New Haven: Yale University Press, 1978.

Hüschen, Heinrich. Das Cantuagium des Heinrich Eger von Kalkar (1328-1408). Beiträge zur rheinischen Musikgeschichte 2. Cologne: Staufen Verlag, 1952.

Jacobus of Liège. Speculum musicae. Edited by Roger Bragard. Corpus Scriptorum de Musica 3. Rome: American Institute of Musicology, 1955-73.

Johannes Affligemensis. De Musica cum tonario. Edited by Joseph Smits van Waesberghe. Corpus Scriptorum de Musica 1. Rome: American Institute of Musicology, 1950.

Lanfranco da Terenzo, G.M. Scintille di musica. [Reproduction of the 1533 edition] Bibliotheca Musica Bononiensis, ser. 2, no. 15. Bologna: Forni, 1970.

Lee, Barbara. "Giovanni Maria Lanfranco's 'Scintille di Musica' and its Relation to 16th-Century Music Theory." Ph.D. diss., Cornell University, 1961.

LeRoux, Sister Mary Protase, R.S.M. "The 'De Harmonica Institutione' and 'Tonarius' of Regino of Prüm." Latin Text with English Translation. Studies in Music 22. Ph.D. diss., Catholic University of America, 1965.

Migne, Jacques Paul, ed. Patrologiae cursus completus: Series latina. Paris, 1844-64; reprint ed., Paris, 1957-66.

Müller, Hans. Die Musik Wilhelms von Hirschau. Wiederherstellung, Übersetzung und Erklärung seines musiktheoretischen Werkes. Frankfurt am Main: B.G. Teubner, 1883.

Music Handbook (Musica enchiriadis). Translated by Léonie Rosenstiel. Colorado College Music Press Translations, no. 7. Colorado Springs: Colorado College Music Press, 1976.

Niemöller, Klaus Wolfgang. Die Musica Gregoriana de Nicolaus Wollick: Opus aureum, Köln 1501, pars I/II. Beiträge zur rheinischen Musikgeschichte 11. Cologne: Staufen Verlag, 1955.

Ornithoparchus, Andreas. Musicae active micrologus, Together with John Dowland's Translation, Andreas Ornithoparchus His Micrologus, or Introduction: Containing the Art of Singing. Edited by Gustave Reese and Steven Ledbetter. New York: Dover Publications, Inc., 1973.

Petrus de Cruce Ambianensi, Tractatus de tonis. Edited by Denis Harbinson. Corpus Scriptorum de Musica 29. Rome: American Institute of Musicology, 1976.

The Practica musicae of Franchinus Gafurius. Translated and edited by Irwin Young. Madison: University of Wisconsin Press, 1969.

Prefatio seu tractatus de cantu in Epistola S. Bernardi et Tractatus Scriptus ab auctore incerto Cisterciense. Edited and translated by Francisco J. Guentner, S.J. Corpus Scriptorum de Musica 24. Rome: American Institute of Musicology, 1974.

Rhau, Georg. Enchiridion utriusque musicae practicae. [Reproduction of the 1538 edition] Edited by Hans Albrecht. Kassel: Bärenreiter Verlag, 1951.

Riemann, Hugo, ed. "Anonymi Introductorium Musicae (2 parts)." Monatshefte für Musikgeschichte 29 (1897), pp. 157-64; 30 (1898), pp. 1-8.

Ruini, Cesarino, ed. Ameri Practica artis musice. Corpus Scriptorum de Musica 25. Rome: American Institute of Musicology, 1975.

Hugo Spechtshart von Reutlingen. Flores musicae omnis cantus gregoriani, 1332. Edited by Carl Beck. Bibliothek des Litterarischen Vereins in Stuttgart 89. Stuttgart, 1868.

Schmid, Hans. Musica et Scolica Enchiriadis una cum aliquibus tractatulis adiunctis. Bayerische Akademie der Wissenschaften Veroeffentlichungen der Musikhistorischen Kommission, Band 3. Munich, 1981.

Seay, Albert, ed. Anonymous Ex Codice Vaticano Lat. 5129. Corpus Scriptorum de Musica 9. Rome: American Institute of Musicology, 1964.

________. Guilielmi Monachi: De preceptis artis musicae. Corpus Scriptorum de Musica 11. Rome: American Institute of Musicology, 1965.

Smits van Waesberghe, Joseph. Aribonis De musica. Corpus Scriptorum de Musica 2. Rome: American Institute of Musicology, 1951.

________. Cymbala. Bells in the Middle Ages. Edition of Texts and Introduction. Musicological Studies and Documents 1. Rome: American Institute of Musicology, 1951.

_______. Guidonis Aretini Micrologus. Corpus Scriptorum de Musica 4. Rome: American Institute of Musicology, 1955.

Sources Readings in Music History. Selected and Annotated by Oliver Strunk. New York: W.W. Norton & Co., 1950.

Steglich, Rudolf. Die Quaestiones in musica: ein Choraltraktat des zentralen Mittelalters und ihr mutmasslicher Verfasser Rudolf von St. Trond (1070-1138). Leipzig, 1911; reprint ed., Wiesbaden: Breitkopf & Härtel, 1970.

Sweeney, Cecily Pauline. "The Musical Treatise Formerly Attributed to John Wylde and the Cistercian Chant Reform." Ph.D. diss., University of California at Los Angeles, 1972.

Tallanderius, Petrus. Lectura. Edited by Albert Seay. Critical Texts, no. 4. Colorado Springs: Colorado College Music Press, 1977.

Tinctoris, Jean. Concerning the Nature and Propriety of Tones. Translated by Albert Seay. Colorado College Music Press Translations, no. 2. Colorado Springs: Colorado College Music Press, 1967.

_______. Dictionary of Musical Terms. An English Translation of Terminorum Musicae Diffinitorium Together with the Latin Text. Translated and annotated by Carl Parrish. London: The Free Press of Glencoe, 1963.

_______. Opera theoretica. Edited by Albert Seay. Corpus Scriptorum de Musica 22. Rome: American Institute of Musicology, 1975.

Tractatus Anonymus de Musica et de Transformatione Specialiter in Quellen zur Transformation der Antiphonen: Tonar- und Rhythmusstudien. Edited by Heinrich Sowa. Kassel: Bärenreiter Verlag, 1935.

Turrell, Frances Berry. "The Isagoge in Musicen of Henry Glarean." Journal of Music Theory 3 (1959), pp. 97-139.

Ugolino of Orvieto. Declaratio Musicae Disciplinae. 3 vols. Edited by Albert Seay. Corpus Scriptorum de Musica 7. Rome: American Institute of Musicology, 1959-62.

Vanneo, Stefano. Recanetum de musica aurea. [Reproduction of the 1533 edition] Edited by Suzanne Clercx. Documenta Musicologica, ser. 1, no. 28. Kassel: Bärenreiter Verlag, 1969.

Venceslaus Philomathes. Musicorum libri quatuor. 3rd ed. Vienna, 1523.

Vivell, P. Cölestin, O.S.B. Commentarius anonymus in Micrologum Guidonis Aretini. Vienna: Alfred Hölder, 1917.

_______. Frutolfi Breviarium de Musica et Tonarius. Vienna: Alfred Hölder, 1919.

Wingell, Richard J. "Anonymous XI (CS III): An Edition, Translation, and Commentary." Ph.D. diss., University of Southern California, 1973.

Wolf, Johannes. "Ein anonymer Musiktraktat des elften bis zwölften Jahrhunderts." Vierteljahrschrift für Musikwissenschaft 9 (1893), pp. 186-234.
Wollick, Nicolaus. Enchiridion musices. [Reproduction of the 1512 edition] Geneva: Minkoff Reprint, 1972.

The Music

Antiphonaire monastique; XIIe siècle: Codex 601 de la Bibliothèque Capitulaire de Lucques. Paléographie musicale 9. Tournai, 1906; reprint ed., Bern: Herbert Lang, 1974.
Antiphonaire monastique; XIIIe siècle: Codex F. 160 de la bibliothèque de la cathedrale de Worcester. Paléographie musicale 12. Tournai, 1922; reprint ed., Bern: Herbert Lang, 1971.
Antiphonale monasticum pro diurnis horis. Paris: Desclée & Co., 1934.
Antiphonale sacrosanctae Romanae ecclesiae. Paris: Desclée & Co., 1949.
Bamberg, Staatsbibliothek lit. 25.
Cambrai, Bibliothèque municipale C 38 (40)
Le Codex VI. 34 de la Bibliothèque capitulaire de Bénévent (XIe-XIIe siècle): Graduel de Bénévent avec prosaire et tropaire. Paléographie musicale 15. Tournai, 1937; reprint ed., Bern: Herbert Lang, 1971.
Le Codex 903 de la Bibliothèque Nationale de Paris (XI^{e}siècle): Graduel de Saint-Yrieix. Paléographie musicale 13. Tournai, 1925; reprint ed., Bern: Herbert Lang, 1971.
Davison, Archibald T. and Willi Apel. Historical Anthology of Music. 2 vols. Rev. ed. Cambridge, Mass.: Harvard University Press, 1970.
Frere, Walter, ed. Antiphonale Sariburiense. A Reproduction in Facsimile of a Manuscript of the Thirteenth Century, with a Dissertation and Analytical Index. London: Plainsong & Mediaeval Music Society, 1901-24; reprint ed., London: Gregg Press Limited, 1966.
________. Graduale Sariburiense. A Reproduction in Facsimile of a Manuscript of the Thirteenth Century, with a Dissertation and Historical Index. London: Bernard Quaritch, 1894; reprint ed., London: Gregg Press Limited, 1966.
Graduale sacrosanctae Romanae ecclesiae. Paris: Desclée & Co., 1952.
Heinrich Isaac: Weltliche Werke. Edited by Johannes Wolf. Denkmäler der Tonkunst in Österreich Jahrg. XIV/1, Band 28. Vienna, 1907.
Liber responsorialis pro festis I. classis. Solesmes, 1895.
The Liber usualis with introduction and rubrics in English. Tournai: Desclée & Co., 1961.

Lipphardt, Walther, ed. Der karolingische Tonar von Metz. Muenster: Aschendorff, 1965.
Les Manuscrits musicaux de Jumièges. Edited by René Jean Hesbert. Monumenta musicae sacrae 2. Macon: Protat frères, 1954.
Musica nova. Edited by H. Colin Slim, with a forward by Edward E. Lowinsky. Monuments of Renaissance Music 1. Chicago: University of Chicago Press, 1964.
Officium hebdomodae sanctae et octavae Paschae. Rome: Desclée & Co., 1962.
Petrucci, Ottaviano. Canti B Numero Cinquanta, Venice 1502. Edited by Helen Hewitt. Chicago: University of Chicago Press, 1967.
_______. Harmonice Musices Odhecaton A. Monuments of Music and Music Literature in Facsimile 10. New York: Broude Brothers, Ltd., 1973.
_______. Harmonice Musices Odhecaton A. Edited by Helen Hewitt. The Mediaeval Academy of America Publication, No. 42. Cambridge, Mass.: The Mediaeval Academy of America, 1942.
_______. Motetti de la corona, Libro secundo. Fossombrone, 1519.
Processionale monasticum ad usum congregationis Gallicae. Solesmes, 1893.
Le Prosaire d'Aix-la-Chapelle: manuscrit 13 du chapitre d'Aix-la-Chapelle. Monumenta musicae sacrae 3. Rouen: Imprimerie rouennaise, 1961.
Schlager, Karlheinz. Alleluia-Melodien 1 bis 1100. Monumenta Monodica Medii Aevi, vol. 7. Kassel: Bärenreiter Verlag, 1968.
Variae preces ex liturgia tum hodierna tum antiqua collectae aut usu receptae. Solesmes, 1901.
Werken van Josquin des Prés. Edited by A. Smijers. Amsterdam: G. Alsbach & Co., 1925- .

Secondary Sources: A Selected Bibliography

Andrews, Frederick S. "Medieval Modal Theory." Ph.D. diss., Cornell University, 1935.
Apel, Willi. Gregorian Chant. 3rd. ed. Indiana: Indiana University Press, 1966.
Atcherson, Walter Thomas. "Modal Theory of Sixteenth-Century German Theorists." Ph.D. diss., Indiana University, 1960.
Atkinson, Charles M. "The Parapteres: Nothi or Not?" The Musical Quarterly 68 (Jan. 1982), pp. 32-59.
Bailey, Terence. The Intonation Formulas of Western Chant. Studies and Texts 28. Toronto: Pontifical Institute of Mediaeval Studies, 1974.
Balmer, Lucie. Tonsystem und Kirchentöne bei Johannes Tinctoris. Bern: Haupt, 1935.
Bartha, Denes. "Studien zum musikalischen Schriftum des 15. Jahrhunderts (2 parts)." Archiv für Musikforschung vol. 1, no. 1 (1936), pp. 59-82; vol. 1, no. 2 (1936), pp. 176-99.

Bergquist, Peter. "Mode and Polyphony around 1500: Theory and Practice." Music Forum 1. Edited by William J. Mitchell and Felix Salzer. New York: Columbia University Press, 1967, pp. 99-161.

Besseler, Heinrich. "Studien zur Musik des Mittelalters." Archiv für Musikwissenschaft 7 (1925), pp. 167-252.

Bomm, Urbanus. Der Wechsel der Modalitätsbestimmung in der Tradition der Messgesänge im IX. bis XIII. Jahrhundert. Einsiedeln: Benziger & Co., 1929.

Bower, Calvin. "Review of Hucbald, Guido, and John on Music." Journal of the American Musicological Society 35 (Spring 1982), pp. 157-67.

Bragard, Roger. "Le Speculum Musicae du Compilateur Jacques de Liège (2 parts)." Musica Disciplina 7 (1953), pp. 59-104; 8 (1954), pp. 1-17.

Bursill-Hall, G.L. Speculative Grammars of the Middle Ages. The Doctrine of Partes Orationis of the Modistae. The Hague: Mouton and Co., 1971.

Chailley, Jacques. "Une nouvelle méthode d'approche pour l'analyse modale du chant grégorien." Speculum musicae artis. Festgabe für Heinrich Husmann zum 60. Geburtstag. Edited by Heinz Becker and Reinhard Gerlach. Munich: W. Fink Verlag, 1970, pp. 85-92.

Cocheril, Dom. "Le 'Tonale Sancti Bernardi' et la définition du 'ton.'" Citeaux, Commentarii Cistercienses 13 (1962), pp. 35-66.

Crocker, Richard. "Hermann's Major Sixth." Journal of the American Musicological Society 25 (1972), pp. 19-37.

________. "A New Source for Medieval Music Theory." Acta Musicologica 39 (July-Dec. 1967), pp. 161-71.

Dahlhaus, Carl. Untersuchungen über die Entstehung der harmonischen Tonalität. Kassel: Bärenreiter Verlag, 1967.

Delalande, Fr. Dominique. Vers la version authentique du Graduel Grégorien: Le Graduel des Prêcheurs. Paris: Les Editions du Cerf, 1949.

Ellsworth, Oliver. "The Origin of the Coniuncta: A Reappraisal." Journal of Music Theory 17 (1973), pp. 86-109.

Fellerer, Karl Gustave. "Die Kölner musiktheoretische Schule des 16. Jahrhunderts." Renaissance-muziek. 1400-1600: Donum Natalicium René Bernard Lenaerts. Louvain: Katholieke Universiteit, Seminarie voor Muziekwetenschap, 1969, pp. 121-30.

________. "Untersuchungen zur Musica des Wilhelm von Hirsau." Miscelanea en homenaje a Monsenor Higinio Anglés. 2 vols. Barcelona, 1958, vol. 1, pp. 239-52.

________. "Zum Musiktraktat des Wilhelm von Hirsau." Festschrift Wilhelm Fischer. Edited by Hans Zingerle. Innsbrucker Beiträge zur Kulturwissenschaft 3. Innsbruck, 1956, pp. 61-70.

Feretti, Paolo M., O.S.B. Estetica gregoriana. Rome: Pontificio Istituto de Musica Sacra, 1934; reprint ed., New York: Da Capo Press, 1977.

_______. Esthétique grégorienne. Paris: Desclée & Co., 1938.

Fleming, Keith. "The Editing of Some Communion Melodies in Medieval Chant Manuscripts." Ph.D. diss., Catholic University of America, 1979.

Gevaert, François Auguste. La mélopée antique dans le chant de l'église latine. 1895; reprint ed., Osnabrück: Otto Zeller, 1967.

Gombosi, Otto. "Studien zur Tonartenlehre des frühen Mittelalters (3 parts)." Acta Musicologica 10 (1938), pp. 149-74; 11 (1939), pp. 28-39, 128-35; 12 (1940), pp. 21-52.

Gümpel, P.K. "Zur Interpretation der Tonus-Definition des Tonale Sancte Bernardi." Akademie der Wissenschaften und der Literatur 2. Wiesbaden: Franz Steiner Verlag, 1959, pp. 25-51.

Gushee, Lawrence. "Questions of Genre in Medieval Treatises on Music." Gattungen der Musik in Einzeldarstellungen: Gedenkschrift Leo Schrade. Edited by Wulf Arlt et al. Bern: Francke Verlag, 1973, pp. 365-433.

Gysin, Hans Peter. "Studien zum Vokabular der Musiktheorie im Mittelalter: Eine linguistische Analyse." Ph.D. diss., University of Basel, 1958.

Handschin, Jacques. Der Toncharakter. Eine Einführung in die Tonpsychologie. Zurich: Atlantis Verlag, 1948.

Hermelink, Siegfried. Dispositiones modorum: die Tonarten in der Musik Palestrinas und seiner Zeitgenossen. Tutzing: H. Schneider, 1960.

Horsley, Imogene. "Fugue and Mode in 16th-Century Vocal Polyphony." Aspects of Medieval and Renaissance Music. Edited by Jan La Rue. New York: W.W. Norton & Co., Inc., 1966, pp. 406-22.

Huglo, Michel. Les Tonaires. Paris: Société Française de Musicologie, 1971.

Hüschen, Heinrich. "Der Modus-Begriff in der Musiktheorie des Mittelalters und der Renaissance." Mittellateinisches Jahrbuch 2 (1965), pp. 224-32.

Jacobsthal, Gustav. Die chromatische Alteration im liturgischen Gesang der abendländischen Kirche. Berlin, 1897; reprint ed., Hildesheim: Georg Olms, 1970.

Jammers, Ewald. "Einige Anmerkungen zur Tonalität des gregorianischen Gesänges." Festschrift Karl Gustav Fellerer, zum 60. Geburtstag. Edited by Heinrich Hüschen. Regensburg: Gustav Bosse Verlag, 1962, pp. 235-44.

Kromolicki, Josef. "Die Lehre von der Transposition in der Musiktheorie des frühen Mittelalters." Festschrift Hermann Kretzschmar zum 70. Geburtstage. Leipzig, 1918; reprint ed., Hildesheim: Georg Olms, 1973, pp. 62-64.

Lowinsky, Edward E. Foreword to Musica nova. Edited by H. Colin Slim. Chicago: The University of Chicago Press, 1964.

________. Tonality and Atonality in Sixteenth-Century Music. Berkeley: University of California Press, 1961.

Mantuani, Josef. "Ein unbekanntes Druckwerk." Mitteilungen des österreichischen Verein für Bibliothekswesen 6. Vienna, 1902.

Marosszeki, S.R. "Les origines du chant cistercien." Analecta sacri ordinis cisterciensis 8 (1952).

Martinez-Göllner, Marie Louise. "Marchettus of Padua and Chromaticism." L'Ars Nova Italiana Del Trecento. Certaldo: Edizioni Centro di Studi Sull 'Ars Nova Italiana Del Trecento, 1969, pp. 187-202.

Meier, Bernhard. "Alte und neue Tonarten, Wesen, und Bedeutung." Renaissance-muziek. 1400-1600: Donum Natalicium René Bernard Lenaerts. Louvain: Katholieke Universiteit, Seminarie voor Muziekwetenschap, 1969, pp. 157-68.

________. Die tonarten der klassischen Vokalpolyphonie, nach den Quellen dargestellt. Utrecht: Oosthock, Scheltema and Holkema, 1974.

Miller, Clement A. "The Dodecachordon: Its Origin and Influence on Renaissance Musical Thought." Musica Disciplina 15 (1961), pp. 155-66.

________. "Gaffurius's Practica Musicae: Origins and Contents." Musica Disciplina 22 (1968), pp. 105-28.

Die Musik in Geschichte und Gegenwart. 14 vols. Edited by Friedrich Blume. Kassel: Bärenreiter Verlag, 1949-68.

The New Grove Dictionary of Music and Musicians. 20 vols. Edited by Stanley Sadie. London: Macmillan Publishers, Ltd., 1980.

Niemöller, Klaus Wolfgang. Nicolaus Wollick (1480-1541) und Sein Musiktraktat. Beiträge zur rheinischen Musikgeschichte 13. Cologne: Arno Volk Verlag, 1956.

________. "Zur tonus-Lehre der italienischen Musiktheorie der ausgehenden Mittelalters." Kirchenmusikalisches Jahrbuch 40 (1956), pp. 23-32.

Oesch, Hans. Berno und Hermann von Reichenau als Musiktheoretiker. Publikationen der schweizerischen Musikforschenden Gesellschaft, ser. 2, vol. 9. Bern: Paul Haupt, 1961.

________. Guido von Arezzo. Publikationen der schweizerischen Musikforschenden Gesellschaft, ser. 2, vol. 4. Bern: Paul Haupt, 1954.

Ortigue, M.J. de. Dictionaire liturgique, historique et théorique de plain-chant et de musique d'église. Paris: Potier, 1954.

Perkins, Leeman L. "Mode and Structure in the Masses of Josquin." Journal of the American Musicological Society 26 (Summer 1973), pp. 189-239.

Planer, John H. "The Ecclesiastical Modes in the Late Eighth Century." Ph.D. diss., University of Michigan, 1970.

Powers, Harold. "The Modality of 'Vestiva i colli.'" Studies in Renaissance and Baroque Music in Honor of Arthur Mendel. Edited by Robert L. Marshall. Kassel/Hackensack, 1974, pp. 31-46.

________. "Tonal Types and Modal Categories." Journal of the American Musicological Society 34 (Fall 1981), pp. 428-70.

Reaney, Gilbert. "Modes in the 14th Century, in Particular in the Music of Guillaume de Machaut." Organicae voces: Festschrift Joseph Smits van Waesberghe. Amsterdam, 1963, pp. 137-43.

________. "The Question of Authorship in the Medieval Treatises." Musica Disciplina 18 (1964), pp. 7-17.

Reese, Gustave. Music in the Middle Ages. New York: W.W. Norton & Co., Inc., 1940.

________. Music in the Renaissance. 2nd ed. New York: W.W. Norton & Co., Inc., 1959.

Reichert, Georg. "Kirchentonart als Formfaktor in der mehrstimmigen Musik des 15. und 16. Jahrhunderts." Die Musikforschung 4 (1951), pp. 35-48.

Schrade, Leo. "Johannes Cochlaeus, Musiktheoretiker in Köln." Beiträge zur rheinischen Musikgeschichte 20. Cologne: Arno Volk Verlag, 1956, pp. 124-32.

Seay, Albert. "The Beginnings of the Coniuncta and Lorenzo Masini's 'L'Antefana.'" L'ars nova italiana del Trecento. Certaldo: Edizioni Centro di Studi Sull 'Ars Nova Italiana Del Trecento, 1969, pp. 187-202.

________. "The Declaratio Musice Discipline of Ugolino of Orvieto: Addenda." Musica Disciplina 11 (1957), pp. 126-33.

________. "The 15th-Century Coniuncta: A Preliminary Study." Aspects of Medieval and Renaissance Music. Edited by Jan LaRue. New York: W.W. Norton and Co., Inc., 1966, pp. 723-37.

________. "Ugolino of Orvieto, Theorist and Composer." Musica Disciplina 9 (1955), pp. 111-66.

Smith, F. Joseph. "Accidentalism in the Fourteenth Century." Revue belge de musicologie 24 (1970), pp. 42-51.

________. "Ars Nova, a Re-definition? Observations in the Light of the Speculum Musicae (2 parts)." Musica Disciplina 18 (1964), pp. 19-36; 19 (1965), pp. 83-98.

________. Jacobi Leodiensis Speculum Musicae II: A Commentary. Musicological Studies 22. New York: The Institute of Mediaeval Music, Ltd., 1970 or 1971.

Smits van Waesberghe, Joseph. De musico-paedagogico et theoretico Guidone Aretino eiusque vita et moribus. Florence: L.S. Olschki, 1953.

________. Muziekgeschiedenis der Middeleeuwen. 1-. Tilburg: W. Bergmans, 1938-.

________. "Some Music Treatises and their Interrelation: A School of Liège c. 1050-1200? (2 parts)." Musica Disciplina 3 (1949), pp. 25-31, 95-118.

Spiess, Lincoln B. "The Diatonic 'Chromaticism' of the Enchiriadis Treatises." Journal of the American Musicological Society 12 (1959), pp. 1-6.

Sweeney, Cecily. "John Wylde and the Musica Guidonis." Musica Disciplina 29 (1975), pp. 43-59.

Treitler, Leo. "Tone System in the Secular Works of Guillaume Dufay." Journal of the American Musicological Society 18 (1965), pp. 131-69.

Vivell, P. Cölestin. "Ein anonymer Kommentar zum Mikrologus des Guido d'Arezzo." Studien und Mitteilungen zur Geschichte des Benediktiner-Ordens und seiner Zweige 35 (1914), pp. 56ff.

________. "Le tonus peregrinus (2 parts)." Revue de chant grégorien 18 (1909), pp. 147-53; 19 (1910), pp. 18-22.

Waddell, Chrysogonus. "The Origin and Early Evolution of the Cistercian Antiphonary: Reflections on Two Cistercian Chant Reforms." The Cistercian Spirit: A Symposium. Edited by M.B. Pennington. Cistercian Studies Series, no. 3. Spencer, Mass., 1970, pp. 190-223.

Wagner, Peter. Einführung in die gregorianischen Melodien, 3 vols. Leipzig: Breitkopf & Härtel, 1911-21; reprint ed., Hildesheim: Georg Olms, 1970.

________. "Zur mittelalterlichen Tonartenlehre." Studien zur Musikgeschichte: Festschrift für Guido Adler zum 75. Geburtstag. Vienna, 1930; reprint ed., Vienna: Universal Edition, 1971, pp. 29-32.

Weakland, Rembert. "Hucbald as Musician and Theorist." The Musical Quarterly 42 (Jan. 1956), pp. 66-84.

Werner, Eric. "The Origin of the Eight Modes of Music. Hebrew Union College Annual 21 (1948), pp. 211-55.

_______. "The Psalmodic Formula Neannoe and its Origins." The Musical Quarterly 28 (1942), pp. 93-99.

Wienpahl, Robert W. "Modality, Monality, and Tonality in the Sixteenth and Seventeenth Centuries, II." Music and Letters 53 (Jan. 1972), pp. 59-73.

________. "Modal Usage in Masses of the Fifteenth Century." Journal of the American Musicological Society 5 (Spring 1952), pp. 37-52.

Index of Chants

General Index

www.ingramcontent.com/pod-product-compliance
Lightning Source LLC
Chambersburg PA
CBHW070842100426
42813CB00003B/715
9780253304605